MAN IN BIOSPHERE

MAN IN BIOSPHERE

A Case Study of Nilgiri Biosphere Reserve

Edittors

ARUN KUMAR SINGH

SURESH PATIL

GYAN GYAN PUBLISHING HOUSE

NEW DELHI-110002

Man in Biosphere : A Case Study of Nilgiri Biosphere Reserve

Rs. 540

ISBN: 81-212-0943-9

Published in 2007 in India by
Gyan Publishing House
5, Ansari Road, Darya Ganj,
New Delhi-110002
Phones : 23282060, 23261060
Fax : 011-23285914
E-mail: books@gyanbooks.com
Website: www.gyanbooks.com

Lasser Type Setting by: Rudra Computer Graphics, Delhi
Printed at : Salasar Imaging System, Delhi

Contents

List of Tables

List of Maps

Foreword

The present volume *Man in Biosphere – A Case Study of Nilgiri Biosphere Reserve* contains research articles undertaken by the members of the Anthropological Survey of India under its Tenth Five Year Plan Project – *Cultural Dimension of Tourism* which was reoriented as *Man in Biosphere*. Nilgiri Biosphere Reserve is one of the important biospheres declared by the Govt. of India in the month of September, 1986 embraces the sanctuary complex of Wynaad, Nagarhole, Bandipur and Mudumalai, the entire forest hill slopes of Nilambur, upper Nilgiri plateau, Silent Valley of Siruvani hills. The total area of the Biosphere Reserve is around 5520 sq.kms. of which 1240 sq.kms. is the core zone, 3239 sq.kms. manipulation zone (forestry) and around 335 sq.kms. manipulation zone (agriculture) and 706 sq.kms. as a restoration zone which is also used as a tourism zone.

Nilgiri Biosphere Reserve possesses different habitat types, unspoilt areas of natural evergreen forest with several dry shrubs, dry and moist deciduous, semi evergreen and wet evergreen forest, evergreen shrubs, grassland and swamps. Nilgiri Biosphere Reserve includes the largest known population of two endangered animal species i.e. the Nilgiri Thar and the lion tailed Macaque and the largest South Indian population of elephant, tiger, gaur, sambar and cheetal and a good number of endemic endangered plants which makes it a rich biodiversity hot spot of the Western Ghat. The Nilgiri Biosphere Reserve is equally rich in cultural diversity and it harbours large number of tribal groups, remarkable for their tradition ways of harmonious use of the environment. The whole exercise deal with two very main aspects – conservation and development. If the biosphere is to be protected, the biodiversity as well the cultural diversity should be maintained so that it becomes sustainable for the future generation to come. The volume consists of different issues, such as anthropogenic threats and conservation of biosphere, eco-tourism and sustainable development, peoples' perception of forest management and biodiversity and sustainable development. The team of research scientists has done commendable work in bringing out this volume, which I hope, will serve as a bridge between biodiversity and cultural diversity. Anthropological Survey of India, a premier institute doing research on bio-social aspect of human population of this country has undertaken this project with a key motto to start a dialogue between the scientific personnel working in the field of biodiversity and cultural diversity so that the biosphere can be sustained in a sustainable manner which, in return, will support life support system for all the species including man. The degradation of the environment specially in the third world country has reached an alarming situation and one has to be very very careful in handling the ecological problem so that development can take place and at the same time environment is not degraded. I congratulate the team of Dr. Arun Kumar Singh and Dr. Suresh Patil and their colleagues for doing the research work on Nilgiri Biosphere Reserve. I am sure, the volume is going to help the researchers, planners, administrators and managers of the forest to understand the biosphere in a better way.

V.R. Rao
Director-in-Charge

Preface

Concern for forest and its surrounding environment is as old as the human civilization. Forest has been the abode of human population for sustenance by utilizing the forest resource and at the same time protecting it through traditional form of forest management. Thus there is a symbiotic relationship between the forest ecosystem and the human population. This symbiotic relationship got strained after the industrial revolution when forest was looked upon as a source of wealth. This attitude changed the total utilitarian pattern and from this period forest degradation started resulting in vanishing of the forest cover from many parts of the earth surface. India was no exception to this change and with the coming of the colonial power forest became the prime target for massive exploitations. Laws were enacted to take full control of the forest resources and reallocation / resettlement of human population started during this period. The so called autochthonous population who were residing in the forest had to bear the brunt very heavily. The village settlements inside forests were relocated at different places where they were under the full control of the forest department for supplying labour in the day to day activity of the department. Baiga Chack, in Madhya Pradesh, is a good example where the villagers were shifted from the dense forest areas to the valley plains resulting changes in land utilization and livelihood pattern. No longer shifting cultivation was allowed by the governance. At a later stage when forest were more exploited, different stake holders started making inroads for timber exploitation, collection and sale of various types of forest produce. Encroachment of forest land started on a massive scale. Forest cover was cleared to accommodate agriculture, mining, industry, and other human induced activities. Whatever pristine ecosystem was left became the target of eco-tourism in the recent years followed by construction of various types of infrastructural support system for the growing tourism industry. People, who were living in this forest ecosystem, became a silent spectator losing all their rights and privileges in the forest ecology.

During the mid 18th century man started thinking loudly regarding the problems of forest conservation and its protection. At the same time ways and means were looked for how to restore the forest ecology so that the degradation of environment is arrested. The journey from Stockholm to Rio de Janeiro forced the civilized society to launch for UNESCO's Man and Biosphere (MAB) programme in 1970. The basic objective of this programme is to minimize man-nature conflict and to protect and conserve the biosphere wherever it is possible in its pristine ecosystem. It also suggested the sustainable development of human population living in and around biospheres and tried to establish a linkage between biodiversity and cultural diversity. Anthropological Survey of India in it's 10th Five year Plan project undertook a detail study on the project 'Cultural dimensions of tourism' which was reoriented as 'Man in Biosphere' project. Under this project the Survey decided to study first three biospheres namely Pachmarhi BR, Nilgiri BR and Sundarban BR out of the fourteen Biosphere Reserves declared by the Govt. of India till date. The issues identified for studies in these biospheres are mainly anthropogenic threats, ecotourism, traditional forest management, resource utilization and sustainable development, rehabilitation issues, etc. This volume entitled ***Man in Biosphere: A Case Study of Nilgiri Biosphere Reserve*** deals with the issues and problems of based on detailed study undertaken by the scientific personals of Southern Regional Centre, Mysore and Head Office, Kolkata.

Of the three biosphere reserves the Nilgiri Biosphere Reserve is the oldest biosphere reserves to be notified by the Government of India : on 1st August 1986 spreading over three southern States viz. Tamil Nadu, Karnataka and Kerala. Primarily located in the Western Ghats of the Indian peninsula Nilgiri BR lies between 10° 50' – 12° 16' N latitude and 76° -77 ° 15' E longitudes. It forms an almost complete ring around the Nilgiri Plateau covering an area of 5520.40 sq. km. The core zone consists of 1240 sq. km. whereas buffer zone (forestry) has an area of 3238.70 sq. km. apart from the forestry zone there is a buffer zone tourism and restoration zone with an area 335.00 sq. km. and 706.40 sq. km. respectively. The districts which fall under Nilgiri BR are Kozhikode, Wayanad, Malappuram and Palakkad in Kerala, Nilgiri, Koimbatore and Sathyamangalam of Tamil Nadu and Chamrajnagar and Mysore districts of Karnataka. This mountain mass is also known as 'Blue Mountains' and is one of the most studied areas from social point of view. However most of the researches are mainly concentrated on the upper elevation of the plateau areas. The important tribes of this area are the Todas, Kotas, Mullu Kudumbas and the one important caste group known as the Badagas. However, study on human interaction with the forest ecosystem is not many. This volume intends to fill up the gap with the basic assumption that conservation and development should go hand to hand.

The first article entitled development of ecotourism, anthropogenic threats and conservation of biosphere in Mudumalai Wildlife life sanctuary by Arun Kumar Singh deals with the problems of anthropogenic threats in the form of tourists flow ion Mudumalai Wildlife life sanctuary and also due three settlements inside the sanctuary. Rehabilitation has become a very important issue where forest dwellers are willing to shift their settlement if proper rehabilitation package is provided by the Government. But irony is that this package is yet to be decided. The second article by K

Ravi and G. V. Ramna deals with ecotourism and sustainable development- a case study of Bandipur National Park. This park is also famous for tiger reserve. To preserve the pristine ecosystem nearly 10 tribal families were rehabilitated on the fringe of Bandipur National Park from the interior areas. The study denotes that the situation of those tribal families has not improved though various development programmes has been implemented. These tribal households at present have not only become homeless and landless but also marginalized in their own habitat. The third article by B. R. Vijayendra and H. M. M. Patel on the same issue, taking Nagarhole National Park as a case study. The national park attracts tourists from around the world and Forest Department, Government of Karnataka has provided infrastructural facilities but not maintained properly. The tribal population living inside the National Park has not benefited much due development ecotourism. However, some of the households has got fringe benefits due to their deployment in the forest department as wage labourers. P. K. Guha in his article Peoples' perception about Forest Management and tourism – a case study of Vokkapuram village, Mudumalai Wildlife Sanctuary deals with the conflict between tradition and modern forms of forest management. Though the village situated in the outscarts of the sanctuary impact of tourism has not been felt as the land has been taken away for the development of resorts and hotels the villagers are primarily dependent on wage labourer. Their dependency on forest has also been reduced to a greater extent though forest still remains an cultural aspect of the tribal society. The last article by Sanchita Ghatak entitled Biodiversity and sustainable development in a fringe village in Mudumalai Wildlife Sanctuary primarily deals with the problem of sustainable development in the village. It is believed that the forest can be well protected if the fringe villages are economically developed so that their dependency on the forest is minimized.

All the articles present case studies of the situation which are prevailing in and around the Nilgiri Biosphere Reserve and tried to explore the human interaction with the forest ecosystem and at the same time it also emphasise how the forest can be conserved and protected so that the people living in and around can have a better life. Ecotourism is one of the solutions but it has top be seen that the benefit of it reaches to the people of that area.

Arun Kumar Singh

Suresh Patil

Introduction

Arun Kumar Singh

Suresh Patil

Concern for environment is as old as human civilization. The old society took sanctity of environment for granted as a necessary pre-condition for the existence of human society. But this situation started changing after the industrial revolution when human society with the help of technologically advance knowledge system started making significant change in the whole environment and this gave the society an understanding that man will be able to modify the environment according to his will and need. Now need based development of the pre-industrial era has been replaced by greed based development which is marked by the rampant consumption of resources by the society. Under this changed scenario the environment is more stressed and degradation has started taking place. At the present era when man has technologically developed at a very higher level and environment is getting degraded at an alarming rate, the very existence of human society is now at a stake. Even then, plunder of nature at the cost of human progress is continuing virtually unabated. We have lost the basic theme of human development or progress wherein the environment is considered as a living entity. This has resulted into serious environmental crisis and forest has become the most vulnerable area on the earth surface which suffered greatly due to human intervention in the form of clearing the forest for various types of crops, mining, industrial development, construction of dams etc. But the situation has to be changed if the human society has to survive. Man at the present juncture has started thinking how to safeguard the environment and at the same time how development can take place. This has led to the initiation of the process of sustainable development where man can indulge in developmental pursuits without damaging the environment and thus ensuring a better future for all the living beings.

Bio-sphere a Concept

The concept of bio-sphere reserve was initiated by the United Nations Educational Scientific and Cultural Organization (UNESCO) in the year 1970 to facilitate resolution of increasing conflict between people and the Protected Areas. Representative parts of natural and cultural landscapes extending over large areas of terrestrial or coastal / marine ecosystems or a combination thereof are designated as Biosphere Reserves. Biosphere Reserves are internationally recognized within the framework of UNESCO's Man and Biosphere (MAB) programme. The UNESCO's framework stipulates that BRs should be representative of a bio-geographic province and should have appropriate zoning system with legally constituted and minimally disturbed core zone. In addition, the site should contain unique and pristine biodiversity, ecosystems and landscape suitable to explore and demonstrate approaches to sustainable development and should be of appropriate size to serve three functions such as conservation, development and logistic support.

It is aimed to bring at least one representative site in the country within each biogeographic province under the network of Biosphere Reserves and ensure their long term protection and conservation by involving various stakeholders. Biosphere Reserves are designated to deal with one of the most important questions of reconciling the conservation of biodiversity, the quest for economic, social development and maintenance of associated cultural values. Conservation of landscapes, ecosystems, species and genetic variations; promote economic development, which is culturally, socially and ecologically sustainable and to provide logistic support for research, monitoring, education and information exchange related to local, national and global issues are important aspects of Biosphere Reserves.

Biosphere Reserves and Protected Areas

There has been suspicion that Biosphere Reserves and Protected Areas are in some senses rivals. In fact, they are complementary to each other. At the site level, a Protected Area or several Protected Areas, will almost always form part of a Biosphere Reserves, although there will often be parts of Biosphere Reserves which are not suitable for Protected Area status. At the policy level, the development of Biosphere Reserves has illuminated thinking about Protected Areas. Thus, while biodiversity conservation is a central feature both of Biosphere Reserves as a whole, and is a necessary condition of a Protected Area, conservation is not necessarily a function of all parts of Biosphere Reserves. Indeed, conservation may be absent altogether within some parts of buffer zone where the emphasis will be on the sustainable use of natural resources – a highly desirable end but not the same as biodiversity conservation.

Present assumption is that if local people and communities living in buffer areas of the Biosphere Reserves are made more productive and economically viable in their own right, then people will reduce their dependence on the regions within core areas. The present interventions, based on the above assumptions are therefore mostly restricted to augmenting alternate livelihood options for the local communities through following approaches :

- Ecosystem protection
- Participatory, democratic structure
- Open communication
- Management responsibility and benefit sharing in relation to traditional use
- Gender equality
- Community responsibility
- Effective conflict resolution
- Traditional right and uses
- Effective monitoring

MAB Programme and Biosphere Reserves

The UN Conference on Environment and Development (1992) led to orientation of MAB programme to the issues of biodiversity, sustainable management of natural resources, capacity building and information and communication on environmental matters. The sites designated and managed under the scheme are representing sites of major biogeographic zones of the world and represent pristine ecosystems, which contain biodiversity elements of great potential for future survival of mankind and needs to be conserved for posterity. Therefore, conservation of Biosphere Reserves should be the responsibility of the world community as a whole. By November, 2000, there were 391 Biosphere Reserves on world network in 94 countries, which includes Nilgiri Biosphere Reserves from India. The world's major ecosystem types and landscapes are represented on this network, which is devoted to conserving biological diversity, promoting research as well as seeking to provide models of sustainable developments in the service of humankind. Participation in the world network is voluntary. It facilitates co-operation and exchanges at regional and international level.

Status of Biosphere Reserves in India

The Indian National Man and Biosphere (MAB) Committee was first constituted in 1972 as a follow up of UNESCO's Man and Biosphere (MAB) programme initiated in 1970s, The MAB programme is co-ordinated, serviced and funded by the Ministry of Environment and Forests (MoEF), Govt. of India, New Delhi. The committee supervises the activities under the programme and encourages interdisciplinary demonstration and training. In the year 1979, a Sub-group of the Indian MAB Committee identified 14 sites in India for being designated as Biosphere Reserves based on which and subsequent advice of the committee, the Government of India have designated 12 Biosphere Reserves till July 2001. The total area under the 12 Biosphere Reserves account for a total geographical area of 53,849.39 km^2 of which 12492 km^2 is core zone. These sites were identified on the basis of their unique biodiversity, naturalness and effectiveness as a conservation unit. At the present 2 more Biosphere Reserves have been added making it 14 in total.

The Problem

(i) The Nilgiri Biosphere Reserve – An Overview

As part of the UNESCO's Man and Biosphere Programme, India launched the Indian National Man and Biosphere Programme in the 1970s to identify areas which are representative of the various biogeographical zones that can be set aside as biosphere reserves. Consequently, the Nilgiris were identified as representative of the Western Ghats. The Department of Science and Technology had constituted a committee under the Chairmanship of Professor Madhav Gadgil of the Indian Institute of Science, Bangalore to survey and demarcate the exact limits of the proposed biosphere reserve in the Nilgiris. As per the first document on this proposed biosphere reserve, the total area demarcated was around 5670 km^2 of which 2020 km^2 were designated as the core zone, 2290 km^2 as manipulation (forestry) zone, 1330 km^2 as manipulation (agriculture) zone and a mere 30 km^2 as restoration zone. Subsequently, the biosphere reserve was established.

Area under the various zones of the Nilgiri Biosphere Reserve

State	*Total (km^2)*	*Core Area (km^2)*	*Manip (km^2)*	*Forestry (km^2)*	*Tourism Restoration (km^2)*
Tami Nadu	2537.6	274.0	2081.5	65.8	116.3
Kerala	455.4	264.5	945.0	0.0	245.9
Karnatake	1527.4	701.8	212.2	269.2	344.2
Total	5520.4	1240.3	3238.7	335.0	706.4

The Nilgiri Biosphere Reserve (NBR) is the first biosphere reserve set up in India under the Indian National Man and Biosphere Programme. It was set up on 1.9.86 vide order number J. 22010/6/86.CSC, Government of India. The NBR is spread over three south Indian states; Tamil Nadu, Kerala and Karnataka and hence under the joint jurisdiction of the three state's forest department. It embraces a complex of Protected Areas and reserved forests including Rajiv Gandhi National park (Nagarhole) and Bandipur (Karnataka), Wynaad, the slopes of Nilambur, Silent valley and

Siruvani Hills (Kerala) and Dr. J Jayalalitha Wildlife Sanctuary (Mudumalai), and Mukurti (Tamil Nadu). Of these Bandipur, Nagarhole and Silent Vally are National Parks. Mudumalai, Wynaad and Mukurti are Wildlife Sanctuaries. Bandipur is a Tiger Reserve and also the single largest Protected Area (974.0 km^2) within the NBR.

The NBR on declaration includes a total area of 5520 km^2. This large area is further divided into a Core Zone (1240km^2) and a buffer zone (4280 km^2) (Anon 1989). The core zone is distributed between Kerala (264.5 km^2), Karnataka (701.8 km^2) and Tamil Nadu (274.0 km^2). The Buffer Zone is further divided into Manipulation (Forestry) Zone (3239 km^2), Manipulation (Tourism) Zone (335 km^2) and Restoration Zone (706 km^2).

(ii) Management : It was originally proposed that there will be five councils / committees to manage the NBR.

(a) Governing Council comprising the higher officials of the three states viz, Chief Secretaries, Chief Conservators of Forests, Directors of Agriculture, four nominees from the Government of India Department of Science and Technology or Department of Environment including the Chairman of the Man and Biosphere Committee and the Technical Director of the Biosphere Reserve who would serve as the Secretary of the Governing Council.

(b) Eco-development Council including all members of the state legislature whose constituencies fall within the biosphere reserve area, all Deputy Commissioners concerned, the Technical Director of the Biosphere Reserve, three Field Directors of the biosphere reserve, Deputy Conservators of Forests involved, Deputy Directors of Agriculture, Horticulture and Animal Husbandry and Deputy Director of Tribal Welfare.

(c) Biosphere Protection and Co-ordination Committee involving Deputy Inspector Generals of Police in charge of forests and wildlife in the three states, the three Field Directors, the concerned Deputy Commissioners and the Technical Director of the Biosphere Reserve.

(d) Management Committee in which the Technical Director, the three Field Directors, Deputy Conservators of Forests, all

Technical Advisers and three Research Scientists nominated by the Chairman, Man and Biosphere committee would be the members.

(e) Research and Monitoring Committee with Chairman of the Man and Biosphere Committee, the three Field Directors, all the Technical Advisers and all the Research Project Heads. The Technical Advisers will be from the departments of soil and water conservation, agriculture, horticulture, animal husbandry, forestry, wildlife management, tribal welfare, eco-development, statistics and data management, finance and public education.

The organizational committee that was originally established included the Chief Conservators of Forests Kerala, Tamil Nadu, and Karnataka as the Nodal / Contact Officers and Departments. Directors of the NBR viz., Conservators of Forests, Udhagamandalam (Ooty, Tamil Nadu), Field Director, Project Tiger (Mysore, Karnataka) and a conservator of Forests (Kerala) together formed the Co-ordination Committee, A 9 member Research Committee with Professor Madhav Gadgil, Indian Institutes of Science, Bangalore as Convener and a 8 member Management Council Chaired by a representative of the Ministry of Environment and Forests, Government of India.

More recently in 1992, the Tamil Nadu State Government has constituted a steering Committee vide GO No. 10 dt. 10.1.92 for preparation and review of action plans covering physical, financial and scientific aspects of the NBR.

(iii) Objectives of Biosphere Reserves

As stated by the Indian National Man and Biosphere Committee Biosphere Reserves are aimed at :

(a) preserving biological diversity,

(b) catalyzing ecologically sound development of the entire region and

(c) generating assured employment for all tribals, rural landless and other weaker segments of the population living in and near the biosphere reserve for the purpose of ecological restoration

(iv) As stated in the 1994 UNESCO's Biosphere Reserve Nomination Form : Biosphere Reserves are designed to play three basic roles in relating to conservation, development and logistic support for comparative research and monitoring.

(a) ***Conservation role*** : Biosphere reserves provide non-conventional protection of indigenous genetic resources, plant and animal species ecosystems and landscapes of value for the conservation of the world's biological diversity.

(b) ***Development role*** : Biosphere Reserves seek to combine conservation concerns with sustainable use of ecosystems, resources through close co-operation with local communities, taking advantage of traditional knowledge, indigenous products and appropriate land management.

(c) ***Logistic role***: Biosphere Reserves are linked through a global network; they provide facilities for research, monitoring, education and training for local purposes as well as for international or regional comparative research and monitoring programmes.

(v) Geography

The 5520 km^2 Nilgiri Biosphere reserve (10^{0}45' – 12 ^{0}15' N latitude and 76^0 – 77^{0}15' E longitude) stretches from Coorg-Wynaad plateau east of Brahmagiri, south to Attapadi-Bolampatti Hills at the northern edge of the Palghat Gap and eastwards into the Talamlai-Hasanur Plateau of the Eastern Ghats.

The NBR is biogeographically part of the Indo-Malayan Realm and an appropriate representative of the topographic and climatic complexity of the Western Ghat – a biodiversity hot-spot in India.

The underlying rocks in the Nilgiri Hills are archaean dating back to 2000 million years BP. The NBR is also representative of some of the oldest hills in India which were uplifted somewhere around 40 million years ago. The present structure of these hills (of the Western Ghats in general) – steep western scarp and a gradual merging with the plateau in the east, is a result of more resent faulting.

The NBR has a remarkable topographic diversity varying from as low as 80 metres (Nilambur plains) to over 2600 metres

(Nilgiri plateau) above MSL. As a result of this topographic complexity and spread, the NBR encompasses a wide range of rainfall zones which receive between 500 and 7000 mm of precipitation annually. The rainfall is generally heavier in the western side averaging 5000 mm. The wet season is June-September though there are summer and occasional winter rains locally within the biosphere reserve. The length of the dry season varies from about a month in the western hills to over six month in the eastern plateau. April-May are the hottest months. Ground temperature below 0°C (frost) is frequent during December-January in the higher hills of Nilgiri.

The varied climatic pattern coupled with a complex relief have given rise to a wide variety of vegetation types viz., scrub in the eastern plains, through dry and moist deciduous forests as that in Mudumalai, evergreen forests as in Silent Valley to mountain forests (shola) and grasslands as found in the Nilgiri plateau.

(vi) Vegetation

The major vegetation types of the NBR are presently in a stage of serious damages due to the influences of modern humans and developmental activities. However the following types of vegetation can be readily identified.

Evergreen forests : These forests are found along the western slopes and valleys of the NBR usually in areas where the annual rainfall is not less than 2000 mm. These forests are further distinguished by altitude and thus we have low elevation evergreen forests (0 – 600 m) characterized by dominant trees in the genera dipterocarpus, Mesua and palaquium. Remnants of these forests are found in New Amarambalam and Muthikulam-Palghat hills.Higher up are the medium elevation evergreen forests (600-1400 m) Consisting of dominants such as cullenia, Mesua and palaquium.These forests occur in Silent Valley, New Amarambalam, Attapadi and Nilambur. A third altitudinal category of evergreen forests viz. the high elevation forest (1400 – 1800 m) is often recognized. This type is however not very distinct if floristic composition as the former two. The last category is the montane or shoal forests which appear in patches above 1800 m. These are characterized by their low stature and montane species such as Schefflera. Shola forests are found on the slopes of almost all the higher hills especially within the Nilgiri district. Secondary stages of evergreen forests and mixed forests are often classified as semi-evergreen forests.

Montane grassland : This vegetation type is found on the higher hills of the southern western Ghats and is a common feature of the NBR too. Extensive cover of short grass all over the slopes dotted with occasional Rhododendron trees is a characteristic. Grassland surround most shoals and the ecolones thus created are important habitats for a variety of organisms especially plants.

Deciduous forests : Deciduous forests are the prevalent of vegetation types in the NBR. Moist deciduous forests areas where the rainfall is around 1500 mm. However over most of the NBR where rainfall is around 1000 mm, dry deciduous forests dominate, often thinned down to form tree savannas by human interference. Climax moist deciduous forests may be seen in the Rajiv Gandhi National Park (Nagarhole) and the western parts of Mudumalai. Much of the Bandipur Tiger reserve shows a typical stand of dry deciduous forests.

Scrub : The eastern margin of the NBR and all along the Moyar River dense scrub jungles occur. These forests are characterized by stunted and thorny trees such as Hardwickia binata and cassia. Rainfall is usually less than 1000 mm.

Plantations : A variety of exotic and native tree plantations cover the landscape of the NBR.

(vii) Biodiversity : The NBR is known for its rich biodiversity. There are 3238 species of angiosperms, 71 species of gymnosperms, 134 species of pteridophytes, 300 species of butterflies and 684 species of vertebrates hitherto reported from this area of the 285 species of vertebrates endemic to the Western Ghats, 156 occur within the NBR. Several species of lower organisms are yet to be discorvered and described.

(a) Flora : Flora of the various forest types in the NBR have been found.

(b) Endemic flora : According to Nayar (1980) there are 141 genera endemic to India, out of which 50 spread over 25 families are endemic to the Western Ghats, 11 genera occurring in the Nilgiri. At the species level, out of the estimated 2100 species of flowering plants endemic to peninsular India, 818 are to be found in the Nilgiri and adjoining areas (Mohanan & Balakrishnan, 1991).

One hundred and thirty two species and 13 varieties of flowering plants are endemic to the NBR which amounts to 4.0 per cent of its total angiosperm flora. Of these, 28 are exclusive to the Kundah Range in the Nilgiris district. The genus Baeolepis with a single species nervosa (Periplocaceae) is restricted to the Nilgiris (Ahmedullah and Nayar, 1986). Endemism is marked in the families Acanthaceae, Balsaminaceae, poaceae and Orchidaceae within the NBR.

(c) **Threatened flora :** Of the 168 species of flowering plants of Tamil Nadu listed as endangered in the Red Data Books, 25 (15%) are exclusive to the Nilgiris. Some of the threatened orchids of this region are Bulbophyllum acutiflorum, B. nodosum, Habenaria denticulate, H. polyodon, Liparis biloba, Spiranthes sinensis, Thrixspermum musciflorum and Vanda wightii (Mohanan and Balakrishnan, 1991).

(d) **Economically important flora :** Sanjappa (1991) recorded 80 species of legumes from Wastern Ghats and a majority of these are from the NBR and adjacent areas.

A large number of medicinal plants also occur in the Nilgiri Biosphere Reserve. About 200 species of medicinal plants have been reported from the NBR of which 24 species are commercially exploited. Due to over exploitation certain species such as Rauvolfia serpentina and saraca asoca have become rare.

(e) In addition, Nilgiris is an important center of speciation and many plant new to science have been discovered and described from the region making it the type locality for a number of species. Silentvalleya (Poaceae), and Kanjaram (Acanthaceae) are two genera recently discovered from this region. Curcuma silentvalleyi, eria tiagii, Hedyotis silentvalleyensis, Hydnocarpus pendulus, Liparis indiraii, Oberonia bisaccata, porpax chandra sekharanii, Robiquetia josephiana, Sauropus saksenianus and Silentvalleya nairii are newly described species.

(f) Certain over-exploited and rare medicinal plants of NBR

Family	*Species*	*Locality*
Araceae	Acorus calamus	Nilgiris
Menispermaceae	Coccinium fenestratum	Silent valley
Zinziberaceae	Curcuma zeoaria	Nilgiris
Droseraceae	Drosera peltata	Nilgiris
Liliaceae	Gloriosa superba	Nilgiris
Ophioglossaceae	Helminthostachys zeylanica	Nilambur
Asclepidaiaceae	Hemidesmus indicus	Nilgiris
		Attapadi
Apiaceae	Heracleum candolleanum	Nilgiris
Lamiaceae	Plectranthus barbatus	Nilgiris
Apocynaceae	Rauvolfia serpennina	Palghat and
Caesalpiniaceae	Saraca asoca	Palghat

(g) Fauna

We know very little about the invertebrates of the NBR except butterflies. Almost all the butterfly species endemic to the Western Ghats also occur within the reserve. The best known animals are however the vertebrates, especially the larger mammals. There are already efforts made towards the protection of endangered and endemic mammals such as the Asian elephant (Elephas maximus), tiger (Panthera tigris), Nilgiri tahr (Hemitragus hylocrius), Nilgiri langur (Presbytisjohnii) and liontailed macaque (Macaca silenus) within the biosphere reserve. A number of little known bats (Chiroptara) and smaller mammals including the clawless otter (Aonyx cinerea), Nilgiri marten (Martes gwatkinsi), civets (Viverra sp.) and the lesser cats (felis sp. exist within the reserve) there is however very little information on their current range and status in the Western Ghats itself. Twelve species of mammals endemic to the Western Ghats are also found here; Mus famulus a rodent being exclusive to this reserve.

Over 300 species of birds are known from the NBR and of the 15 species endemic to the Western Ghats. Except the whitebreasted laughing thrush (Garrulax jerdoni), All species are found in the biosphere reserve. And of the 14 species, the Nilgiri laughing thrush (Garrulax cachinnans) is exclusive to the higher hills of the Nilgiris. The Nilgiri wood pigeon (Columba elphinstonii) listed as globally endangered is found frequently within the reserve.

Some of the uncommon migratory birds that visit the Western Ghats during from the Himalayas such as the woodcock (Scolopax rusticola), bluechat (Erithacus) and brownbreasted flycatcher (Muscicapa muttui) are found most often within the NBR.

Amongst the lower vertebrates a number of little known amphibians, reptiles and fish exist in the NBR. 39 species of fish, 31 species of amphibians and 60 species of reptiles endemic to the Western Ghats also occur within the biosphere reserve. Of these, 24 are hitherto known only from the NBR.

There are at least 300 marsh crocodiles (Crocodylus palustris) distributed in the major water of the reserve. Of these the Moyar river has the most substantial population.It must also be emphasized that this is the largest intact naturally breeding population of crocodiles anywhere in south India. Other endangered reptiles viz., the Indian rock python (python molurus) and king cobra (Ophiophagus Hannah) are frequently sighted within the NBR.

A list of fish, amphibians and reptiles hitherto known only from the NBR.

Fish	*Amphibians*	*Reptiles*
Danio neilgheriensis	Ichthyophis longicephalus	Cnemaspis
Hypselobarbus	Ansonia rubigina	Cnemaspis sisparensis
Puntius bovanicus	Bufo silentvalleyensis	Scincella bilineatrss
Puntius melanostigma	Micrixalus thampii	Typhlops tindalli
Neolissochilus wynaadensis		Rhabdops olivaceous
Garra Mcclellendi		Melanophidium bilineatum
Noema cheilus sinuatus		Plecturus guentheri
Noema cheilus striatus		

(Contd.)

(Contd.)

Fish	*Amphibians*	*Reptiles*
Mystus punctatus		
Silurus wynaadensis		
Clarias dayi		
Glyptothorax anandalei		

(h) Human diversity

The NBR is also the home of several human communities such as the Cholanaickas, Todas, Paniyans, Kurichiyans, Mullukurumbans, Adiyans, Kurumbas, Jenukurumbas, Kadu Kurumbas, Betta Kurumbas, Urali Kurumbas, Edanadan Chettis, Wyaadan Chettis, Mandatan Chettis, Kurichyans, Karimpalans, Kaders, Pathiyans, Kanaladis, Adiyans, Kattunayakans, Aranadans, Mudugas, Sholagas, Kotas, Panjari Yeravas, Pani Teravas, Irujas and Alars.

The pastoral Todas immigrated into the Nilgiris during the 2nd Century BC. Along with them probably came the first domestic cattle and buffaloes. (It is believed that some of the currently free ranging feral buffaloes in the Upper Nilgiris are those left behind by the Todas). During the 8th century AD, huntergatherers and shifting cultivators including Kotas, Kurumbas and Irulas entered the biosphere reserves. However, the most important event of human immigration that has had a permanent bearing on the landscape of the Nilgiris is that of the Badagas during the 15th century AD. Further infilteration of humans from the plains of Malabar, Coimbatore and Mysore have added to the population of the biosphere reserve. As per the 1991 census, there are 704, 827 people in the Nilgiris district.

Kerala part of NBR, especially the Wynaad district gives shelter to the maximum number of tribes both scheduled and unscheduled followed by Tamil Nadu and Karnataka. The approximately 2,00,000 tribal population within the NBR is distributed as follows : Kerala 1,50,000, Tamil Nadu 330,000 and Karnataka 170, 000.

Map-1

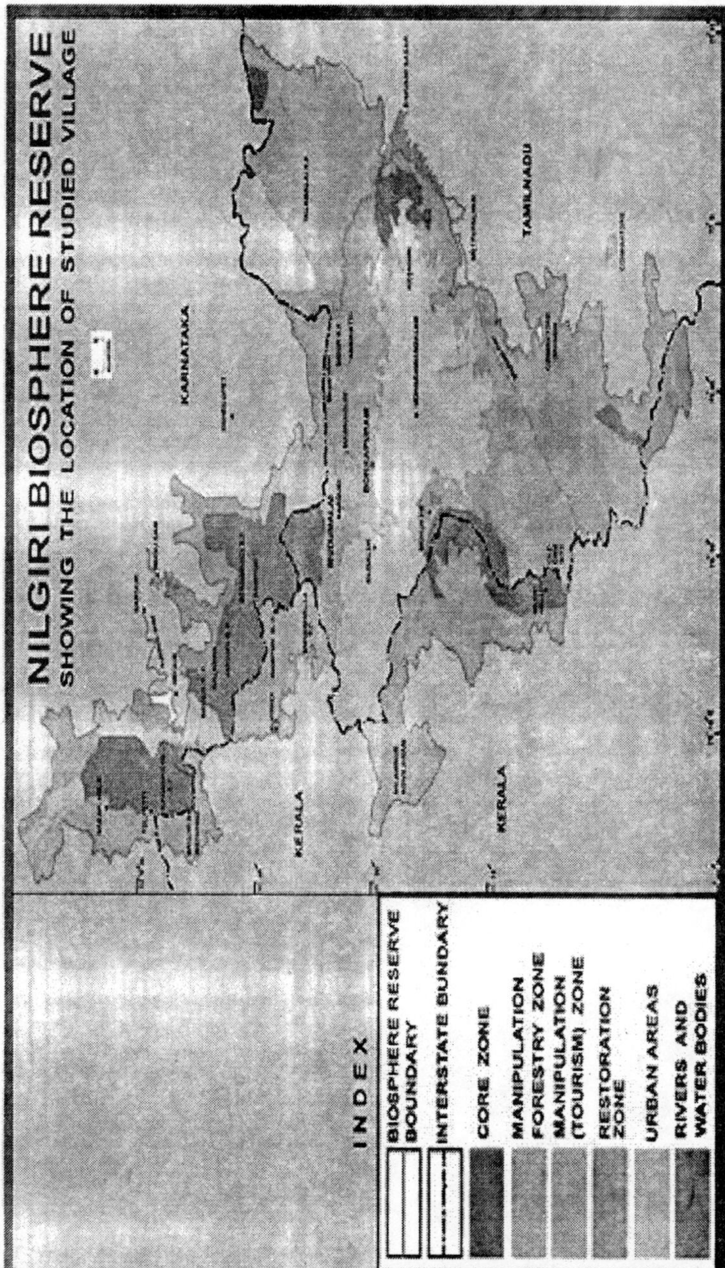
NILGIRI BIOSPHERE RESERVE
SHOWING THE LOCATION OF STUDIED VILLAGE
KARNATAKA
KERALA
KERALA
TAMILNADU
INDEX
BIOSPHERE RESERVE BOUNDARY
INTERSTATE BUNDARY
CORE ZONE
MANIPULATION FORESTRY ZONE
MANIPULATION (TOURISM) ZONE
RESTORATION ZONE
URBAN AREAS
RIVERS AND WATER BODIES

1

Development of Eco-tourism, Anthropogenic Threats and Conservation of Biosphere in Mudumalai Wildlife Sanctuary, Nilgiri Biosphere Reserve

Arun Kumar Singh

Mudumalai : The Oldest Sanctuary of the State

The word 'Mudumalai' means Ancient Mountain. Mudumalai tract is exceedingly rich in wildlife harboring a bewildering variety of animals which include one of the largest populations of elephants in the state, one of the well reserved populations of carnivores and a variety of other animals such as Black Back, Sambhar, Chital, Indian Gour etc. The array of avifauna, reptilian and amphibian fauna of this region is equally impressive. In due recognition of the tremendous biological potential of the region and with the view to provide better protection to wildlife, Mudumalai Wildlife Sanctuary was carved out of this region.During 1977 when the administration of Mudumalai Wildlife Sanctuary was brought under the Wildlife Warden. The 321 km^2 sanctuary area had the following territorial arrangement (Fig. 1).

The sanctuary is surrounded by Bandipur Wildlife Sanctuary of Karnataka on the northern side and by Wynaad Sanctuary of Kerala on its north-western side, cultivated private lands border the southern boundary while on the east lies the Segur Range of Nilgiris north Division. The sanctuary is characterized by various type of forests. Within its limited confines, the area encompasses four botanically distinct tracts. While the western Benne block is represented by rich growth of southern sub-tropical semi evergreen forests, the eastern part constituting Avarallah RF is of scrub growth, the typical of the southern high level thorn forest. The central habitat comprising the Theppakadu and Mudumalai blocks consists of both moist and dry deciduous forest with medium sized trees.

Table 1.1 Mudumalai Wildlife Sanctuary: Range Division

Range	*Head Quarters*	*Area (ha)*
Mudumalai	Kargudi	9660
Kargudi	"	5460
Theppakadu	Theppakadu	8945
Maninagudi	Masinagudi	8035
	Total	**32100**

The terrain is even with a few hillocks scattered about. An idea of Mudumalai country can be gained from the viewpoint on Dodakal Gudda located behind the Upper Kargudi rest house (1007 m). This point commands a panoramic view of the Wynaad on the west, Mysore Plateau on the north and the lofty bluish Nilgiri mountain on the southern side. Moyarbetta with its summit at 1266 m is highest peak in the sanctuary and is better known as Morgan betta, after Major Morgan who spent much of his life from 1853 in Mudumalai in connection with the management of teak forests and who was reported to have stayed in a hut on top of the peak. The grave of Morgan in brick and motor lied on the right side of the road as one goes from Sylvan Lodge to Theppakadu reception center.

The sanctuary area was segregated into four blocks each further divided into several compartments for the purpose of management and working of the forests. At the time of constitution of the blocks, they contained the following extant of forests.

Table 1.2 Mudumalai Wildlife Sanctuary: Block Division

Block	*Area (ha)*	*Compartments*	*No. of compartments*
Theppakadu	7197	1-14	14
Mudumalai	8016	15-28	14
Benne	4613	29-39	21
Dodahatti	6835	Not divided as it has been declared as wilderness zone	

Mudumalai was the stage for intense exploitation of timber wealth for nearly a century commencing from 1850. It was also a popular hunting ground upto the period when Nilgiri Game and Fish Preservation Act was enacted in 1879. The area where wild life was shot indiscriminately spelling doom to all forms of wild life before the implementation of the Act, soon recovered and had supported a thriving and viable stock of animals and birds. The Game Association also took other steps like closing the trunk road between Thorapalli and Theppakadu and a 100 yard strip on either side of the road to shooting in order to discourage motor car poaching. Despite about 21 sq. miles of Mudumalai Range having been declared as on sanctuary in 1940 the area suffered a brief setback during the later part of the Second World War, when the South East Area Command set up a jungle warfare training camp in Kargudi. However, peace returned to the sanctuary with the ending of war.

When the sanctuary was expanded in 1958 to an area of 318.7 sq. km. four checking stations were formed for controlling poaching and shooting of wildlife : near Thorapalli and Kakkanhallah on the Gudalur-Mysore Road, near Masinagudi on the Theppakadu-Masinagudi road and on the interstate boarder on Gudalar-Saltan Battery Road. All these checkposts continue to exist to check the movement of forest produce and to contain the menace of poachers.

Mudumalai remains one of the most popular and largely visited sanctuary in the state. A glimpse of the tourist arrival at the Sanctuary during the last few years would prove the point.

Table 1.3 Details of Visitors Arrival at Mudumalai Wildlife Sanctuary

Year	*Domestic*	*Foreign*	*Total*	*Total revenue (Rs)*
1995-96	87516	7429	94945	2433392
1996-97	91677	9929	101606	2740643
1997-98	82600	8818	91418	2504343
1998-99	528	Nil	528	13798
1999-00	72528	1891	74419	2006381
2000-01	75045	1776	76821	2158651
2001-02	101419	1910	103329	2886172
2002-03	101638	655	101293	2934580

The predominately deciduous forest interspersed with Vayals in the tourism zone provide greater visibility during dry months followed by abundant herbaceous and grass growth in the premonsoon periods thus offering scope for the best wildlife sightings to the tourists who throng the sanctuary through out the year which in effect suggests that there is no closed season in Mudumalai. However the sanctuary is kept closed to tourists during the periods of drought which is usually between February and April when the flow in Moyar river becomes thin, the storage in water holes recede and the area become dry and highly vulnerable to fire.

The relatively easy access of the sanctuary is one reason for its growing popularity. The sanctuary is virtually bisected by the interstate Oty-Mysore highway and could be approached with equal ease from both ends. It is well served by public transport system including inter-state buses. Other modes of transport are easily available for tourists.

At the sanctuary either a vehicle ride or elephant ride or both facilitate forest traverse combined with wildlife viewing. Van rides cover longer distances and possibly more closer approach to wild life animals. The visitors experience in the sanctuary is enhanced by sheer abundance of herbivores like chital, sambhar, occasional back buck and mega herbivores like gour and elephants. When they ride along the narrow roads through the Mudumalai sanctuary which is one of the protected area in the state carnivore sighting is reported to be frequent. Instances are not uncommon that after a ride, tourist groups return to the reception center with joy and register their admiration of the sanctuary and its wildlife.

The sturdy machans were once existent around the major waterholes providing chance to the interested tourists to sit on and watch the forest quietly, which was most productive during summer as most wild animals congregate around the water sources. These viewpoints fabricated on treetops gave way to permanent observation or watch tower at various locations over years enabling the visitors to sit and observe wildlife. The Chief Ministers Watch Tower overlooking the Mayor Falls offer the most enchanting view of the Moyar river cascading in the midst of greenery. Other breath taking viewpoint is Avarallah R F that throws a wider view of the Great Mayor Gorge running 16.5 km from west to east from Chief Minister watch tower to Palathathipatti with its precipitous ridges separating the sanctuary from Karnataka State, that provides a glimpse of one of the deepest water falls of the district, Sigur Falls (86 m).

Forest of Nilgiri Wynaad

The whole of erstwhile Mudumalai and Cherambady ranges and a small area in the north-western corner of the Sigur Range comprises the Nilgiri-Wynaad forests. The average altitude of this tract is about 1000 m. These areas receive their principal precipitation from the south-west monsoon and the total annual rainfall ranges from under 1000 m. as its most part of Doddavatti block as well as in some parts of Mudumalai Block to about 4500 mm in some parts of Charambady range. Depending on the amount of annual rainfall, various sub types of the most deciduous and dry deciduous teak forests occur in different parts of this tract. In areas of high rainfall patches of evergreen and semi evergreen forest occur. The more important types are :

West Coast Tropical Evergreen Forest: These forests occur in small patches in Benne Compartment 31 and comparatively larger patches in the Cherambady range. These are some of the best forest areas both from the point of view of vegetation diversity, high growth as well as luxuriant in the entire state. These areas with above 4500 mm of annual precipitation perhaps receives the highest rainfall in the whole of Tamil Nadu. All tree species that are typical of evergreen forests are represented here. Many storey are recognized along with a great variety of under growth.

West Coast Semi-evergreen Forest : The semi-evergreen forests occur as ecotone zones, between the West Coast tropical evergreen forests and the mixed deciduous forest, as well as isolated patches of greater or lesser extent in the moistest situations in the southern moist mixed deciduous forests. All these areas are generally small in extent and occur sandwiched between the evergreen and the mixed deciduous forest, there is little that is distinctive in it. Indeed, its general characteristics are intermediate in nature between those two types of forest and its floristic is an admixture of them. The same evergreen forest occur in parts of Benne block and the Cherambady range.

Southern Moist Mixed Deciduous Forest : In the Mudumalai and Cherambady ranges, areas receiving annual rainfall ranging from 200 cm to 300 cm with a prolonged dry season due to poor precipitation in the winter month bear this type of forests. The forest, though luxuxiant in growth in entirely leafness during the dry months prior to the south-west monsoon. This is typical of the Nilgiri-Wynaad and its height growth often exceeds 30 meters although there is a great range of variation depending on the quantum of precipitation. These forests carry a variety of economically valuable trees including rosewood, teak, vengai, Terminalias etc.

Southern Secondary Moist Mixed Deciduous Forests : Many areas in the Cherambady range and some in the Benne block of the erstwhile Mudumalai range, which receive rainfall increase of 200 cm per annum, support a mixed deciduous type of forest although the quantum and distribution of rainfall would suggest at least semi-evergreen type as the climax vegetation.

Dry Teak Forest : This forest type is very distinctive from the others that are prevalent in the Nilgiri Wynaad. It is more open than the other types and the height growth is generally poor, being about 10 meters. There is dense undergrowth of tall grasses and in the more favorable localities, lantana an introduced weed is met with. The grasses dry up during dry months resulting in severe annual surface fire in which much of the shrubby undergrowth, whose dry leafs and turing add to the inflammable material, also get burnt wholly or partly. These recurrent arrival fires keep down the vegetation to the lower order that the climatic conditions would warrant. The effect of the fire is reflected in the floristic, for most of the characteristics species which are predominant here are known to survive in localities burnt down by surface fire. The reckless over exploitation of these forests in the past, prior to the period when they were brought under systematic management, also had resulted in lasting gaps which formed the nuclei for the invasion of grasses and weeds, which assisted by the periodic fires, had aggressively spread over the area causing further regression of the vegetation. Teak is an important constituent of these dry teak forest, forming, as it does nearly pure patches in small area and occurring at the other extreme as an occasional component. This type of forest occurs over much of the Dodda Katti block and over considerable area of Mudumalai and Theppakadu blocks.

Secondary grassland : In the Cherambady range which experiences very heavy rainfall, large tracts of grassland extending over several hundred of acres amidst woodlands is a conspicuous feature of the landscape. These lands experience grazing besides annual surface fires. The deep letarite soil gets badly eroded in areas where grazing is rampart and in such areas, the dwarf date palm occurs gregariously amidst the grasses. Often a degraded scrub is met with in the form of savannah. Local inquires about the occasional occurrence of the vestiges of large stumps in the grasslands reveal that these grasslands were the cumulative result of biotic influences of fire and grazing preceded by indiscriminate cutting of trees, which clothed the area in the past.

Teak Plantation of Mudumalai : Establishment of teak plantation as part of teak management in Mudumalai were formed between 1863 and 1875. Not brought under proper thinning they carried an excessive numbers of stems per area for their age thus resulting in unsatisfactory development of the stems. Several small experimental plantations were made on carefully selected sites along roadsides in Mudumalai and Theppakadu Blocks between 1918 and 1922 and some of them have grown well.

Annual planting over small areas had been carried on since 1924 continuously excepting for a short break from 1945 to 1947 during the war years. A regular age gradation is therefore available from 1924 to 1944. Growth in the teak plantations of Mudumalai range being not as good as in the moister regions where teak is grown commonly, the plantations remained open, in the early years. This resulted in overrunning of gaps with weeds chiefly tall grass. The general height growth of the plantations is poor though satisfactory girth is noticed.

Mudumalai Wildlife Sanctuary: Nature-Culture Interface: Linkages between the indigenous people and ecosystem of Nilgiris had been long, intimate and harmonious. For all the local communities the hills were (and are) life giving and sacred. The social organizations of these communities were woven around the management of their environment. Their cultural elaborations were taking place primarily through interaction with their immediate neighborhood. The depended on their immediate natural catchments and reservoirs for their survival and consequently had a genuine stake in conserving their habitat.

Most of the social and cultural practices of the local communities of Nilgiris are traceable to the usage and practice of natural resource. The intensive shola grass land eco-complex of the Nilgiri hills has been a well known sanctuary for the buffalo herds in the past. Both for the Todas and the Badgas, these herds meant subsistence and livelihood or "banda badhuku" and never inseparable. This linkage continues to be fondly recalled in all the prayers. These prayers refer to the bearing of the buffalo calves, yield of milk, filtering of ghee, thick mass of buttermilk, sprouting of new grass, springing forth of water, abundance of honey, ripening of fruits, bursting forth of pulses, and millets, and the subduring of illnesses and diseases. The Toda prayer and the Badaga conservations identify all the samples of trees and thickets, steams and swamps, slopes and summits and peaks and pastures in the neighbourhood and wish them well.

While the Kurumbas always treat the earth and soil as 'Bhooma Thai' or the earth mother, the Badagas went one step further and termed the forest cover as the locks of hair of the "*somi or god*". The Jade Somi or the god of the forest is propitiated once a year with a fire walking ceremony. The fire of the ceremony is made with traditional fire sticks with honey pounded, over the firewood. In the olden days, it is said that a buffalo calf is made to cross over the firewood instead of humans. It is meant to recall the shifting of the pasturage from one side to another to suit the dictates of the season.

The biodiversity in each micro-zone of the Nilgiri hills is also illustrated in the way Badagas perform a gratitude ceremony at the end of their calendar year. Five distinct species of flowers known as kappu hoo or conservation flowers are thrown over the roofs of their houses and their ancestral spirits are propitiated on the occasion for all the environmental protection they have received during the past year. These flowers have differed from zone to zone even within the limits of the hills.

The factor of domestic animal biodiversity is also evident in the Nilgiri environment. The Todas, Badagas and Kotas give salt to the buffaloes and cattle almost two times during the year. The grass turning tasteless after heavy rains or after being frostbitten is said to be made good by offing salt to the animals. Usually the Badaga ceremony is more elaborate than the Toda and the Kota ones. Water courses are also purified during these observances.

The interface between the human and biodiversity is still reflected in the world view of the traditional Nilgiri people. Whether it is the Badaga 'bana – gudi' or the Kurmba 'devar kadu' the sacredness of the environment is still part of their ethos, virtually adhered to in their cultural practices. The Todas too transmit their heritage and no better example can be offered other than their naming ceremony of the newborn. Anytime between the first and the third month on a full moon day, the Toda child is turned to the sky which is followed by the naming ceremony. The child first exposure to the Universe and its elements should take place in the process of their buffaloes at the break of the down. Blessing is offered for the child to see the sky, the moon, stars, the sun, the dairy of buffaloes and so on.

Table 1.4 Conservation of Forestry in Nilgiris

	Area (km^2)	*Core Zone*	*Manipulation Zone*	*Tourism Zone*
Nilgiris Biosphere Reserve Mudumalia WL & NP	321.1	96.0 (29.90)	163.1 (50.77)	62.0 (19.31)

Anti-poaching Efforts in Nilgiri

As the forest of Nilgiri is endowed with rich wildlife and in such as the forest areas have common frontiers with the neighbouring states of Kerala and Karnataka, wildlife becomes susceptible for illegal hunting. In order to stop the illegal hunting practices, the Department has initiated several measures. Historically the high altitude forests in the district were brought under strict surveillance so as to minimize the impact of interstate poaching gangs. One of the examples of the early anti poaching initiatives was the employment of the tribal men to guard the vulnerable points that were difficult to be perambulated by field staff on a regular basis. Forest Dept. has established antipoaching network covering some of the most sensitive wildlife populated tracts of the district which otherwise are inaccessible and are inspected by the field staff in a less frequent manner. In such location permanent camps came to be established by deploying the tribal youth who are familiar with the terrain with the mandate to intensively walk about the areas, keep constant vigil so as to contain poaching in an effective manner. These camps work round the clock where the campers are provided with communication facility in form of wireless and the arms and ammunition required to counter any poaching gang. The communication enables the inmate of the camp to reach the range headquarters immediately seeking additional contingent of staff in case of emergencies. The antipoaching staff is given the specific task of covering certain extent of the forest beat extending approx about 10 km^2 which is regularly done by camp inmates. Known widely as the Mudumalai model this system was put in force around 1999 which is still in operation.

To ensure wholehearted involvement of the local tribal youth in this task, the Department meets the living expenses of the campers by providing their daily ration during the work time besides giving them their daily wages. To provide extra strength to the temporary workers engaged in these camps, the Department has covered the daily wages under the Jantha group insurance scheme. This system has brought down the poaching pressure throughout the forest areas in the Nilgiri by supplementing the efforts of the field staff (Sekar, T: 2004).

Ecological Setting of Mudumalai

Physical Setting: Geology and Physiography

Nilgiri Wynaad in general and Mudumalai in particular has been a place for living of the different tribal groups and non-tribal population since long time. Each population has been struggling to survive in their particular ecological setting with the help of their own cultural know how. In this process somewhere they have modified the physical landscape or somewhere they have adopted it for better survival. Keeping this in mind the present exercise deals with physical and cultural landscape of man in Mudumalai. Since man is an integral part of the complex Nilgiri ecosystem, not a single environmental factor is without some relevance to human aspects and vice-versa (Hockings : 1989 : 20).

Mudumalai is located between $76^{0}24'$ and $76^{0}36'$ longitude and $11^{0}42'$ latitude on the meeting point of the Eastern and Western Ghats. These two mountain ranges run parallel along the coast of the Arabian Sea and Bay of Bengal. Lower in elevation Mudumalai forming a part of Nilgiri plateau has an undulating topography with an average height of 1000 meters from the mean sea level. Surrounded by Berambadi Reserve Forest in the north, Bandipur Reserve Forest in the east, Srimadurai and Cherumuli Revenue villages in the south and Benne Reserved Forest in the west this area is sparely populated with human settlements at Teppakadu, Kargudi, Thorapalli and nearly 11 settlements located in the wet lands between Namkond Betta in the north to Bosepara in the south.

Geologically Mudumalai belongs to archcan continental landmass of Indian peninsula composed of pre-cambrian mainly metamorphic rocks (Gneisses, Charnrockites, Crystalline Schist's). Due to continental drift of the Indian shield which until Jurassic times was a part of ancient Gondwanaland and coincident with the Himalayan arogenis during the Cretaceous and Tertiary periods, geotectonic movements in the southern Deccan resulted in its fragmentation and in vertical dislocations along the faults which later on become the course of rivers of the area. Physiographically Mudumalai has three uprising. These uprising are followed by board depression through which streams flow. The first uprising is on northern portion forming Daddakatti Mukku peak with an elevation of 1053 meters from the sea level. This peak forms a dividing range between the north flowing river and the south flowing river with slope towards west. The important stream is Doddakatti Halla and Dodda Halla. South of these two streams the second uprise occurs which again forms a chain of four ridges such as Angattibath Betla (1181 meters from sea level) followed by Jainbari Betta (1146 meters) a spur of a height of 1130 meters from mean sea level and lastly Boli Gudde with a peak of 1075 meters. These four continuous uprising forms another divide for the hill streams south of Angattibath Betta and there is another uprising with a height of 1188 meters from mean sea level. This uprising along with another one uprising located little east decides the course of the hill streams. Because from here there are two slopes one towards the east which becomes the course of Imbar Halla which originates near the uprising with a height of 1081 metres flows towards east and meet the Kekkan Halla which is a tributary of Moyar River. On the extreme western head of this hill stream is located the first wetland of Mudumalai with a settlements of Panekolli, Japur Hulkalu and Mandakamola. Moving east of these settlements there lies a big swampy land which was under cultivation prior to 1988 after which the forest department is not allowing cultivation. South of this, there is another uprise with a height of 1094 metres. South of this uprise the hillstream flows towards south-east forming the second wetland Mudumalai with settlements of Mandekerai, Vetta Vayal and Nagampalli. South of the second wetland there is another spur of 1058 meters from the mean seal level which again acts as a dividing line between the hill streams following towards south forming the third wetland of Mudumalai. This wetland can be approached from

Thorappali which connects the settlements of Nambikunnu, Linganakolli, Kelakolli, Ninganakolli and Pilakoli while the other settlements of Kuvakolli and Kallangeri can be approached from Bosepara.

Drainage : Drainage lines hold particular significance in the study area. Not only do they provide redeeming topographic breaks in the general undulating topography and provide sub-regional or even local uniqueness and individuality to the different landmarks but also govern to a great extent, the human occupance of land, particularly the settlements (Singh, R.L. 1968). The surface of Mudumalai is undulating and hence the hill streams which use to carry off their drainage meander with comparatively gentle fall through rounded forested hills or uplands. If we look at Map-3 then three drainage pattern emerges each of them following towards three different directions. The first drainage pattern which originates around the hill of Daddakali Mukku flow towards west draining the water of the northern Mudumalai with two important hill streams Doddak and Dodda Halla. These two streams join together at a spur (890 meter msl) moves towards west and meet Marvin Halla at the spur of 878 meter msl moves further west and joins Nugu Hole which is a tributary of River Kaveri. The second drainage line originating from the south of the chain of spur like Angattibath Betta in the west to Jainbari Betta in east moves downwards till Panakolli settlement and from here moves towards east taking the name of Imbar Halla. Imbar Hall draining the water of central Mudumalai meets Kekkan Halla near Pundenkeri Gudda peak. Kekkan Hella meets Moyar River further east. This drainage system forms the second important and biggest wet land of Mudumalai village. The third drainage system which originates on the western border of the Mudumalai village moves east forming the third wetland of the village fanning out towards east and taking the name of Bidar Halla. Near the spur of 879 meter msl. Hamballa Todu joins Bidar Halla which later flows towards south-east and meet Moyar River south of Abhayaranyam Forest Rest House. Apart from these three drainage system there are numerous small streams which originates on the wooded slopes and disappears in the swamps of Mudumalai.

Climate : Climate along with its two important variable temperature and rainfall forms life support system for any region and Mudumalai is no exception. The climate of Mudumalai is characterised by a rhythms of seasons which is produced by the south-west and north-east monsoon. On the basis of this phenomena of monsoon winds four seasons or periods can be observed in Mudumalai: the North East (NE) monsoon period from December to March, the first inter-monsoon period from April to May, the South West monsoon period (SW) from June to September and the second inter -monsoon period from October to November (Hockings, Paul : 1989). Before we go into the details of the four seasons Table 1.5 is being given to show the minimum and maximum temperature and rainfall which is recorded at Gudalur.

Table 1.5 Temperature and Rainfall

	Month	*Max Tem*	*Min Temp (in centigrade)*	*Ranifall (cm)*
II	April	30.0	16.3	52.8
	May	30.9	14.7	8.2
III	June	25.5	17.0	238.4
	July	23.8	16.1	417.4
	August	24.6	15.7	248.1
	September	25.9	15.4	74.9
IV	October	25.0	15.34	226.4
	November	25.5	13.8	38.8
I	December	26.5	9.7	9.6
	January	28.5	10.4	0.0
	February	29.2	11.4	0.0
	March	31.0	12.0	6.8

North East monsoon period (December to March) : During this period Mudumalai falls within the northern hemispheric trade wind belt which result into fair weather condition with temperature tending to raise with minimum or no rainfall. From

December to March the Temperature varies between 26^{0}C (Minimum) to 31°C (maximum). Mudumalai experiences hot season during this period and hence the Sanctuary is closed. This year the Sanctuary was closed from 1st March to 15th April 2005. The first intermonsoon period (April – May) : Climatalogically this period is transitional in nature because in April NE monsoon gradually disintegate while the SW monsoon gets slowly established. The maximum temperature remains at 30°C with occasional pre-monsoon shower. These pre-monsoon help the temperature to fall. However these two months are also hot month. But as the seasons (from tourists points of view) starts Madumalai Wildlife Sanctuary gears up to receive the tourist flow from the surrounding regions because the surrounding Coimbatore plain or Malabar remains hot during this period. After long hot spell and rainless period the first shower in April give relief to the local people specially the Mandadan Chettis who starts their agricultural operation for cultivating paddy. The surrounding tea estates get bumper crops of tea as the plucking is maximum. The rainfall also acts as a decisive for the coffee growers because it is also known as coffee blossom showers.

The southwest monsoon period (June – September) : After May there is a major change in the weather condition due to onset or burst of SW monsoon over the Mudumalai. During this period the monsoon winds originating from the southern hemisphere moves towards north-east evaporating large quantity of water while crossing Arabian Sea and bursts on the slopes of Nilgiri Wynaad after crossing the Western Ghat. Due to the monsoon winds of Bay of Bengal Nilgiri Wynaad also receives rainfall. Due to heavy rainfall temperature goes down considerably and July -August suppose to have the lowest temperature (23°C to 24°C). On the other hand July receives the highest rainfall of the year (417 mm). The heavy rainfall which starts from the month of June continues upto September. Thus this period from June to September can be termed as the rainy seasons in Mudumalai. The forest of Mudumalai becomes lush green. The paddy fields becomes green and coffee plants become laden with green berries.

The second Inter-monsoon period (Oct.-Nov.) : During this period rain fade away though in the month of October

Mudumalai gets rain due to retreating monsoon. Temperature has a tendency to increase due to position of the sun in the southern hemisphere. Temperature during this period remains at about 25°C (maximum).

Soil : Geographically speaking soil of Mudumalai can be classified into two broad category. Wet land and Dry land. In wetland soil loam contain is high and it is wet throughout the year. These soil are mainly located in the flat low land areas of Mudumalai distributed along the hill streams. Due to heavy rainfall the finer particles of soil particularly the clay colloids are carried down to the foot of the hills and gets deposited due to poor drainage resulting in the formation of the wetland with swampy character. These swamps are dried up by the Chettis and now have become fertile land for cultivation of paddy during the rainy season where as vegetable in the dry period with the help of well or lift irrigation. Dry land soil is generally red in colour where sand contain is very high. In Mudumalai nearly 98.79% of the soil fall in this category where as only 1.2% in under wetland soil.

Cultural Setting

Cultural landscape is the artificial landscape that a community create on the surface of the earth crust by inhabiting it. Every inhabited area has a cultural landscape fashioned from the physical landscape and each uniquely reflects the culture that created it. Landscape mirrors culture and much can be learned about the community by looking at the cultural landscape which the group has created (Jordan & Rowntree :1982) . The content of cultural landscape are its settlement pattern and landuse pattern. We will try to discus these two important variables specially in the light of ecological change which the group / community are bringing on the land surface due to its long occupation.

Man's distribution on the village map of Mudumalai has three locations where concentration of population can be seen. The first concentration is along the location of the wetlands, second concentration near Kargudi and the third concentration is near Teppakadu. The first concentration has a mixed population where the Mandadan Chettis lives with the Paniyan, in the second location Paniyan are not found, Katu Naicken and Irula are found. In the

Table 1.6 People and Settlement

Sl No.	*Year*	*No of Household*	*Total population*		
			Person	*Male*	*Female*
1.	1921	113	603	363	240
2.	1941	129	572	325	247
3.	1951	141	841	476	365
4.	1961	--	-	-	-
5.	1971	-	916	486	430
6.	1981	-	-	-	-
7.	1991	-	1342	695	647
8.	2001	325	1411	709	702

Table 1.7 Mudumalai: Growth of Population in Ratio Percentum

Sl No.	*Year*	*Percentage*	*Male*	*Female*
1.	1921	10.60	11.80	9.10
2.	1941	10.06	10.04	9.40
3.	1951	14.70	15.50	13.88
4.	1941	-	-	-
5.	1971	16.11	15.90	16.30
6.	1981	-	-	-
7.	1991	23.60	22.75	24.60
8.	2001	24.80	23.20	26.70

third location, Katunaicken, Betta Kumba and Irula are found. If we look at the historical aspect of the population distribution it can be noticed that the tribal population: Paniyan, Katunaicken, Betta Kurumba and Irula group have been living in the Nilgiri Wynaad where as the Mandadan Chettis have come from outside and have settled long back and today they have become the local inhabitant of the region sharing their way of life with the Paniyan tribal group. However for understanding the population growth we have constructed two tables. Table 1.6 and 1.7 on the basis of data collected from the census records of Nilgiri district from 1921 onwards. We do not have the population figures for 1931, 1961 and 1981 as these are not available with the Taluk office. In Table 1.6 we have presented the population on male and female as recorded in the census records. But Table 1.7 is constructed on the basis of Table 1.6 showing the increase of population in different census period in ratio percentage. Following considerations appear to emerge from the examination of Table 1.7.

(a) In the year 1941 growth of population of Mudumalai village has come down negligible due to various disease. Malaria is very common in Nilgiri Wynaad.

(b) 1951 census period has recorded an increase of nearly 4.70% over the period of 1921 which was marked by opening up the Mudumalai reserve forest for timber exploitation and tribal people were brought here to work in the forest.

(c) The upward growth trend continue to move upward in 1971. However from 1991 the population has a sharp increase due to development of Teppakadu as a tourist center as well as Chettis population also increased due to natural process.

(d) The sex ratio is 990 female per 1000 males for 1991 which is supposed to be high. This is mainly due to the fact that the population residing in Mudumalai mainly lives with their family as the economy is traditional in nature.

Though the population of Mudumalai is living under constant threat of being evicted the growth of population is said to be satisfactory.

Table 1.8 Distribution of Population According to Location

Sl No.	Location	OR House (surveyed)	Total population	Male	Female
1.	Wetland No. 1	21	131	75	56
2.	Wetland No. 2	45	203	102	101
3.	Wetland No. 3	18	77	45	32
4.	Kargudi	12	48	26	22
5.	Teppakadu / A paddi	31	144	66	78
6.	Teppakadu / Light paddy	46	180	91	89
7.	Teppakadu Anna paddi	60	233	116	117
8.	Total	233	1016	521	495

Table 1.9 Population According to Location in Ratio Percentum

Sl. No.	Location	ORHouse (surveyed)	Total population	Male	Female
1.	Wetland No. 1	25.75	22.93	22.26	23.63
2.	Wetland No. 2	19.71	19.98	19.57	20.40
3.	Wetland No. 3	19.31	17.71	17.46	19.97
4.	Kargudi	13.30	14.17	14.39	15.76
5.	Teppakadu / A paddi	9.0	12.89	12.66	12.89
6.	Teppakadu / Light padi	7.72	7.58	8.63	6.46
7.	Teppakadu Anna padi	5.15	4.72	4.99	4.44
8.	Total				

Note : ORH = Occupied Residential House

Following considerations may be noted after looking at table 1.9

(a) Teppakadu Anna Padi ranks first having 25.75 % of the total household surveyed in Mudumalai village. Teppakadu Light

Padi ranks second with 19.71% of the household while Wetland No. 2 ranks third with 19.31 % of the household surveyed. Teppakadu Anna Padi and Teppakadu Light Padi are tribal dominated settlements where as Wetland no. 2 is dominated by the Mandadan Chettis.

(b) From total population point of view Teppakadu Anna Padi ranks first with 22.93% the total surveyed population in Mudumalai followed by 19.98% of the Wetland no. 2. On the third position remains Teppakadu Light Padi.

Communities in Mudumalai

Table 1.10 Mudumalai Caste / Communities Population

Sl. No.	*Caste/community*	*Total*	*Male*	*Female*	*Remarks*
1.	Mandadan Chettis	265	133	132	
2.	Paniyan	161	95	66	
3.	Betta Kurumbas	441	216	225	
4.	Kattu Naicken	107	54	53	
5.	Irula	42	23	19	
	Total	1016	521	495	

Table 1.11 Mudumalai Caste / Community-wise Population in Ratio Percentum

Sl No.	*Caste/community*	*Total*	*Male*	*Female*	*Remarks*
1.	Mandadan Chettis	43.40	41.45	45.45	
2.	Paniyan	26.08	25.52	26.66	
3.	Betta Kurumbas	15.84	18.23	13.83	
4.	Kattu Naicken	10.53	10.36	10.70	
5.	Irula	4.13	4.41	3.83	
	Total	-	-	-	

Nilgiri Wynaad in general and Mudumalai in particular is sparsely populated area of the Nilgiri district. According to 2001 the total population of Mudumalai is 1141 of which 709 are males and 702 are females. The total geographical area is 188.86 sq.km. So density of population comes to about 7.50 person per km^2 where as Gudalar Taluk density comes to about 136.02 person per km^2. The reason for being sparsely populated is this that Mudumalai is covered with thick forest where agricultural land is less. Whatever agricultural land are available agriculture is difficult to practice due to the unfavourable environmental conditions. Secondly Mudumalai forms a part of the Nilgiri Biosphere Reserve and human habitation is not allowed. However 37.3 of the total population are scheduled tribe. Apart from these tribal population Mandadan Chettis forms the major caste population of Mudumalai village. We are presenting below a brief account of the communities in Mudumalai village.

Betta Kurumbas : Among the tribal groups living in Mudumalai Betta Kurumbas ranks first. According to Household survey 43.40 of the total population is of the Betta Kurumbas who lives in the Teppakadu settlement near the Mudumalai Wild Life Sanctuary Reception Centre. Betta Kurumbas are also known as wood cutting Kurumbas. Betta Kurumbas were brought to Teppakadu by the forest department for clearing the forest and transporting the wood to other places. Today they live in Forest built houses in Teppakadu settlement doing cooli work in Gudalur area. Cutting of wood is completely banned after 1986 so for them there is no work in forest department after 1986.

Paniyan: Second largest tribal group in Mudumalai are the Paniyan who live along with the Mandadan Chettis doing mostly agriculture labour. As they have no agriculture land they were bonded labour of the mandadan chettis. After the abolition of bonded labour system they have become free to work any where. Due to the close binding with Chettis, the Paniyan still stick with the Mandadan Chettis household. Only difference is this that the Mandadan Chettis has to pay in cash for the labour the Paniyan gives to the Mandadan Chettis household. Of the surveyed household Paniyan consists 15.84% of the total population. Paniyan are dark skinned tribes short in structure with broad nose and curly or wavy hair. Socially they are considered to be lowest in the hierarchical order.

The word Paniyan means labour and they believe that their original occupation was agriculture and even today they do bulk of the agricultural work of the Chettis. The woman collect variety of tuber and roots from the forest for their subsistence. The Paniyan live in group and their settlements are found near the Chettis household or land given by the Chettis or other type of Government land.

Kattu Naicken : Kattu Naicken were brought to Teppakadu by the Briteshers to work in the forest department specially as a Mahaut or elephant keeper, trainer and even the elephant trapper. The total population of Kattu Naicken at jeppakadu settlement is 107 spread in two areas-A Padi and Light Padi. Kattu Naicken have the system of traditional headman known as Maran who use to take all the social decision. Generally the family is nucleus however joint family has also been found where married adult live together with their parents though cooking is done individually. Presently work in the forest department is sinking which has forced the Kattu Naicken to go for cooli work near Gudalur or Masinagudi.

Irula : Irula only form 4.41% of total tribal population of Mudumalai village and are scattered in settlements ; Kargudi and Teppakadu. Through they are important tribe of Nilgiri but in Gudatur their presence is not significant. Basically they were shifting cultivators but now they do daily wage in the forest as and when work is available and also go out for cooli work. One Irula family of Kargudi has planted tea in Bosepara area of Srimadurai village.

Mandadan Chettis : Apart from the above stated four tribal population, Mandadan Chettis which falls into backward caste are the wetland cultivators of Nilgiri Wynaad concentrated into the wetlands of Mudumalai forms nearly 25.52% of the total surveyed population. Mandadan Chettis are hardworking farmers of the wetland where they grow paddy with the help of their Paniyan labourers. Mandadan Chettis are settled in Mudumalai. Nellakota, Cherumulli, Devala, Padantarai and Gudalur Revenue villages of Gudalur Taluk of Nilgiri district. They construct their houses on the upland so that they can keep watch on their agricultural field. Mandadan Chettis speak corrupt Canarese follow the Makkatayam (inheritance of property and rights through son) law. At present they speak Tamil also. Paddy is the main crop of the Mandadan

Chettis followed by ragi. They grow different kinds of vegetables and banana in their wetlands. At present ginger is becoming very important cash crop of the village. They are very hospitable and are looking forward for a good future in Gudalur though outcast by the migrant population who have come to work in the plantation agriculture.

Land and Land Use : In the ecological setting land and land utilization pattern is the most important component because it forms the basis of economic and social life of people living in that particular space. At the same time land is the most important components of the life support system and its use and misuse is directly related with the development of the people concern. We will not go into the details of the model for land use, however we will focus on land and its utilization by the people of Mudumalai village. However it must be noted that the people of Mudumalai have two type of economic opportunities : One who live in Teppakadui and Kargudi settlements and have no scope of agriculture as they do not have land where as the people who are living in the wetland areas who are primarily dependent on agriculture.

Table 1.12 Land Classification

Sl. No	*Classification*	*Area in ha*	*%*	*Remarks*
1.	Reserve Forest	18649.20	98.77	
2.	Assessed Dry	34.16	0.18	
3.	Poromboke	5.12	0.02	
4.	Total	18688.57	98.97	
5.	Royatwari Patta	165.73	0.87	Wetland 'Nanje'
6.	Royatwari Patta	26.59	0.13	Dry land 'Punje'
	G. Total	**18880.89**		

Land in Mudumalai has two basic classification Patta land and non-Patta land or forest lease land. At the present moment non-Patta land or forest lease land do not exist because forest department has suspended giving lease to the people of wetland from 1986. So the people of wetland has to depend on Patta land only. Patta land has two classification – Wetland and dry-land. Wetland are those land which remains wet throughout the year and with high level of clay content where as dry land are dry throughout the year with high level of sand content. In Table 1.12 land classification has been presented. Following considerations appear to emerge from the analysis of Table 1.12

(a) As we have stated above the land of Mudumalai may be divided into two class : Government land and Royatwari Land.

(b) Government land has three classification : Reserve forest, Assessed Dry or Anaadinam and Poramboke.

(c) Reserve forest concide with the Mudumalai Wild Life Sanctuary. Mudumalai Wild Life Sanctuary extends upto Nellakotta village of Gudalur Taluk and Masinagudi village of Ooty Taluk. However the present study is confined only to Mudumalai revenue village of Gudalur Taluk.

(d) Royatwari Patta land are those land from where Government use to collect land tax. It has two classification : Royatwari Patta land – Wetland or locally known as 'Nanje' and Royatwari Patta land – Dry land locally known as 'Punje'.

(e) Reserve Forest occupies nearly 98.77 of the total land of Mudumalai village. This is mainly due to the Mudumalai Wild Life Sanctuary and National Park. Mudumalai Wild Life Sanctuary forest is the best forest of Tamil Nadu. Drained by several hill streams and the undulating landscape support good growth of forest. Due to this features it has declared as a part of Nilgiri Biosphere Reserve.

(f) In the Government land category second comes Assessed dry land. Assessed dry land are those lands which has been assessed but tax is not collected. Generally Govt. houses and other building falls under this category. It has nearly 34.16 ha of land (0.18%) under it uses. Locally it is called as Annadinam and it has been encroached at many places for cultivation of plantation crop specially coffee.

(g) Under the Poramboke category percentage of land is very negligible: 0.02 Under this category roads generally fall. Apart from forest roads no other road are allowed to be built. As the state highway (Ooty-Mysore) crosses through the Wild Life Sanctuary it acts as a starting point for various forest roads. There are three important forest all weather roads which originates from three different points from Ooty-Maysore Road like, Teppakadu and Kargudi and the Thorapalli road in the east while on the western side Bosepara acts as an originating point for forest roads which connects the three wetlands and terminate near Mudumalai forest Rest House.

(h) As we have mentioned earlier apart from Government land there are Royatwari Patta land which has two categories: Wetland locally called 'Nanje' and dry land locally known as 'Punje'. Wetlands are the most fertile land of the village Mudumalai. Spread over in 3 patches wetland are formed in the valley bottom where particles of good soil is deposited by the hill streams coming down from the surrounding hills. Paddy is the main crop because they are rainfed area. However wherever water is available through hill streams or dug well local vegetable are grown followed by banana and ginger. The wet land are in the possession of Mandadan Chettis who do agriculture with the help of Paniyan tribal labourer braving wildlife. Mandadan Chettis work hard to get their crops. Apart from Royatwari Patta wetland there was forest lease wetland where paddy was grown by the Chittis. But forest department has stopped the practice of giving lease from 1986. These wetland have been transformed into elephant grass land. Royatwari patta wet land has a total area of 165.73 hectare which come to 0.87% of the total geographical land of Mudumalai Revenue village.

(i) Royatwari Patta dry land locally called as 'Punje' has a very negligible area under its occupation that is 0.13% of the total geographical area of Mudumalai village. Dry land are generally occupied by the house sites and kitchen garden where vegetables are grown

Mudumalai revenue village though covered by thick forest forming a part of Madumalai Wildlife Sanctuary and National Park has no diversified land use pattern. Due to restriction imposed by the Forest Department growth of agriculture is not encouraging here. Forest Department wants to shift the population of Mudumalai to some other place in Gudalur Taluk but when, only future can say. But it is certain, the Mandadan Chettis and the tribal population living in the Sanctuary are the most suffer due to this uncertainty.

Anthropogenic Threats: Development of Eco-Tourism

The Mudumalai Wild Life Sanctuary under which the Mudumalai revenue village falls is one of the largest protected areas for biological conservation in the Western Ghat region of Tamil Nadu. Being a part of Nilgiri Biosphere Reserve it is also a global biodiversity hot spot. The Sanctuary supports rich floral and fauna species diversity. There is increasing threats to the virgin forest cover of this Sanctuary due to location of 4 villages on the southern boundary with increasing plantation agriculture. The Sanctuary has in itself 5 settlements : Kargudi, Teppakadu and 3 wetlands where 11 settlements are located with approximate 233 household fully depended on Mudumalai Wild Life Sanctuary for their day to day livelihood. Apart from the settled settlements there is a continuous threat due to increasing number of tourist visiting the Wild Life Sanctuary. Here we will try to deal with these threats firstly by looking into the development of eco- tourism in Mudumalai and secondly by looking into the settled population which lives in the Sanctuary itself.

Eco-Tourism has been flourishing as an industry for the last few decades. Eco-Tourism is seen as a boon for the developing country where less explored diversity of wildlife and landscape all attract tourists from all over the globe. Eco-Tourism at the one hand is bringing the process of development to the area but at the same time uncontrolled growth of Eco-Tourism has done significant environmental and social damages.

Mudumalai Wild Life Sanctuary and National Park is located in Gudalur Taluk of Nilgiri District of Tamilnadu. The Nilgiris – one of the oldest mountain ranges, older than the Himalayas is located at the trijunction of Tamil Nadu, Kerala and Karnataka and is a part of the Western Ghat. Ooty the queen of Hill station is the district headquarter. There are 3 more tourist spots : Coonor – 19 km from Ooty, Kotagiri 31 km from Ooty and Gudalur 50 km from Ooty making the Nilgiris the most visited area of South India. Nilgiris is India's first biosphere. It has been declared as one of the 14 hot spots of the world due to its unique bio-diversity. Rolling grassland, dense shoals, waterfalls, streams, lakes, vast expanses of tea and coffee plantation, interspersed with vegetable gardens and golden rice fields, spectacular viewpoints, vast expense of virgin forest, fabulous trekking trails, spell binding sunrise and sunset, pollution free atmosphere, mist, clouds, fog, clear sky, Nilgiris present a truly breathtaking view of nature. Among the many tourist sites which are visited by tourist Mudumalai Wildlife Sanctuary is the most important. It can be visited from Ooty itself on local site seeing programme or the tourist can stay at Masinagudi or Gudalur and visit the Sanctuary. Apart from these, forest department has Rest Houses with moderate facility at Teppakadu and Masinagudi where the tourist can stay and enjoy the nature calmly and quietly.

Gudalur is a town of the same named Taluk and is a land of cultural trinity because people from Karnataka, Kerala and Tamil Nadu have made there home in Gudalur apart from the tribal population like Paniyan, Kurumbas, Irulas etc. Gudalur is at the foot hills of the Nilgiris 50 km. west of Ooty on Ooty Mysore highway. Mudumalai Wildlife Sanctuary starts at a distance of 6 km from Gudalur however the reception Center is located at Teppakadu 17 km away on the northern side of Gudalur town again on Ooty Mysore highway.

Mudumalai Wildlife Sanctuary(MWS) is located where the Nilgiri Hills the offshoot of the Western Ghats meet the Eastern Ghats. The MWS has varied type of landforms : flat land, undulating park land, open grass land, swamps, valleys and nullas. The Moyar River which flows on the south-eastern side of the Mudumalai Revenue village collects almost half of the water of the Sanctuary and move towards east and meet the Bhavani River down the hills. Bhavani River moves further and meets River Carvery north of Erode.

Tourist Infrastructure at Mudumalai Wildlife Sanctuary and its surrounding areas

One of the aim of the Biosphere Reserve is to promote tourism so that a general awareness can be created among the common people for biodiversity protection and conservation. Tourist flow has to be properly supported by development of infrastructure like hotel accommodation, better means of transport system etc. At the same time attention must be given so that there is no adverse effect of tourism on the flora, fauna and local inhabitants of the tourist spot. So along with developing awareness among the Tourist the primary objective of the forest managers is to see that the Sanctuary provides a safe and proper habitat for the wildlife. Forest department has increased its control on tourism in the form of regulated tourism in the Wildlife Sanctuary. Number of Tourists visiting the Sanctuary is increasing day by day as Mudumalai Wildlife Sanctuary is located on the Ooty-Mysore highway and can be easily approachable from Ooty and Mysore the two important destination in South India for domestic tourists and foreign tourists. To meet the requirements let us look at the infrastructure available in the Sanctuary and also at Gudalur and Masinagudi.

Table 1.13 Forest Department Managed RH / Lodges etc. at Teppakadu

1. Abhayarainiam RH*	4 suits (Double Beds)
2. Abhayarainiam RH*	4 suits (Double Beds)
3. Sylvan Lodge*	4 suits (Double Beds)
4. Teppakaddu Log house*	4 suits (Double Beds)
5. Minivet Dormitory	8 Beds
6. Morgan Dormitory	8 Beds
7. Peacock Dormitory	50 Beds
At Masinagudi	
1. Masinagudi RH	4 Suits (Double Beds)
2. Masinagudi Log House	4 Suits (Double Beds)
Government of Tamil Nadu	
1. Hotal Tamil Nadu (With Restaurant)	4 Suits (Double Beds)
(European Toilet system with Restaurant).	8 Beds

Table 1.14 Private Hotels / Lodges at Gudalur

Sl No. 1	*Name of the Hotel / Lodge (2)*	*Accommodation*		
		Single Bed Room	*Double Bed Room*	*Total beds*
1.	Rock Garden Holiday Resort *		6	12
2.	Star Lodge		8	21
3.	Charms Lodge		6	12
4.	Surya Lodge		7	14
5.	Nilgiri Holiday Resort	4	6	16
6.	Hotel Dwaraka *	1	4	9
7.	Venus Lodge *	15	13	44
8.	Hotel Anusuya *	8	15	38
9.	Darsan International	13	13	39
10.	Hill View Lodge	7	13	34
11.	Everest Lodge	1	5	12
12.	Reney Lodge	9	11	33
13.	Blue Hill Lodge	21	17	60
14.	Hotel Maharani *	5	20	54
15.	SS Lodge		11	26
	Total			**424**

* Restaurants attached.

Apart from the above there are nearly 3 Resorts and 5 hotels lodges in Masinagudi and 8 Resorts in Bokkapuran very near to Masinagudi

(a) Looking at Table 14 .1 it can be stated that all together there are 122 beds available in Government sectors Rest House / Hotel which are located in the Mudumalai Wild Life Sanctuary itself. There are restaurants attached with the Rest House / Hotel. Booking are done at Ooty as well Mudumalai Wild Life Sanctuary reception centers.

(b) In the private sector 424 beds are available (except Masinagudi area) located at Gudalur which is 17 km away from the Mudumalai Wild Life Sanctuary reception center. Out of 15 Hotels / Lodges only 5 have restaurant facilities. The accommodation in the private sector are moderate in type.

(c) At Mudumalai Wild Life Sanctuary 5 vehicles are available to the tourists to take them inside the Sanctuary on prescribed route and time.

(d) At Teppakadu reception center Forest department provide 2-4 elephants daily for jolly ride for the tourist in the morning and evening.

(e) STD facility is available at Teppakadu along with bus stand from where the tourist can go to Ooty as well as Mysore and Calicut etc.

(f) At Gudalur there is a Cinema Hall and number of eating as well as shopping centers where tourists can spent time.

(g) Taxi and Jeep are available at Gudalur or Teppakadu itself for quick transport.

Growth of Tourist at Mudumalai Wild Life Sanctuary

Located at the foothills of Nilgiri Mountain Mudumalai WS has attracted tourist from India and abroad due to its luxurious growth of forest, diverse flora and fauna and favourable climate.

Table 1.15 Growth of Tourism in Mudumalai Wildlife Sanctuary

Sl. No.	*Year*	*Domestic*	*Foreign*	*Total*	*Remark (Revenue card)Rs.*
1.	1995-96	87516	7249	94765	2433392
2.	1996-97	91677	9929	101606	2740643
3.	1997-98	82600	8818	91418	2504343
4.	1998-99	528	Nil	528	13798
5.	1999-00	72528	1891	74419	2006381
6.	2000-01	75045	1776	76821	2158651
7.	2001-2002	101419	1910	103329	2886172
8.	2002-2003	101638	655	101293	2934580
9.	2003-2004	111389	648	112037	3856287
10.	Total	724340	32876	757216	19125188

Source : Office of the Wild Life Warden, Mudumalai Wild Life Sanctuary, Ooty.

Table 1.15 indicates the growth of Tourist flow to MWS during different periods. It can be noticed that in the year 1998-99 tourist visiting to MWS is very low. This is mainly due to the drought condition when the MWS was closed for tourist. On the basis of Table 1.15 we have prepared Table 1.16 in Ratio per centum for better understanding.

Table 1.16 Growth of Tourist in Ratio Percentum

Sl. No.	*Year*	*Domestic*	*Foreign*	*Remark*
1.	1995-96	12.08	22.04	9.87
2.	1996-97	12.65	30.00	13.41
3.	1997-98	11.40	26.82	12.07
4.	1998-99	0.07	-	0.06

(Contd.)

(Contd.)

Sl. No.	*Year*	*Domestic*	*Foreign*	*Remark*
5.	1999-00	10.01	5.75	9.82
6.	2000-01	10.36	5.40	10.14
7.	2001-02	14.00	5.80	13.64
8.	2002-03	14.03	1.99	13.37
9.	2003-04	15.37	1.97	14.79

Following consideration emerges if we analyse Table 1.16 and Fig 1.14.

(a) Total number of Tourists have increased but the curve demonstrates two or three important features : From 1995-96 to 1997-98 there is a marginal increase in tourist visiting MWS but during the period 1998-99 there is a sharp decline. This is mainly due to the fact that MWS was closed for tourist due to severe drought. After 1998-99 there is again a sharp increase and the trend continued up to 2003-2004.

(b) Domestic tourist also tend to visit Mudumalai during this period with a sharp decline of tourist growth during 1998-99. However the Domestic tourist growth has a higher rate in comparison to total growth and foreign tourists.

(c) Foreign tourist has an even growth pattern because before 1998-99 there is a peak growth 30% but when it decline during the period 1998-99 and it failed to attain that growth rate. However after 2001-2002 there is again a sharp decline in tourist growth rate. Local enquiry revels that foreign tourists visiting Mudumalai Wildlife Sanctuary prefers to stay at various Resorts which have come up around Masinagudi and Bokkapuram. It may be noted that Masinagudi is only 5 km away from Teppakadu.

Nature and Pattern of Tourist in MWS : Tourist visiting MWS are coming from different destination in India and abroad. We have interviewed 92 tourist for this purpose. Result are as follows.

Table 1.17 Type of Tourist

Sl No.	*State / Foreign*	*No.*	*%*
1.	Kerala	36	39.13
2.	Karnataka	9	9.78
3.	Tamilnadu	14	15.21
4.	OTS	5	5.43
5.	Foreign	28	30.43
	Total	92	

OTS = Other than three states

Table 1.17 has been prepared on the basis of interview taken from 92 tourists who have visited MWS from different destination. It can be observed that Kerala ranks first with 39.13% of the total tourist visiting Mudumalai Wild Life Sanctuary. Kerala tourists are closely followed by foreign tourists who form 30.43% of the total tourist visiting Mudumalai Wild Life Sanctuary. Tourist from Tamil Nadu forms only 15.21% of the tourist coming to Mudumalai Wild Life Sanctuary though it is located in Tamil Nadu state. Tourist from Karnataka has also a poor percentage because most of the tourists from Karnataka prefers to stay at Bandipur National Forest which is closely located to Mudumalai Wild Life Sanctuary. The percentage is only 9.78%. From other than three state not much tourist visit Mudumalai Wild Life Sanctuary.

Table 1.18 shows that highest number of tourist visiting Mudumalai Wild Life Sanctuary falls under the age group 30-44 years. Tamil Nadu ranks first followed by Karnataka and Foreign tourists.

Tourist visiting Mudumalai Wild Life Sanctuary prefers to visit in group (42.39%) because it is more convenient for them.

Being a Wild Life Sanctuary Mudumalai is being visited by all the three major religious group people to have a view of the nature. However according to the Table 1.19 36.95% of the

Table 1.18 Showing the Percentage of Different Age Groups

Sl. No.	Age Groups	Kerala		Karnataka		Tamilnadu		Other states		Foreign	
		Total	*%*	*Total*	*%*	*Total*	*%*	*Total*	*%*	*Total*	*%*
1.	0-15	-	-	-	-	1	7.14	-	-	-	-
2.	16-29	14	38.80	2	22.22		-	2	40.00	20	
3.	30-44	18	50.00	6	66.66	11	78.57	3	60.00	4	
4.	45-59	4	11.11	1	11.11	2	14.28			3	
5.	60+		-		-		-		-	1	
	Total	**36**		**9**		**14**		**5**		**28**	

tourists visited Mudumalai are Hindu. Hindu are followed by Christian. Muslim comes last in this regard.

Table 1.19 Showing the Composition of the Tourist

Sl. No.	*Location / State*	*Alone*	*Group*	*Family*	*Remark*
1.	Kerala	8	11	17	
2.	Karnataka	1	1	7	
3.	Tamil Nadu	3	3	8	
4.	Other States	1	1	3	
5.	Foreign	4.	23	1	
6.	Total	17 (18.47)	39 (42.39)	36 (39.13)	

Table 1.20 Tourist Flow according to Religion

Sl. No.	*Religion*	*Total No. Tourist*	*%*	*Remark*
1.	Hindu	34	36.95	
2.	Muslim	21	22.82	
3.	Christian	32	34.78	
4.	Total	92		

Table 1.21 Reasons for Selecting Mudumalai as Tourist Spot

Sl. No.	*Reasons*	*Total*	*%*	*Remark*
1.	Natural Beauty	65	70.65	
2.	Adventure	1	1.08	
3.	Historical	2	2.17	
4.	Other Reasons	24	26.08	

With reference to Table 1.21 it can be safely assumed that more than 70% of the tourists visiting Mudumalai comes here to enjoy the natural beauty. Being one of the best managed forest of South India Mudumalai is famous for its flora and fauna. On the basis of data of Table 1.21 we have prepared Table 1.22 showing break up on state wise with the given reason for selecting Mudumalai as a place of visit as tourist destination. Following consideration appears to emerge from examining Table 1.22.

Table 1.22 Showing Reason for Selection State-wise

Sl No.	State	Reason	Total	%
1.	Kerala	Natural Beauty	33	91.66
		Historical	1	2.77
		Other Reason	2	5.55
		Total	**36**	-
2.	Karnataka	Natural Beauty	8	88.88
		Historical	1	11.11
		Total	**9**	-
3.	Tamil Nadu	Natural Beauty	14	100
		Total	**14**	-
4.	Other than 3 states	Natural Beauty	5	100
5.	Foreign	Natural Beauty	5	17.85
		Adventure	1	3.57
		Other Reason	22	78.57
		Total	**28**	-
6.	**Total**		**92**	

With regard to Indian tourists coming from all the states of South India. Natural Beauty is the main cause for selecting Mudumalai as a place for destination. However Tamil Nadu ranks first with 100% of tourist come to Mudumalai for enjoining the natural beauty. Tamil Nadu is closely followed by Kerala with 91.66% and Karnataka with 88.88%. In case of foreign tourists other reason comes first with 78.57% where and natural beauty have 17.85% of the tourists in its fold. 3.57% tourists comes to Mudumalai for adventure purpose.

Table 1.23 Problems Faced by Tourists

Sl.No.	*Problems Faced*	*Total*	*%*
1.	Language	42	45.65
2.	Transport	14	15.21
3.	Accommodation	7	7.60
4.	Food	4	4.34
5.	Clearances / Hygienic	5	5.43
6.	No Problem	22	21.73
7.	Total	92	

Table 1.23 has been prepared to show the problems faced by tourist who are visiting Mudumalai Wildlife Sanctuary. 45.65% of the tourist have stated that language is a problem and they felt difficulty in communicating with the people in Mudumalai. 21.73% of the tourists have returned with satisfaction as they not faced any problem. 15.21% of the tourist have stated that transport is a problem because local buses operating from Ooty Gudalur are overcrowded and long distance buses like Ooty to Mysore also does not stop at Mudumalai if seats are not vacant. Jeep services are available but they are not comfortable. On the basis of Table 1.23 we have prepared Table 1.24 to show the details of the problems faced by tourists coming from different destination. Following conclusions can be made from Table 1.24

(a) In case of language foreign tourists are the worst sufferer because 85.71% of the tourists has complains about language problem. Karanataka ranks second with 44.44% followed by tourists coming from other than three states whose percentage is 40.00%. As the Sanctuary is located in Tamil Nadu language problem faced by the tourists from this state is 14.28%. It may be noted that forest official posted at Mudumalai faced difficulty in speaking other language like

English or Hindi. If tourism has to be promoted this is the area where attention has to be paid.

(b) The second problem which the tourist have faced is transport and Tamil Nadu ranks first (35.71%) in this regard. Though located in Tamil Nadu it is difficult to reach Mudumalai from any destination of Tamilnadu due to it isolated location. Kerala ranks second (19.44%) in this regard followed by Other Than Three States. Only Karnataka has the lowest percentage (11.11%) because Mudumalai is easier to reach from Bangalore or Mysore.

Table 1.24

Sl. No.	*State*	*Problems*	*Total*	*%*	*Remarks*
1.	Kerala	Language	10	27.77	
		Transport	7	19.44	
		Accommodation	7	19.44	
		Food	2	5.55	
		Cleanliness / Hygienic	3	8.33	
		No Problem	7	19.44	
		Total	36		
2.	Karanataka	Language	4	44.44	
		Transport	1	11.21	
		Accommodation			
		Food			
		Cleaniness / Hygienic			
		No Problem	4	44.44	
		Total	9		
3.	Tamil Nadu	Language	2	14.28	
		Transport	5	35.71	
		Accommodation			
		Food	1	7.14	
		Cleaniness / Hygienic			
		No Problem	6	42.85	
		Total	14		
4.	Other 3 State	Language	2	40.00	

(Contd.)

(Contd.)

Sl. No.	*State*	*Problems*	*Total*	*%*	*Remarks*
		Transport	1	20.00	
		Accommodation			
		Food	1	20.00	
		Cleanliness / Hygienic	1	20.00	
		No Problem (50)			
		Total	5		
5.	Foreign	Language	24	85.71	
		Transport			
		Accommodation			
		Food			
		Cleanliness / Hygienic	1	3.57	
		No Problem	3	10.71	
		Total			

(c) In the category of accommodation tourists coming from Kerala are the only who faces problem. 19.44% of tourists have stated that they faced problem in getting accommodation.

(d) With regard to food tourists coming from 03S (other than 3 states) ranks first with 20% followed by tourists from Tamilnadu (7.14%) and Kerala (5.55%).

(e) Regarding cleanliness / hygienic tourists coming from 03S have problem followed by Kerala where as Tourists coming from Karnataka and Tamil Nadu have not complain on this front. Foreign tourists have also complained about cleanliness and hygienic condition specially at the eating establishment. It may be noted that there is one shop serving tea and coffee in front of Reception center at Mudumalai.

(f) Whether a tourist destination is good or bad it depends on the satisfaction of the tourists. If a tourist returns with no problem than it can be assumed that the tourist destination has all the necessary ingredients for a good tourist spot. 44.44% of the tourists coming from Karnataka have stated that they did not face any problem at Mudumalai Wildlife

Sanctuary closely followed by the tourists of Tamil Nadu (42.85%). 19.44% of the tourists of Kerala has stated that they are satisfied. Foreign tourists have also stated that they did not faced any problem though there percentage is 10.71%.

Mudumalai Wildlife Sanctuary (MWS) is a popular destination for the tourists and with this Forest Department has to cope up in making the visit of tourists rememberable by adopting conservational methods so that the flora and fauna is not damaged.

Anthropogenic Threats : Human Settlements

Man has been the greatest wonderer. He has traveled from one place to another in search of food, water and shelter for himself and for his animal also. At some occasion he has also moved from one place to the other for security reason or in search of work. Some time he has been transported by agents as a labourer to distant place. In Mudumalai Wildlife Sanctuary human settlement has grown mainly due to two reasons. One group of people are the Mandadan Chettis who are supposed to have migrated to this area from Karnataka during the time of Muslim invasion and settled down here with the blessing of the Raja of Nilambur who had granted them patta land.They are spread in the 7 villages of Gudalur Taluk east of Needle rock. This peak and its hill ranges are the dividing line between the Mandadan Chettis and Wynaad Chettis. The other groups are the tribal population who are the original settler of the region but at Teppakadu and Kargudi these tribal people were brought by the Forest Department at different periods of time to work in the forest as cooli , Mhaut etc. Thus we will try to deal with these settlements in detail separately :

Mandadan Chettis : Their Land and Economy

Mandadan Chettis migrated from Karnataka and settled down at Mudumalai Revenue village in three wetlands. These wetlands are located mostly on the south central part of Mudumalai village mainly formed by the tributaries of Bidar Halla. The hill streams originating from the hills slow down at the valley bottom leave the fine particulars of soil thus forming wetland. These wetlands are fertile land where paddy is grown by the Mandadan

Chettis. During the summer months they grow vegetables and ginger as a cash crop where water is available. According to Mudumalai Panchyat office there are approximately 210 Households of Mandadan Chettis spread over in 15 hamlets of Mudumalai village. In Table 1.25 we have presented the data on households located in different hamlets of Mudumalai village.

Table 1.25 Hamlets and Household

Sl. No.	*Name of the Hamlets*	*No. of house hold*	*%*
1.	Mandagamulla	4	1.90
2.	Puliyalam	10	4.76
3.	Kapur	9	4.28
4.	Panamkolly	6	2.85
5.	Gudivail	5	2.38
6.	Puliyalam	2	0.95
7.	Nagampally	32	15.23
8.	Vattavayal	3	1.42
9.	Mandakarai	42	20.00
10.	Muthukully	74	35.23
11.	Mudumalai	1	0.47
12.	Gundahalam	4	1.90
13.	Nellakarai	14	6.66
14.	Cheruvattur	2	0.95
15.	Nemganokolly	2	0.95
		210	

It can be observed that out of the 210 household nearly 74 household are located in Muthukully hamlet with a percentage of 35.23%. Muthukully is followed by Mandakarai hamlet with 20.00% and again Nagampally 15.23%. According to Taluk office 165.73 hectares of patta wetland is being cultivated by the Mandadan Chettis which requires intensive labour and animal energy. The he-buffalo is the main source of animal energy. It has been reported that nearly 186.0 hectares of wetland were given to the Chettis as forest lease land in the past which has been discontinued after 1986. The Chettis society is facing enormous difficulty in sustaining themselves in Mudumalai village. There movement is controlled by the chain gate at Bosepur and Thorapally. They are not permitted free movement of their agricultural produce. Every time they have to pay tax to the Forest Department. With no proper educational infrastructure the children has to walk through the dense forest to reach Bosepara. Government is unable to decide how to rehabilitate the Chettis population because in Biosphere Reserve no settlement is allowed. The whole population is under siege of the forest department.

Tribal population at Kargudi and Teppakadu: Apart from the settlements which have grown around the wetland there are two settlements which are existing at Mudumalai they are the Kargudi settlement and Teppakadu settlement. These two settlements consists of tribal households of Paniyan, Kattu Naicken, Betta Kurumba and Irula. These tribal people where brought by the forest department at different period of time to work in the various jobs of the forest like clearing, cutting, transporting of wood from forest to other place. Today these settlements have become permanent settlements though work in the forest has gone down. We will deal each of these settlements separately.

Kargudi : Located on Ooty-Mysore state highway on the left side of the Moyar River Kargudi has 12 households of 48 people with 26 males and 22 females. The population consists of Paniyan, Kattu Naicken, Betta Kurumba and Irula. In the past they were getting work in the forest on daily wage basis but at present no work. They go out for work as a cooli at different estates in and around Gudalur. They live in forest built quarters in a very bad condition. Only one Irula family has managed to get one acre of tea plantation near Bosepara in Srimadurai village. In the past they also used to collect minor forest produce but now it has been completely banned. They are looking forward towards the forest department for rehabilitation.

Table 1.26 Kargudi : Demography

Sl. No.	*No. of h.h*	*Total pop.*	*Male*	*Female*	*Occupation*	*Remark*
1.	12	48	26	22	Coli	

Only Tribal population who are permanently living at Kargudi.

Teppakadu : Located at the junction of Ooty-Mysore Road and Teppakadu – Masinagudi Road on the left bank of Moyar River. Teppakadu is an important location in Mudumalai Wildlife Sanctuary because it has Reception center, 3 important places of stay, post office and a STD center. We have not surveyed the population which stay in Forest Department Quarters. We have concentrated in 3 settlements of Teppakadu where the tribal population resides. The 3 settlements are : A Padi, Light Padi and Anna Padi. All these settlements are multi tribal. The houses are mainly built by village Panchyat with assistance from the forest department.

(a) **A padi :** Located on the western side of the Tourist Reception center A Padi consists of 17 households of Kattu Naickan and 14 households of Betta Kurumba. Other details are as follows :

Table 1.27 A padi Settlement

Sl. No.	*Name of the tribal*	*No. of H. Holds*	*Total Pop.*	*Male*	*Female*
1.	Kattu Naicken	17	78	37	41
2.	Betta Kurumba	14	66	29	37
	Total	31	144	66	78

From the above table it can be seen that Kattu Naickan consists of 54.16% of the total population and accordingly 54.83% of household belongs to Kattu Naickan where as 45.16% of the household belongs to Betta Kurumba.

Table 1.28 House Types

Sl. No.	Name of the Tribe	Type of houses FBH	PBH	SBH	Total
1.	Kattu Naicken	3	8	6	17
2.	Betta Kurumba	-	14	-	14
3.	Total	3	22	6	31

Note : FBH = Forest Built House, PBH = Panchyat Built House, SBH = Self Built House.

Table 1.28 gives a figure on type of houses occupied by the tribal population of A Paddi of Teppakadu. On the basis of this Table 1.29 has been prepared showing the percentage. It can be seen from this table that 70.96% of houses are built by Village Panchyat where as 9.67% of houses are built by Forest Department. As the population has grown the tribal people here have constructed their own houses and its percentage is 19.35%. One of the Betta Kurumba is also running a shop of daily uses in his house.

Table 1.29 Occupation

Sl. No.	Name of the Tribe	Type of houses FBH	PBH	SBH	Total
1.	Kattu Naicken	17.64	47.05	35.29	
2.	Betta Kurumba	-	100.00	-	
	Total	9.67	7.96	-	

On the occupational front more than 50% of the households are dependent on cooli work. Let us examine the table below.

Table 1.30 Occupation

Sl. No.	*Name of the Tube*	*Occupation*		
		Working of Forest Dept.	*Working of Cooli*	*Total*
1.	Kattu Naicken	6	11	17
2.	Batta Kurumba	3	11	14
	Total	**9**	**22**	**31**

Out of the total 31 households 9 are working in Forest Department as Mahaut and Kavadi (Asst. to Mahaut) and 22 are working as Cooli. On the basis of Table 1.30 we have prepared Table 1.31 in. Ratio Percentage.

Table 1.31 Occupation in Ratio Percentage

Sl. No.	*Name of the Tribal*	*Occupation*	
		Working Forest Dept.	*Working as Cooli*
1.	Kattu Naickan	66.66	50.00
2.	Betta Kurumba	33.00	50.00
	Total		

Table 1.31 states that 66.66% of Kattu Naicken households are working in Forest Department where as 33.33% of the Betta Kurumba households are dependent on Forest work. However both the tribal households share equal percentage in the category working as Cooli. If we look at the total share than it can be noticed that 70.96 of the households are dependent on cooli work where as 29.03% are dependent on the Forest Department for work. It is observed that the household who have job in Forest Department are well off economically.

Table 1.32 Demography and Occupation

Sl. No. 1	Population		%
a.	Total person	180	
b.	Male	91	
c.	Female	89	

Sl. No. 2	Type of House		%
a.	Self Built House	8	17.39
b.	Panchyat Built House	38	82.60
	Total	**46**	

Sl. No. 3	Occupation		%
a.	Government Job	12	26.08
b.	Private Job	3	6.52
c.	Cooli Work	31	67.39
	Total	**46**	

Light Padi : Located on the eastern side of Ooty-Mysore Highway and back side of the Tamil Nadu Hotel Light Padi is the second largest tribal settlement of Teppakadu settled by single tribe Betta Kurumba. At Teppakadu they were settled to do work in the forest specially during the British period. After independence the system continued till 1986 and after 1994 there is completely no work in the forest. However very few Betta Kurumba are engaged in peripheral forest work like Mahaut etc. For better understanding we are presenting the following table on Light Padi.

Following considerations appear to emerge from Table 1.32.

(a) Total population of Light Padi is 180 with 91 males and 89 females. The houses are located in liner pattern. All the houses have electricity that's why it is known as Light Padi.

(b) 82.60 of the houses are constructed by Village Panchyat where as 17.39 are Self Built Houses. Forest Department has not constructed any house at Light Padi. However Forest Department claims that Village Panchyat has constructed the house up to plinth level and rest portion has been constructed by the Forest Department.

Table 1.33 Community, House, Occupation

	Sl. No.	Community	Population		
			Total Pop.	Male	Female
[A]	1.	Betta Kurumba	190	93	97
	2.	Kattu Naickan	25	16	9
	3.	Irula	16	7	9
	4.	Malasor	34	20	14
		Total	**265**	**136**	**129**

	Sl. No.	House	Total No.	%
[B]	1.	Self Built House	5	8.19
	2.	Forest Dep. Built House	31	50.81
	3.	Panchyat Built House	25	40.98
		Total	**61**	

(Contd.)

(Contd.)

	Sl. No.	*Occupation*		
[C]	1.	Working in Forest Dept.	24	39.34
	2.	Other Service	4	6.55
	3.	Working as Cooli	33	54.09
		Total	**61**	

(c) On the occupation front Light Padi has 26.08 of the household who are dependent on work in forest department in different way like Mahaut, Kavadi etc. 6.52% household is dependent on private jobs like forest guide and other petty work. The remaining household that is 67.39% are going to work as cooli in different areas like Masinagudi and Gudalur.

Through the people of Light Padi are aware of their economic plight but they have no option to work on. They have complained that even forest department are not engaging them for cooli work but they are bringing laborers from Gudalur. Women Self Help Group (WSHG) is working in the settlement with little success. The women are ready to do any work if it is offered to them. But the situation is not good and they look towards future with dismay.

Anna Padi : Anna Padi is located in between Teppakadu-Masinagudi Road and Moyar River very near to the elephant camp. One has to cross the Moyar River to reach Anna Padi. It is a multi tribal populated settlement where Betta Kurumba are dominant group followed by Kattu Naicken and Irula. We also find a community known as Malasor who have come from the plain of Tamil Nadu and settled here. For detail information we have prepared Table 1.33.

Table 1.33 presents a crude picture of the 3 variable : population, houses and occupation. It may be noted that total population of Anna Padi is 265 persons with 136 male and 129 female which is concentrated into 61 houses built by forest department, village Panchyat and by their own. It can also be noted that 33 households are dependent on cooli work where as 24 households are dependent on work provided by forest department where as only 4 households are doing other service. On the basis of Table 1.33 we have prepared Table 1.34 showing the ratio percentum.

Following considerations appear to emerge from Table 1.34

(a) Betta Kurumba with 71.69% of the total population of Anna Padi ranks first followed by Malasorr a non-tribal community 12.83%. Kattu Naicken and Irula does not from a significant group though there percentage are 9.43% and 6.03% respectively.

Table 1.34 Community, House and Occupation (Ratio Percentum)

	Sl. No.	Community	Population		
			Total Pop.	Male	Female
[A]	1.	Betta Kurumba	71.69	68.38	75.19
	2.	Kattu Naicken	9.43	11.76	6.97
	3.	Irula	6.03	5.14	6.97
	4.	Malasorr	12.83	14.70	10.85
		Total			

	Sl. No.	House	Total	%
[B]	1.	Self Built House	5	8.19
	2.	Forest Dept. House	31	50.81
	3.	Panchyat Built House	25	40.98
		Total		

	Sl. No.	Occupation	Total No.	%
[C]	1.	Working in Forest Dept.	24	39.34
	2.	Other service	4	6.55
	3.	Working as Cooli	33	50.09

(b) In Anna Padi Forest Department has provided maximum numbers of houses with 50.81% which is closely followed by 40.98% built by the Village Panchyat. Self Built house percentage is as low as 8.19%.

(c) Dwindling work in the forest have forced the household to go more and more for cooli work and hence the ratio percentage under this occupation is as high as 50.09%. 39.34% of the household are still dependent on Forest Department for work. 6.55% of the household is dependent on other service like working as daily wage worker in hotels at Masinagudi etc.

Forest Managers are of the opinion that anthropogenic threats specially in the form of rapid and uncontrolled tourism as well as human population residing in the sanctuary is becoming stronger these days. The fall out of these anthropogenic threats are : growing population level in the sanctuary as well problems created by encroaching forest land for cultivation, grazing of domestic animals in the forest, poaching of wildlife and timber smuggling and uncontrolled flow of tourist. However forest department is trying to handle these problems in its own way.

Conservation of Biosphere

In the previous paragraphs we have dealt with the anthropogenic threats faced by Mudumalai Wildlife Sanctuary in the form of flow of tourists at the one hand and on the other hand there has been 3 human settlements in the Sanctuary itself like the Mandadan Chettis settled in around the wetlands situated on the south-eastern-western portion of the village and 2 tribal settlements at Kargudi and Teppakadu. So the conservation efforts taken by the forest department which is the custodian of the Mudumalai Wildlife Sanctuary can be divided into two parts: (a) conservation for the tourists and (b) for the human settlements. We will deal with these two practices separately. But before that it is necessary to discuss the zonation of Mudumalai Wildlife Sanctuary because conservation efforts are done according to zonation. According to the Working Plan which is in operation now Mudumalai Wild Life Sanctuary is divided into the following zones:

(a) National Park area or the wilderness zone or the core zone
(b) Integrated Forest zone or Integrated zone
(c) Experimental zone
(d) Tourism zone
(e) Buffer zone.

(a) National Park area or the Wildness zone or the Core zone: This zone covers the northern part of the sanctuary and it is the least disturbed area. This zone is also called as sanctum sanctorum where there is no settlements, no grazing, and no exploitation of any kind. The vegetation is preserved in its pristine purity. This zone is bordered on the north, east and west by vast Wilderness zone of Bandipur Tiger Project and on the south by the Buffer zone and Integrated Forest zone of Mudumalai Wild Life Sanctuary.

(b) Integrated Zone : Parts of Benne and Mudumalai Reserve Forest are mudded in this zone. In this zone regeneration programme for grass and bamboo and maintenance of teak plantation are done.

(c) Experimental Zone : On the eastern part of the Mudumalai Wildlife Sanctuary covering the Avarahall Reserve Forest falls under this zone. Madurai University has established an Asia Elephant Research Centre in this zone.

(d) Tourism Zone : This zone covers parts of Mudumalai and Moyar Reserve forest. Ombetta road, Kakanalla Mudumalai Road, Cross ant road, Teppakadu – Mudumalai Road and Mandradiyar Avenue are the road were tourists are taken for seeing Wildlife.

(e) Buffer Zone : The entire Moyar Reserve Forest except the tract south of Teppakadu – Masinagudi road traversed by Mandradiyar Avenue is treated as Buffer zone. This zone is open for grazing. Forest department plans to stop grazing in a phase manner.

Apart from the conservation efforts by the forest department there is a provision for periodic closure of Tourism zone and thus Sanctuary is closed for tourism. During this period no tourist is allowed. This year MWS was declared closed for tourists from 1-3-05 to 15-4-05. This period depends on the overall condition of the Mudumalai Wildlife Sanctuary. If there is a severe drought than the Sanctuary remains closed for a longer period. Tourists are allowed only on a decided route and this is strictly followed. The following routes are in operation for tourists tour in the Sanctuary:

(a) Mandradiyar Avenue

(b) Ombetta Vayal Mudumalai – Thorapally

(c) Teppakadu – Mudumalai – Punnagiri Crosscut Road

(d) Circular Route – Kakkanhalla – Mudumalai – Teppakadu routes.

For general awareness for tourist Forest Department has put a big poster / hording known as Eco-Commandments.

(a) Entry in the Sanctuary with permission during the specified hours only.
(b) Wildlife sighting is a matter of chance.
(c) Inform all the sightings and appreciate the habitat also.
(d) Wear dark clothes so as to be inconspicuous and merge with the surroundings.
(e) Maintain absolute silence during van and elephant rides for better sighting.
(f) Do not kindle fire in the forest and do not smoke in the sanctuary.
(g) Entry on foot, campfires, messes, cooking, littering in the sanctuary is prohibited.
(h) Do not get down from the vehicle.
(i) Use of spotlights, fast driving, blowing of horn prohibited.
(j) Bathing, washing and fishing in the river is prohibited.
(k) Shouting, teasing, chasing or feeding animals are prohibited.
(l) Consumption of alcoholic drinks and carrying of arms in the sanctuary are strictly prohibited.
(m) Disposable plastic bags, cups, plates, PET bottles are banned.
(n) Keep Nilgiri plastic free.
(o) Harvest rain water.

It may be noted that Wildlife sanctuaries play an important role in the development of tourism and thereby to create awareness among the people but primary objective of the Wildlife sanctuary is to preserve the pristine ecosystem: flora and fauna for the future generation. If tourism has to be developed in the Wildlife sanctuary it should be so that the ecosystem is maintained because they support the life system.

Resettlement of the human settlement of Mudumalai Wildlife Sanctuary

As discussed earlier that there are 3 settlements in the MWS which has to be rehabilitated suitably so that Mudumalai Wildlife

Sanctuary becomes free from human intervention. This is important from habitat point of view. A scheme for rehabilitation of forest settlements has been prepared 40 years back and is still laying with the government for implementation. Vigorous efforts should be made so that the people are freed from the mental agony of uncertainty. It may be noted that the people of the 3 settlements are willing to move out if proper rehabilitation is given.

Nilgiri Biosphere in general and Mudumalai Wildlife Sanctuary in particular is one of the well studied Wildlife Sanctuary of our country. But a detail geographical and ecological work from human perspective is lacking. However, conservation of the biosphere of Mudumalai Wildlife Sanctuary can be achieved through adequate awareness among the community living inside the sanctuary, effective legal enforcement for encroachers and poachers and well equipped and motivated personal who can manage the forest in a better way. Equally important is to control the tourist flow in the Sanctuary area so that the ecosystem is not damaged. The motto should be to stop the decay of environment

References

Aiyappan, Aijenipalti. 1948 Report on the Socio – Economic conditions of the Aboriginal Tribes of the Province of Madras, Government Press, Madras.

Desai, Mamata & Raha, Manis Kumar. 2004 The Dying Earth, Peoples Action Nature Reaction, ACP Publication, Kolkata.

Hockings, Paul. 1980 Ancient Hindu Refugees, Badga Social History (1550 – 1975), Vikash Publishing House, New Delhi.

Hockings , Paul. 1989 Blue Mountains, Oxford University Press, Delhi.

Hockings, Paul. 1997 Blue Mountains Revisited, Cultural Studies on the Nilgiri Hills, Oxford University Press, Delhi.

Jordan, Terry,G & Rowntree , Lester. 1982 The Human Mosaic : A Thematic Introduction to Cultural Geography, Hatter & Row Publishers, New York.

Khoshoo, T.N. 1986 Environment Priorities in India and Sustainable Development, Indian Science Congress, Delhi.

Krishnan, Rajan: 2002 When the Kurinji Blooms, Orient Longman Pvt. Ltd. New Delhi.

Sekar, T. 2004 Forest History of Nilgiris, Tamilnadu Forest Department, Chennai.

Sharma, Archana. 1987 Resources and Human Well-Being. Indian Science Congress, Calcutta.

Singh, Arun Kumar. 1991 Ecology and Land use Pattern in Gudalur Taluk : A Geographical Study, An. SI, Calcutta.

Singh, R.L. 1986 India : Regional Studies, IGU, Calcutta.

Spate, OHK. 1954 India and Pakistan, Methuean & Co. London.

Thruston, Edgar 1909 Caste and Tribes of Southern India, Government Press, Madras.

Walker, Anthony R. 1998 Between Tradition and Modernity and other. Essays on the Toda of South India, BR Publishing Corporation, Delhi.

Reports :

Equations : July – December 2003, Documentation Update, Bangalore.

Equations : January 2003, Weighing the Ghats on a Development Scale, The Case of Tourism in Goa, India, Bangalore.

Equations : May 2004, Resisting the Sell – Out of the Sunderban Biosphere Reserve, Bangalore.

Management Plan For 1978 – 79 to 1987 – 88, Mudumalai Wildlife Sanctuary, Office of the Wildlife Warden, Ooty.

Mantramurti, A., 2000 Ethnographic Study of Tribes Kattu Nayakans and Paliyars in Tamil Nadu, Project Report of Directorate of Tribal Research and Development, M. Plada, Ooty.

Map-1

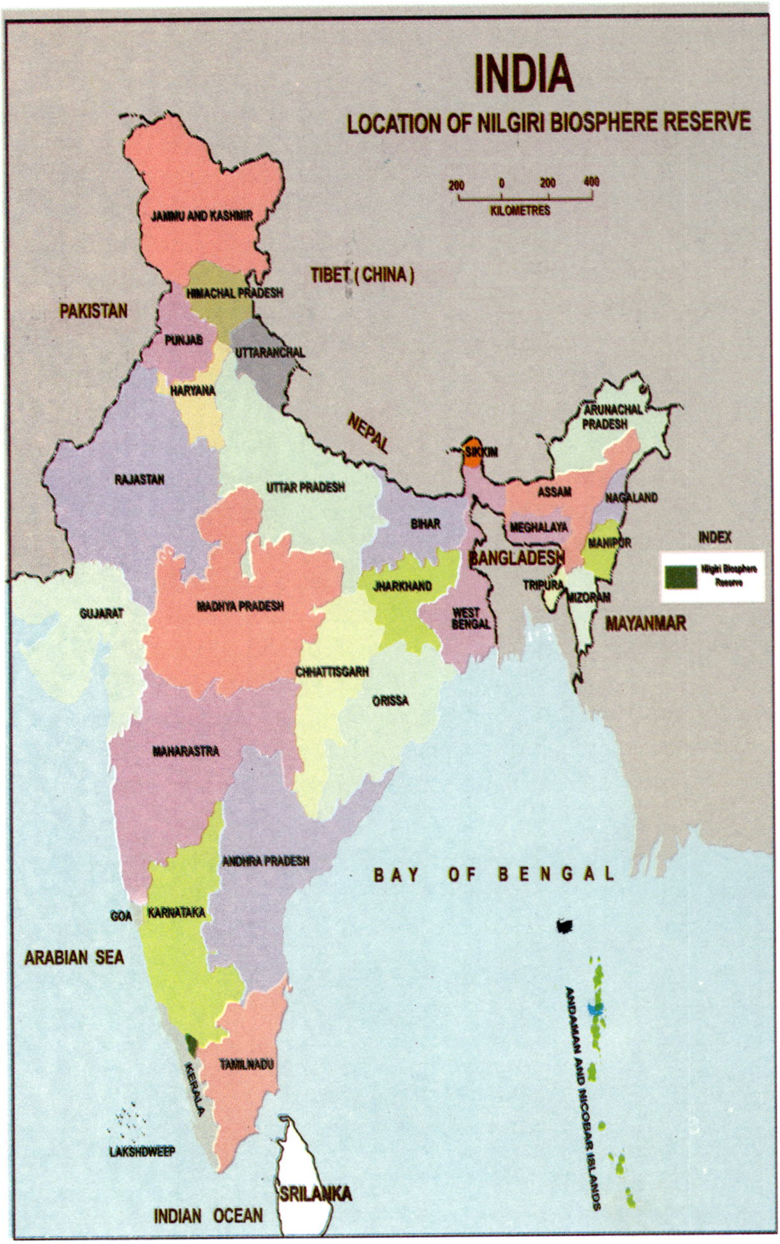
INDIA
LOCATION OF NILGIRI BIOSPHERE RESERVE
200 0 200 400
KILOMETRES
JAMMU AND KASHMIR
TIBET (CHINA)
HIMACHAL PRADESH
PAKISTAN
PUNJAB
UTTARANCHAL
HARYANA
NEPAL
ARUNACHAL PRADESH
SIKKIM
RAJASTAN
UTTAR PRADESH
ASSAM
NAGALAND
BIHAR
MEGHALAYA
INDEX
BANGLADESH
MANIPUR
Nilgiri Biosphere Reserve
JHARKHAND
TRIPURA
GUJARAT
MADHYA PRADESH
WEST BENGAL
MIZORAM
MAYANMAR
CHHATTISGARH
ORISSA
MAHARASTRA
ANDHRA PRADESH
BAY OF BENGAL
GOA
KARNATAKA
ARABIAN SEA
ANDAMAN AND NICOBAR ISLANDS
KERALA
TAMILNADU
LAKSHDWEEP
SRILANKA
INDIAN OCEAN

Map-2

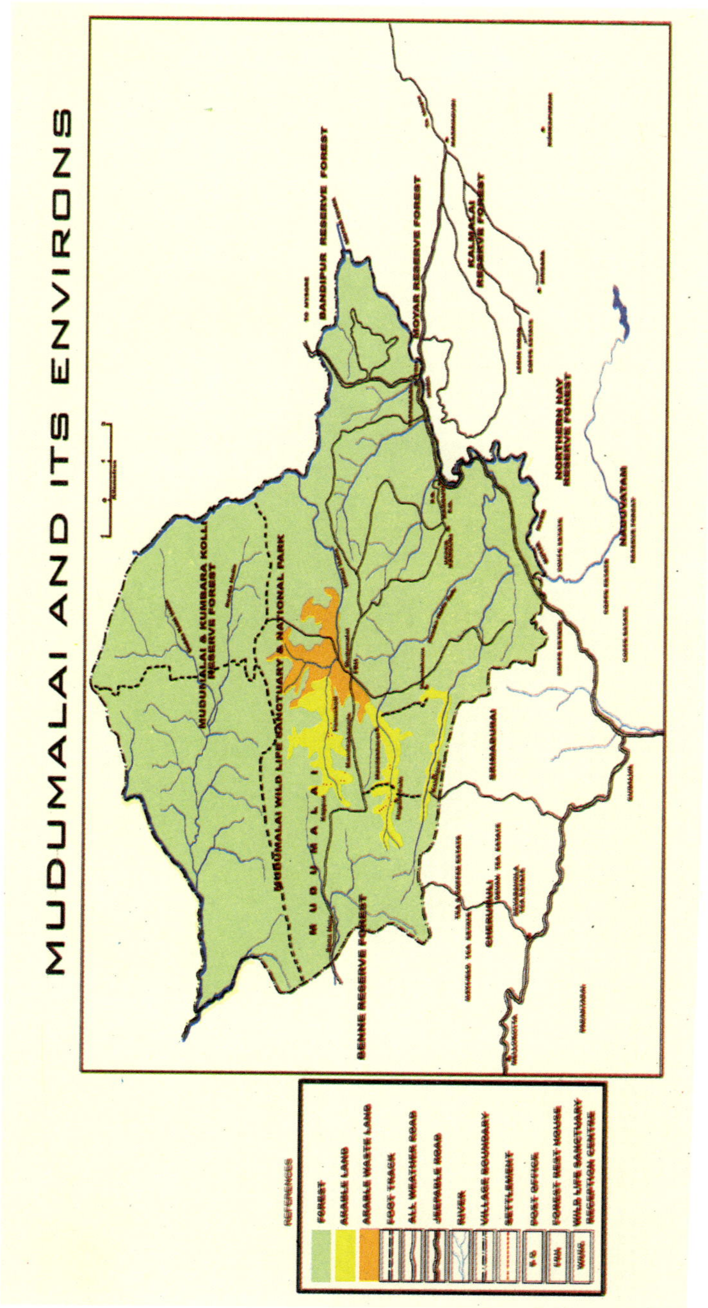
MUDUMALAI AND ITS ENVIRONS
BANDIPUR RESERVE FOREST
MOYAR RESERVE FOREST
NORTHERN HAY RESERVE FOREST
MUDUMALAI & KUMBARA KOLLI RESERVE FOREST
MUDUMALAI WILD LIFE SANCTUARY & NATIONAL PARK
MUDUMALAI
BENNE RESERVE FOREST
SRIMADURAI
NADUVATAM
REFERENCES
FOREST
ARABLE LAND
ARABLE WASTE LAND
FOOT TRACK
ALL WEATHER ROAD
JEEPABLE ROAD
RIVER
VILLAGE BOUNDARY
SETTLEMENT
POST OFFICE
FOREST REST HOUSE
WILD LIFE SANCTUARY RECEPTION CENTRE

Map-3

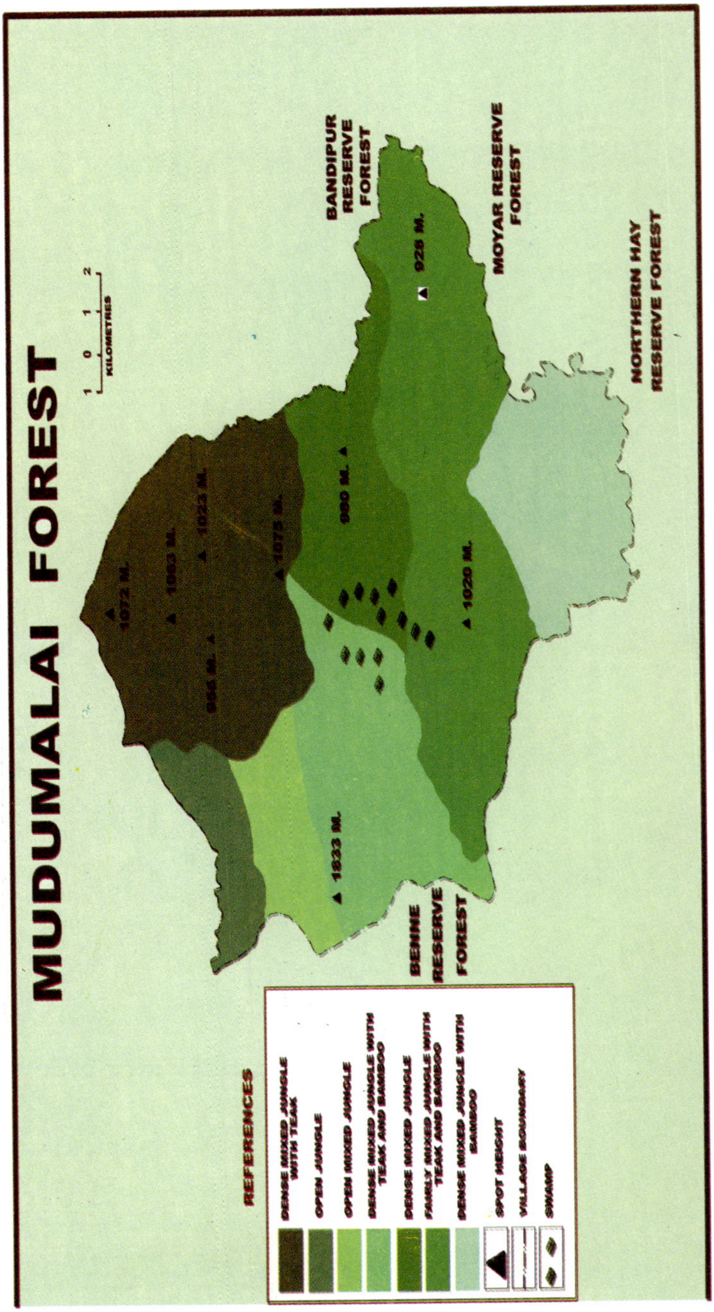
MUDUMALAI FOREST
1 0 1 2
KILOMETRES
BANDIPUR RESERVE FOREST
MOYAR RESERVE FOREST
NORTHERN HAY RESERVE FOREST
BENNE RESERVE FOREST
1063 M.
1023 M.
1075 M.
964 M.
990 M.
926 M.
1020 M.
REFERENCES
DENSE MIXED JUNGLE WITH TEAK
OPEN JUNGLE
OPEN MIXED JUNGLE
DENSE MIXED JUNGLE WITH TEAK AND BAMBOO
DENSE MIXED JUNGLE
FAIRLY MIXED JUNGLE WITH TEAK AND BAMBOO
DENSE MIXED JUNGLE WITH BAMBOO
SPOT HEIGHT
VILLAGE BOUNDARY
SWAMP

Plate 1.1 Inside Mudumalai Wildlife Sanctuary

Plate 1.2 Settlement in Mudumalai Wildlife Sanctuary

Plate 1.3 Cattle Grazing Inside Mudumalai Wildlife Sanctuary

Plate1.4 Agriculture Fields Inside Mudumalai Wildlife Sanctuary

Plate 1.5 Agricultural Fields Inside Mudumalai Wildlife Sanctuary

Plate 1. 6 Reception Centre Mudumalai Wildlife Sanctuary, Teppakaddu

Plate 7. Paniyan in Mudumalai Wildlife Sanctuary

Map-4

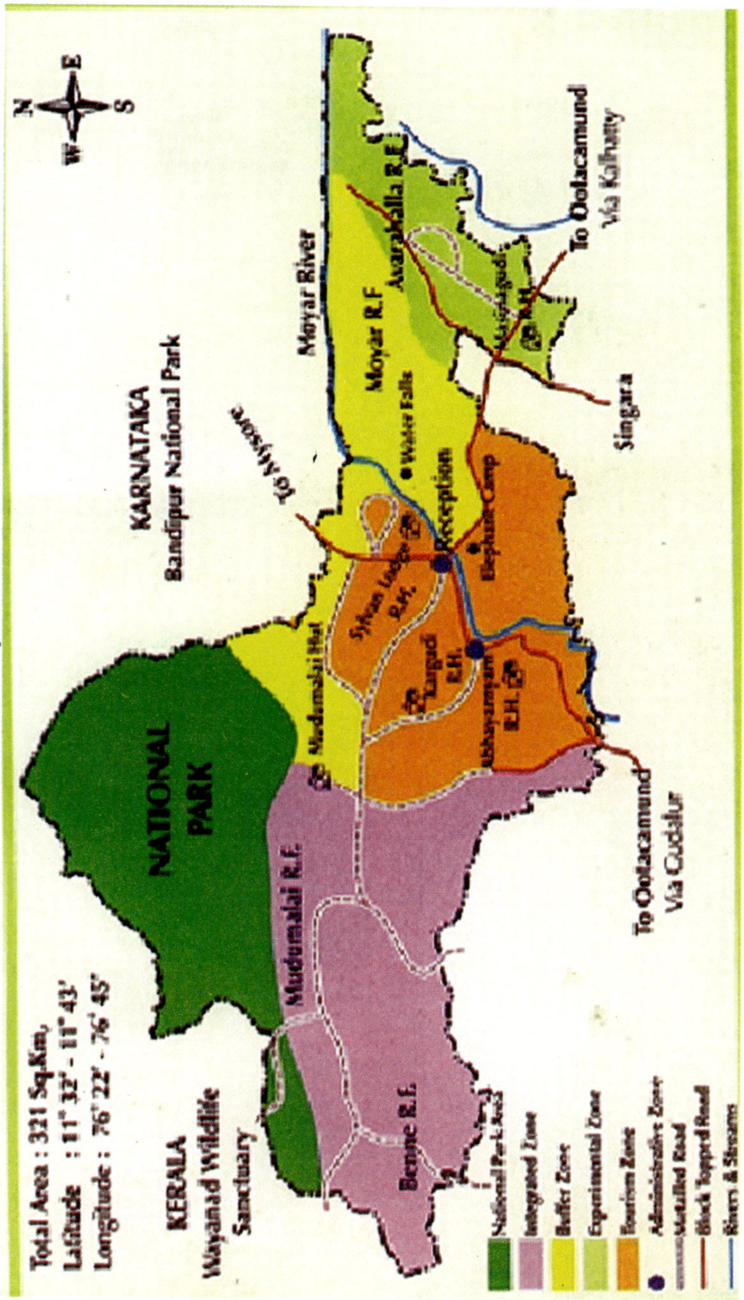
Total Area : 321 Sq.Km.
Latitude : 11° 32' - 11° 43'
Longitude : 76° 22' - 76° 45'
KERALA
Wayanad Wildlife Sanctuary
NATIONAL PARK
KARNATAKA
Bandipur National Park
To Mysore
Moyar River
Moyar R.F
Avarahalla R.F.
Water Falls
Reception
Elephant Camp
Sylvan Lodge R.H.
Kargudi R.H.
Abhayaranyam R.H.
Mudumalai Hut
Mudumalai R.F.
Benne R.F.
Singara
To Ootacamund Via Kalhatty
To Ootacamund Via Gudalur
National Park Area
Integrated Zone
Buffer Zone
Experimental Zone
Tourism Zone
Administrative Zone
Metalled Road
Black Topped Road
Rivers & Streams

2

Eco-tourism and Sustainable Development: A Case Study of Bandipur National Park

K. Ravi and G.V. Raman

Introduction

Tourism is a leisure activity which presupposes its opposite, namely regulated and organized work; tourism relationships arise from a movement of people to, and their stay in, various destinations; the journey and stay are to, and in, sites which are outside the normal places of residence and work; a substantial proportion of the population of modern societies engages in such tourist practices. There are many types of tourism and ecotourism is one of them.

Ecotourism is "a form of tourism inspired primarily by the natural history of an area, including its indigenous cultures" (Ziffer 1989)

"Ecotourism has many definitions; but generally these revolve around the idea of leisure travel that has the object of enjoying features of what is seen as the natural environment in a way that has minimal negative consequences for the environment. Ecotourism is generally taken to include a socio-cultural element, the intention of seeing and interacting with people whose customs and appearance seem exotic and attractive and doing so in away that respects and benefits them. More loosely, ecotourists are people who travel to enjoy features of the environment among attractive exotic people in ways that are responsible environmentally and beneficial socio-culturally" (Paige West and James. G. Carrier, 483: 2004).

The key elements of ecotourism include:

1. A natural environment as its prime attraction.
2. An optimum number of environment friendly visitors
3. Activities which do not have any serious impacts on the ecosystem.
4. Positive involvement of the local communities.

What is Environmentally sustainable development? "Environmentally sustainable development is defined as meeting present needs in an harmonious interchange without harm for future opportunity (Colby, 1990:3). His five paradigm models conclude with eco-development that tries to attain a positive relationship between human society and nature through more thoughtful application of human industry toward socio-ecological development, economic development and environmental management.

Need and Importance of the Study

The important tourist areas in the Nilgiri Biosphere Reserve are twelve in number. These areas attract many tourists from different parts of the country and also from abroad. The forest department has given attention for development of tourism with infrastructural facilities to the tourists such as comfortable accommodations like guest houses, dormitories, resorts and cottages. These facilities have lead to an increase in the number of tourists. Forest department employed local tribal people as forest guards, fire watchers, guides and also workers at dormitories, guest houses, resorts and cottages.

Area of Study

The Bandipur National Park occupies a special place in the country's efforts towards natural conservation. The entire area of this national park now constitutes a part of the Nilgiri Biosphere Reserve, one of India's most extensive tracts of protected forest area designated as Tiger Reserve in 1973. In 1974 intention was declared under the Wildlife Protection Act to notify it as a National Park.

There are very few studies done on impact of ecotourism on tribal communities. This is one of the reasons for taking up this study. Most of the studies have been conducted by Dept. of Forests and Ecological Sciences. Hence there is a need to study from an anthropological perspective.

Issues

1. In order to know the specific impacts of ecotourism on the tribes of the area, whom does ecotourism development actually benefit, how can deleterious impacts be minimized, how tourism can be used as an effective tool to improve the quality of life of the local tribals and the world view of tribal communities.
2. Whether the revenues from ecotourism channeled into conservation and local development needs.
3. How the ecotourism developmental activities would improve the economy of the local communities.
4. What is the extent of local peoples participation in conservation and developmental activities. In this context it may be mentioned that anthropological research documents local knowledge and practices that influence the selection and the maintenance of crop varieties and the conservation of rare and endangered species in protected areas. Anthropologists can describe the increasing importance of participation of local people in conservation programmes Orlove (1996:329).
5. Obstacles to conservation and sustainable development will be highlighted in the study.
6. What are the ecotourism developmental programmes introduced by government in the context of conservation.
7. The role of NGOs in motivating tribals in the context of educating them in conservation.
8. Tourists views about the area, accommodation, problems and their thoughts, feelings and experiences on visiting the Bandipur National Park.

Keeping in view of the above mentioned issues into consideration, the recent study is undertaken.

Specific Objectives

1. To study the dynamics of development of National Park and tourism in the area.
2. To project positive and negative impacts of ecotourism on local tribal communities and to suggest the ways and means to minimize the negative impacts and to make the positive impacts more meaningful.
3. To draw perceptions of the tourists towards the area and the infrastructural facilities extended by the forest department for promotion of tourism in the area.
4. To study obstacles that are instrumental for conservation and sustainable development.
5. To study the tribals and sustainable development in the rehabilitated village.
6. To study the tribal situation in the traditional village.
7. To explore the opportunities for achieving ecologically sustainable development with the growth of tourism in the area.

Methodology

The Bandipur National Park which comes under Nilgiri Biosphere Reserve and ecotourist spot in Karnataka is selected for the study. The main tribal communities are the Jenu Kuruba, the Betta or Kadu Kuruba and the Soliga inhabiting the area.

Field work was conducted in the year 2005 for about 2 months. A standard ethnographic approach including observation, schedule, interview guide, key informant interview case studies were employed to collect both qualitative and quantitative data. Local tribal communities, tourists, forest officials, teachers and other local officials were interviewed.

Structured interviews were conducted among individuals belonging to the following categories:

The first category included tribals who are heads of the households of the rehabilitated village. They were interviewed on their way of life, impact of tourism and conservation practices in relation to sustainable development.

The second category included tribals inhabiting the traditional village. They were interviewed to know their socio-economic conditions.

The third category included employed tribals working in the Bandipur National Park, forest officials, local teachers and other officials who were interviewed.

The fourth category included the tourists who have visited Bandipur National Park. In this category one hundred tourists were interviewed.

Data was also collected on risk perceptions on sustainable developmental activities in ecotourism area. Formal interviews were conducted with forest officials, local tribals and teachers to get information on risk perceptions.

Secondary data was also collected by examining government documents from the forest department, tourists brochures and journals.

Geography

The total area of the Nilgiri Biosphere Reserve is 5,520 square kilometers. It is located in the Western Ghats between 76°-77°15'E and 11°15' – 12°15'N. The Nilgiri Biosphere Reserve comprises parts of Tamil Nadu, Kerala and Karnataka. The annual rainfall of the reserve ranges from 500 mm to 7000 mm with temperature ranging from 0°C during winter to 41°C during summer.

The Nilgiri Biosphere Reserve falls under the bio-geographic region of the Malabar rain forest. The Mudumalai Wildlife Sanctuary, Wyanad Wildlife Sanctuary, Bandipur National Park, Nagarhole National Park, Mukurth National Park and Silent Valley are the present protected areas present within this reserve. The total geographical area of Nilgiri Biosphere Reserve is 5520.40 square kms, of which 2537.60 sq.kms. lies in the State of Tamil Nadu, 1455.40 sq.kms in Kerala and 1527.40 sq.kms. in Karnataka. The Karnataka portion of Nilgiri Biosphere Reserve comprises the Bandipur National Park and the Nagarhole National Park which is a unique bio-geographic region.

Bandipur National Park is one of the Tiger Reserves in India. It was a sanctuary started in the year 1931 and designated as a National Park in the year 1973 under project Tiger. It was notified in 1974 as a National Park under wildlife protection Act. It is a famous wildlife tourism center known for its rich flora and fauna and also for the complex biotic pressures deleterious to its conservation and protection.

Location and Boundary

Half way between the Mysore Ooty highway where the Deccan Platean rises to meet the wrinkled folds of the Western Ghat Mountains, lies one of India's famous wildlife reserve, the Bandipur National Park. It is situated within Chamarajanagar district of Karnataka State. It is located between the longitude 76°12'17" and 76°51'32" East and in between the latitude 11°35'34" and 11°57'02" North (Source: Bandipur National Park – Project Tiger Brochure). It is contiguous to Madumalai Wildlife Sanctuary of Tamil Nadu to the south and Wynad Wildlife Sanctuary of Kerala to the South West. To the North side of the Tiger Reserve lies the vast stretches of cultivable lands. To the west lies the cultivable lands of Kerala habitation to a distance of 8 kms separated by Kannegala stream. To the South West lies the Major Irrigation Project Kabini Reservoir, which forms the barrier between this Tiger Reserve and Sri Rajiv Gandhi National Park – Nagarhole.

Bandipur is situated in midway on Mysore-Ooty highway and is exactly 80 kms. from Mysore as well as from Ooty, with adequate transport facilities. The nearest railway station at Nanjangud which is 55 kms. from Bandipur and the nearest airport is Bangalore which is 220 kms. from Bandipur. The National Park is connected by Mysore Calicut road which passes through the Park via Moolehole; and the rural roads from Hediyala to Chikkabargi and H.D. Kote to N.Begur and connects the network of forest roads inside the Park. (*Source*: Action Plan Report on Project Tiger: Bandipur Tiger Reserve).

The whole area included in the National Park is considered to be core area as per the principles of Wildlife Protection Act, but, there is no buffer forest areas around the National Park to receive and absorb the dependency pressures of the people inhabiting close to it. As such, the fringe forests of the park are exposed to pressures of the people. In order to check the dependency pressures and also to enrich the fringe forests by ecorestoration works, the fringe of the park towards northern side abutting villages has been demarcated as buffer zone, and an area of 82 sq. kms. has been set aside for tourism and one sq.km for administrative purpose within the park. Thus the demarcation of zones in the Park are as follows: (See Table:1)

Table 2.1 Demarcation of Zones in Bandipur National Park

Sl.No.	*Name of the Zone*	*Area in sq.kms*	*Percentage*
1.	Core zone or wilderness zone	523.00	60.40
2.	Buffer zone	274.00	30.00
3.	Tourism zone	82.00	9.50
4.	Administrative zone	1.00	0.10
	Total	880.00	100.00

Source: Action Plan Report on Project Tiger: Bandipur Tiger Reserve.

Climate

The climate is salubrious and it is distinguishable into three seasons in this Park. Summer season starts from mid of February and ends by May end; rainy season from June to October with breaks in the month of September i.e. between South West and North East monsoon; and winter season from November to mid February. The temperature of the Park is usually moderate. The average annual temperature is around 24°C and the maximum temperate is 29.5°C in summer. The nights are cold during winter in areas like Bandipur, Moolehole and Himavad Gopalaswamy Hills with temperature coming down to 8°C at H.G. Hills. The sun is fairly hot in summer.

The forests which come under the Bandipur National Park area receives rainfall both from South West and North East monsoons. The major rainfall is from June to August from South West monsoon and a portion in the months of October and November from North East monsoon. The rainfall varies from 625 mm to 1250 mm with the lowest precipitation in the eastern portion of the Reserve at Moyar and highest in western zone at Kalere. At times, heavy rains are being received in October and November due to cyclonic weather conditions.

Topography and Rivers

The Bandipur is located at the foothills of the Western Ghats. The land is undulating and is broken by chains of hills and flat topped hillocks and water courses. The highest peak is Gopalaswamy hills having an altitude of 1454.5 meters above mean sea level and lowest is along the Kannegala Stream about 680 meters above mean sea level. The reserve is drained by Kabini, Nugu and Moyar rivers and their tributaries like Kannegalahole, Hebbahalla and Kekkanahalla. The Moyar river falls into picturesque gorge popularly known as 'Mysore ditch', which is 260 meters deep forming one of the most beautiful features of the landscape over looking the famous Nilgiri mountains. If forms the southern border of Karnataka along with Tamil Nadu. The Nugu river flows cross cutting the reserve in the middle across which there is a reservoir at Beerwal which provides a perennial water source. The Kabini river forms the western and north-west boundaries of this reserve across which lies a major irrigation dam at Beechanahally and its back-waters provide perennial water source to the wild animals and especially to the elephants during pinch period. (*Source*: Action Plan Report on Project Tiger: Bandipur National Park).

Vegetation and Types of Forests

The forest in the Bandipur Tiger Reserves are of deciduous types and show variation which are rich in their composition. In the eastern part of the Reserve lies the scrub forests while the central portion is found to be of dry deciduous type and the western part of the park is moist deciduous. The vegetation in the park varies from scrub type to moist mixed deciduous type according to the variation in rainfall from east to west. However, the scrub types of vegetation is due to degradation in the fringes of the park all along the northern boundary on account of the pressure of dependency.

Flora

The flora of this area include Teak (Thega, Tectona grandis) which grows naturally in this part of the Western Ghats, while the other dry deciduous trees common in this area are the highly valued sandal (*shreegandha*, Santalum album), *'honne'* (Pterocarpus marsupium), Terminalia species (especially alale (T. chebula), *Thaare* (T.bellarica) and Maththi (T.Tomentosa), *dindagar* (Anogeissus latifolia), which is the dominant species is most areas, *nelli* (Phylanthus emblica), *paadri* (Stereospurmum tetragonum) bende (Kydia caycinae)

Trees which are found in the more moist mixed deciduous forests include the dark rosewood (beete, Dalbergia latifolia), one of the most costliest and finest timbers in the world. Adjacent to pools and water courses, Yetthega (Adina cordifolia) and kadambolu (Mitragyna parviflora) are common. Places where the ground is more open and moist, i.e., around swampy patches, *bangore* (Randia uliginosa) and Kamulu (Careya arborea) are the common trees found. Bamboos are seen scattered through out the Park. The main palm of Bandipur is *eechalu* (Phoenix humilis) found on hill slopes and in hollows. The *kitul* palm (*baini*, Caryota urens), whose pith is converted into sago, is not as common here as it is elsewhere in the Western Ghats. Common among shrubs in the drier parts of Bandipur are species such as *jeevadhele* or *chumbulu* (Erythroxylon monogynum) and *band harike* (Dodonaca viscosa). (Nima Manjrekar - 2001)

Fauna

The Bandipur National Park has a variety of mammals, birds and reptiles. The herbivorous mammals found in the park are elephant, gaur, sambar, chital or spotted deer, muntjae or barking deer, mouse deer, four horned antelope, wild boar, grey langur, bonnet macaque, slender loris, blacknaped hare, porcupine, Indian giant squirrel, common giant flying squirrel, three striped palm squirrel. The carnivorous mammals found in the Park are tiger, leopard, leopard cat, jungle cat, rusty spotted cat, common palm civet, small Indian civet, sloth bear, *dhole* or Asiatic wild dog, stripped hyena, golden jackal, common mongoose, striped necked mongoose, ruddy mongoose, smooth Indian otter, Indian pangolin etc.

There are more than 230 species of birds which have been identified inhabiting Bandipur National Park by ornithologists. Some of the important groups found in the park include herons, storks, ducks, kites, egrets, eagles, partridges, quails, falcons, wild fowls, sandpipers, lapwings, pigeons, doves, parakeets, owls, cuckoos, swifts, nightjars, bee-eaters, barbets, woodpeckers, larks, kingfishers, swallows, shrikes, drongos, mynas, minivets, orioles, bulbuls, babblers, flycatchers, thrushes, chats, warblers, tits, nuthatches, wagtails, flower peckers, sunbirds and munias.

The reptiles found in the Bandipur National Park are marsh crocodile, starred tortoise, Indian pond terrapin, common Indian monitor, Indian chemeleon, southern green Calotes, forest calotes, skinks, geckos, spectacled cobra, Russell's viper, common rat snake, common krait, Indian python, checkered keel back, green whip snake, common Indian bronze back, flying snake, wolf snake, trinket snake etc.

Population of wild animals according to the 2002 census of Wild Animals in Bandipur National Park area, is as follows:

Tigers	78 to 82
Panthers	80 to 88
Gaur	2400 to 2600
Elephants	1950 to 2100
Spotted Dears	8200 to 8400
Sambars	2200 to 2500
Wild dogs	170 to 200
Sloth bears	60 to 70

Other animals include langurs, jungle cats, jackal, four horned antelopes, porcupines, wild bears, hares, cobras, pythons, vipers, tortoise etc.

About the People Living Around Bandipur National Park

Before we talk about the people living around Bandipur National Park we need to get acquainted with a few technical terms used by the forests department. For instance, impact zone is the zone having influence of people within the park; while the zone impacted outside the park by the creation of the protected area is called impacted zone. The people mostly depend on the fringe forests (i.e.,) the area demarcated as buffer) of this National Park for grazing of cattle, collection of fuel wood, collection of non-timber forest produce and also small timber for agricultural implements and house constructions. This dependency without an alternative is the root cause for illicit activities causing impact on the wildlife and its habitat. About three to four kilometers radius of the forest all along the boundary inside the park is facing the pressure of the people and their cattle and is subjected for gradual degradation. The said impact zone is about 310 sq kms in area.

The impacted zone stretches to a distance of five kms all along the boundary outside the Park. People living within a radius of five kms outside the Park have been impacted by the creation of this National Park, as they are facing the pressure of wildlife depredating into their agricultural fields and villages causing crop damages, cattle kills, human injury and deaths in addition to legally forcing the people to keep away from the National Park on which they are depending to meet their requirements since time immemorial.

The villages falling within the impacted zone have been identified by the forest department basing on their location with reference to the boundary of the park and also basing on the impact being faced by the people from the protected area. These are the villages which are again causing impact on the park and affecting the fauna and its habitat.

The human habitation is confined to only northern region and to west for a short distance all along the boundary. Both these surroundings are thickly populated by agricultural communities. The landless people live on labour in agricultural fields and forests. The tribal communities namely the Betta/ Kadu Kuruba, the Jenu Kuruba and the Soliga are concentrated in proximity to the park as they have been rehabilitated and forced to settle at the allotted colonies after shifting from the protect area and other forest areas submerged in Kabini reservoir. There are about 200 villages around the National Park with a population of about 1,60,000 individuals according to 1991 census (which includes Scheduled Tribes, Scheduled Castes, Backward Classes and other communities).

Reportedly, there is no settlement in Bandipur National Park except the tribal in Bandipur village. The settlement at Bandipur was in the administrative zone and the tribal people started showing increase with the socio-economic facilities provided by the Government in addition to improved availability of labour in this park. This increased population was observed to be exerting pressure on the wildlife habitat for fuel wood and in collection of non–timber forest produce. For realizing this pressure, the 100 tribal families living in Bandipur were rehabilitated at Melakamanahalli Colony and Karemala outside the park with the provision of housing and one hectare of land for cultivation to each tribal family with an outlay of Rs. 100 lakhs. This project was in progress upto 1996-97.

The other non-tribal communities living in the affected zone are the dominant Veerashaivas (Lingayats) an agricultural community, followed by Nayakas (Parivars, a Backward Community) Kurubagowdas (cattle graziers cum farmers) Scheduled Castes like Adi- Karnataka, and other communities like Brahmans and Vysyas, in small number.

For the present study Melakamanahalli Tribal Colony was taken as the rehabilitated village and Chennaikattai as the traditional village. Melakamanahalli Tribal Colony comes under the Mangala Gram Panchayat while Chennaikattai comes under the Hangala Gram Panchayat. Both the villages which were taken for the study come under Gundulpet Taluk of Chamarajanagar district. Melakamanahalli Tribal colony is inhabited by the Betta / Kadu Kuruba and the Jenu Kuruba while the Chennaikattai is a mono-ethnic village inhabited by the Soligas. A brief ethnographic profile of all the three tribal communities will be brought into relief with an idea to know about their respective cultures.

Jenu Kuruba

The Jenu Kuruba are a community of food gatherers and honey collectors. The prefixing word *jenu* means honey and the word *Kuruba* indicate the community name. According to Thurston (1909) "The Kurumba or Kuruba are the modern representative of the ancient Kurubas or Pallavas". Misra (1979) has described in detail about this community. He (Ibid) quoting Aiyappan mentioned that "the Kuruba is the name of the large shepherd community of the Karnataka plateau. They speak Kannada. In Mysore they are divided into Uru Kuruba and Kadu Kuruba. Kadu Kuraba are further divided into Betta Kuruba and Jenu Kuruba" (Misra 1979 cited by Gupta : 2003). Misra (Ibid) goes on to say, "sufficient authentic information is lacking in correlating the present Kuruba, Jenu Kuraba and Betta Kuruba with the Pallava dynasty. We do not know whether these groups are the offshoots of the same stock. The Jenu Kuruba, though they live near each other, show marked differences." They inhabit the plateau and hilly areas which has moderate climate, low humidity, thin forest and medium rainfall.

The total population of Jenu Kuruba in Karnataka according to 1981 census was 34,746. It may be noted that their population was only 6696 in 1971 before removal of Area Restriction of Scheduled Groups. They are concentrated in Mysore, Chamarajanagar and Kodagu districts. They have their own dialect called Jenu Nudi and use Kannada script. The Jenu Kuruba are categorized as a Primitive Tribal Group (PTG) among the Scheduled Tribes of Karnataka.

The Jenu Kuruba are nonvegetarian and eat pork but abstain from taking beef. Ragi is their staple cereal, but on festivities they eat rice. In the past they used to take wild roots and tubers regularly which is on the wane of late. Consanguinal of alcoholic drinks is occasional among them. The Jenu Kuruba are an endogamous tribe. Consanguinal cross cousin marriages are common among them with a social sanction to marry one's father's sister's daughter, mother's brother's daughter and elder sister's daughter. Marriage by negotiation is the usual form of marriage while monogamy is the norm. Marriage by elopement is also permitted but such marriages are declining in the recent past. The *Thali* made of copper or silver and toe-rings are the symbols of marriage for a woman. Reportedly, there is neither payment of dowry nor bride price in the community. Residence of marriage is virilocal, followed by a neolocal rule of residence. Junior sororate is permissible if the first wife do not have children. Divorce is permitted but this has to be adjudicated by their own panchayat. Children in the event of their parents divorce are a liability to the father. Reportedly, widows, widowers, male and female divorcees are allowed to remarry.

Traditionally the Jenu Kuruba live in nuclear families. But with the establishment of new tribal colonies by the government, it is not always possible for the new couple to establish a separate dwelling immediately as they used to do earlier when they were engaged in food gathering and led a nomadic life. Hence, a few vertically extended families also exist. Property is equally shared by all sons while the eldest son succeeds to the office of his father. The Jenu Kuruba women participate in agricultural operation, cattle rearing, in collection of non-timber forest produce, and fire wood, thus contributing to the family income. They participate in social activities and also work as labourers. During the festival of Paduldamma and Kambdamma (village deities). The women are not allowed to perform pooja and they are restricted entry into the sanctum sanctorum.

The first delivery takes place in the parental house of the woman. Birth pollution is observed for twelve days. On the twelfth day, they smear the walls and floor with cowdung and after observance of purificatory rituals, the child and the mother are taken inside the house. Naming ceremony is also performed on the twelfth day. In some cases, it is done after three months. Tonsuring ceremony is performed for a boy when he is five or six years old. The maternal uncle takes the boy on his lap and cuts the hair symbolically which is later completed by a barber.

Among the Jenu Kuruba, a girl on attaining puberty, takes bath on alternate day for one month and made to sit in a hut made of leaves. After completion of one month, she is given a purificatory bath. Marriage rituals are performed at the bride's residence.

When a death takes place among the Jenu Kuruba, the corpse is given a bath and laid on a bier (*chatta*) and placed in a north-south direction, with the head facing south and taken to the burial ground. After placing the body in the grave, the eldest son puts a handful of mud into the grave and this is followed by others. It is informed that women also go to the burial ground. Milk is poured on the grave on the third day. Final obsequies called *tithi* are performed on the 12th day for termination of death pollution.

The Jenu Kuruba are traditionally food gatherers from their traditional nomadic life, they have switched over to a sedentary life. They were rehabilitated by the government in tribal colonies with allotment of a few acres of land to the displaced families. Presently they are engaged in collection of non-timber forest produce and labourers in the forest operations.

The Jenu Kuraba have their traditional tribal councils headed by a Yajamana and members who are community elders. These tribal councils adjudicate disputes related to land, petty quarrels, cases of adultery and desertion. The guilty is punished by imposition of fine in cash. Apart from their traditional tribal councils, the members are also part of the statutory village panchayats.

The Jenu Kuruba follow local form of Hinduism. They worship deities namely Chikkamma, Soddamma and Handhigrayamma. The village deities are Pataldaramma, Periyapattanalamma and Kammbadamma. They appease Pataldaramma and Kammbadamma for rains and good yields respectively and Periyapattanalamma for protection of the village by sacrificing sheep, goats and chicken. The Jenu Kuruba also worship deities namely Bellamari, Honnoorhatti, Billoorumari and Nerajettha. Now a days they are also worshipping Someswara. They used to have their own priest, but, of late they are employing a local Jangama as their priest but he would not enter their houses but conduct the rituals only at the Mandapams. They celebrate festivals such as Ugadi, Gowri, Habba and Deepavali.

Kadu Kuruba

The Kadu Kuruba are also referred to as Betta Kuruba. The name Kadu Kuruba and Betta Kuruba have been derived from the words *kadu* meaning forest, and *betta* meaning hill. The Kadu Kuruba are concentrated in the Mysore and Chamarajanagar districts of Karnataka. According to the 1981 census their population is 209,677. They speak in their own dialect among themselves, which seems to be similar to that of Kannada. They speak Kannada with others and use the Kannada script. The Kadu Kuruba women can be identified by their distinctive way of adorning the sari.

The Kadu Kuruba have exogamous clans such as 'Ane' (elephant), Bevina (neem tree) and Kolli (Fire brand). But of late, these divisions are not identifiable. Reportedly, cross-cousin and maternal uncle-niece marriages are prevalent among them. The Kadu Kuruba are monogamous. They follow patrilocal rule of residence. Divorce is permissible for reasons like adultery and maladjustment. Widow, widower and divorcee remarriages are allowed. They mostly live in nuclear families and follow male equigeniture rule of inheritance. However, succession right is transcended to the eldest son. The Kadu Kuruba women participate in all domestic, social and economic activities. The birth of the first child takes place at the natal home of the mother, away from the main house. Birth pollution is observed for seven days, while post-natal restrictions are observed for three to five months. Tonsure ceremony for children is observed after completion of one year of age. Marriage is performed at the bridegroom's residence, wherein the bride and the bridegroom exchange areca nut and betel leaves and the bridegroom ties a *thali* around the neck of the bride. The dead are burried in a lying posture and pollution is observed for ten days. Obsequies called *thithi* are performed on the 11th day.

The primary occupations of the Kadu Kuruba are agriculture, agricultural labour, forest labour, basket making and rolling of beedis (Singh K.S. 1996). Some of them have received agricultural lands from the government on their rehabilitation. The Kadu Kuruba participate in operations to trap wild elephants and often get killed while handling and riding them (Singh : ibid).

The hereditary headman of their traditional tribal council is called megala or *moopadadu* or *yajman*. Their traditional council adjudicates intercommunity disputes and imposes cash fines on those who violate social norms. They profess local form of Hinduism and have faith in local deities like Tavaragatta Madapa, Basaveswara, Bella Mariamma, Kota Mariamma. They have their own sacred specialists. The Kadu Kuruba render folksongs on the occasion of Ugadi and other local festivals.

Water sources and burial grounds are shared with their neighbouring communities like the Jenu Kuruba. They use magic, sorcery and witchcraft for the treatment of ailments. Of late, they have started availing modern medical facilities.

Soliga/Soligaru

The Soliga / Soligaru are concentrated in the hilly tracts of Mysore and Chamarajanagar districts of Karnataka which are covered with forests and experience heavy rainfall. According to the 1981 census, their total population in Karnataka returned as Soligaru is 16,390. The Soligaru speak among themselves in a dialect of the Kannada language and use Kannada script.

According to Singh (1994), the Soliga have five divisions, namely Urali, Kadu, Male, Urubathi or Dasayya or Burude and Pujari. These subdivisions are differentiated on the basis of territory, language and social structure. There are clans (*kulal*) like Chalakiri, Suraru, Belli, Teneru and Haleru, and there exists a hierarchy among these clans groups, which help in determining the offices of tribal councils (Singh ibid). Nanjundayya and Iyer (1930) reported four endogamous divisions among the Soliga, namely Urali, Male, Kadu and Urubatti which are further divided into exogamous clans like Ajuru, Jungalur, Belloru, Surena, and Teneru. Endogamy is practiced by them at group level and exogamy at clan level. Cross-cousin marriages are preferred by the Soliga. They practise adult marriage and generally arrange alliances through negotiation. Marriage by elopement is also allowed in the community. The symbols of a married woman are a pendant and toe-rings. It is customary to pay twelve rupees and fifty paise as bride price by them. Divorce is accorded if asked for on grounds of adultery and maladjustment. The remarriage of widows, widowers and divorcees is permitted among the Soliga. They follow male equigeniture rule of inheritance while succession to an office is transcended to the eldest son. The Soliga women fetch water, collect fuel wood and tubers and take part in social and ritual activities. The Soliga observe childhood rite of naming and also perform puberty rites for girls. When a marriage is preceded by an elopement, the newly wed couple hosts a community feast later for social sanction and recognition of their marriage. For a negotiated marriage, some rituals are performed elaborately. They cremate the dead and ancestors are worshipped annually.

The traditional occupation of the Soliga was shifting cultivation. In addition, they collect non-timber forest produce. Of late, they have taken up forest and agricultural labour. Very few among them have taken up settled cultivation which is in an incipient stage.

The Soliga follow Hinduism. They worship community deities like Karaya, Kyatadevaru, Jadeswamy, Chikkadevamma, Doddamathai, Basaweswara and other deities. Mehadeswar is their regional deity. Sacred specialist from the Lingayat community and from their own community serve them. They observe their traditional festivals like Rotti Habba and Mane Devera Habba. Basketry is the craft of these people in some areas.

A Brief History of The Bandipur National Park

Bandipur has a long and distinguished history. Right from the commencement of the 20th century, the need to conserve wildlife was felt in the Princely State of Mysore, and the Mysore Game and Forest Preservation Regulation was passed. In the year 1931, about 90 sq.kms. sanctuary was carved out in the Chamarajanagar State Forest, but soon it was realised that it was very small for effective conservation and in the year 1941 the Venugopala Wildlife Park was constituted, extending over an area of 800 sq.kms. right from the Moyar river forming the natural southern border of the state towards the Nilgiris, northwards towards Gundlupet to include the Gopalaswamy Betta. The park was named after Venugopala, the deity of the shrine on the hill top, worshipped by the former Maharajas of Mysore. Bandipur, the 60 sq.kms. sanctum sanctorum of the park, has long been famous for its faunal richness, and in it, no forestry operations have been permitted, so that in spite of its dominantly deciduous complexion it still holds many magnificent trees.

The Park as of now comprises most of the forests of the old Venugopala Park and covers about 880 sq.kms. The present core has been shifted outside the old sanctum of Bandipur to comparatively primitive forests, including parts of the Begur, Ainurmarigudi, Beerambadi, Katwal and Bandipur Reserve Forests. (Nima Manjrekar: 2001).

Management of Ecotourism Spot

It is informed that the Park is systematically managed by the Field Director, with the Deputy Director being in charge overall, duly assisted by two Assistant Wild Life Wardens, 9 Park Wardens, 23 Foresters, 98 Forest Guards, and a number of watchers. In addition to the task force, tribals are engaged to assist the staff in anti-poaching and anti-smuggling squads, and in prevention of forest fires. The entire park is connected by wireless network and walkie-talkies are provided to the staff to assist them in protecting the park more efficiently. The park is also well equipped with armoury. (*Sources* : Brochure on Bandipura National Park – Project Tiger).

Infrastructural Facility

A well connected network of roads within the Park ensures quick mobility and each Park Warden is equipped with a fast moving vehicle. The focus of management in the Park is on wildlife conservation, and hence, forestry operations have been completely stopped ever since the area was declared as a Tiger Reserve. A 53 kilometer elephant proof trench has been excavated along certain areas of the Park's perimeter to minimise crop raiding by elephants in the agricultural fields just outside the Park.

For wildlife viewing for the tourists, vehicles are available. Elephant rides are also arranged to go into the forests adjoining the tourist complex at Bandipur. The Park has a salubrous climate, with three seasons: summer, monsoon and winter. Anytime between April and October is the ideal time to visit the Park. The tourism zone with an area of 82 sq.kms. is earmarked for spreading the message among the people to preserve the flora and fauna and the rich heritage of the country. The administrative zone with an area of one sq.km. is earmarked for tourist lodges, staff quarters and administrative offices.

Visiting hours for the park is from 6.00 A.M. to 9.00 A.M. in the forenoon and from 3.30 P.M. to 6.30 P.M. in the afternoons. For entry into the park an adult is charged Rs. 50/- and a child Rs. 25/- for persons of Indian nationality, while for foreigners an adult is charged Rs. 150/- and a child Rs. 25/-. For an elephant ride in the park Rs.50/- is charged per head for a ride lasting for about 20 minutes.

Table 2.2 Accommodations in Bandipur National Park

	For Indians	*For Foreigners*
1. a. Gajendra VIP Suites I & II	Rs. 1500/-	Rs. 2,500/- per suite per day
b.Gajendra Suites III & IV	Rs. 450/- day	Rs. 800/- per suite per
2. Mayura Cottage I & II	Rs. 450/- per day	Rs. 800/- per cottage

(Contd.)

(Contd. Table 2.2)

	For Indians	For Foreigners
3. Papiha Cottage I & II	Rs. 450/-	Rs. 800/- per cottage per day
4. Kokila Cottage I & II	Rs. 450/-	Rs. 800/- per cottage per day
5. Harini Suites I & II	Rs. 300/-	Rs. 500/- per suite per day
6. Chital Suites I & II	Rs. 300/-	Rs. 500/- per suite per day
7. Vanashri Suites I & II	Rs. 300/-	Rs. 500/- per suite per day
8. Vanaranjani Cottage I&II	Rs. 300/- per day	Rs. 500/- per cottage
9. Dormitory – 6 beds	Rs. 300/- per day	
10. Dormitory – 10 beds	Rs. 500/- per day	
11. Dormitroy – 20 beds	Rs. 1000/- per day	

Accommodation is available for the tourists within the tourist complex. Cottages and suites are double bedded. Tarrif for different types of suites cottages and dormitories are mentioned in Table 2.2:

Food for the tourists is prepared on placement of order in all the suites /cottages / dormitories mentioned above.

Bandipur National Park is approachable by road. From Bangalore the distance to the Park is 220 kms. and from either Mysore or Ooty it is 80 kms. The nearest airports are Bangalore and Coimbatore. State transport bus services are available from Bangalore, Mysore and Ooty. Karnataka State Tourism Development Corporation's luxury buses are available from Bangalore and Mysore. The nearby tourist spots from Bandipur are (1) Himavad Gopalaswamy hill and temple is 15 kms and (2) Mudumalai Wild Life Sanctionary 12 kms.

Socio-Economic Background of the Tribals employed in Bandipur National Park

About 20 tribal households were taken for the study where in a member or two from each household are employed in Bandipur National Park to draw the impact of tourism. Out of 20 tribal households taken for the study, 11 households belong to **Betta/**

Kadu Kuruba, five households to Jenu Kuruba and four households to Soliga tribal community. (See Table :2.3). The population of 11 Betta/Kadu Kuruba households is 40 of which 23 are males and 17 are females; the population of five Jenu Kuruba households is 22 of which 9 are males and 13 are females and the population of four Soliga household is 14, of which 10 are males and four are females.

Table 2.3 Tribals Employed in Bandipur National Park, No. of Households and Their Tribe-wise and Sex-wise Population

S. No.	*Tribe*	*No. of Households*	*No. of Persons employed*	*Population*		
				Male	female	Total
1.	Betta/Kadu Kuruba	11	12	23	17	40
2.	Jenu Kuruba	5	5	9	13	22
3.	Soliga	4	4	10	4	14
	TOTAL	20	21	42	34	76

There are 12 persons from 11 Betta/Kadu Kuruba households, five persons from five Jenu Kuruba households and four persons from four Soliga households employed in Bandipur National Park. This may speak of economic dominance of the Betta/Kadu Kuruba in employment in the National Park among the tribals. They (Betta/Kadu Kuruba) are also educationally better off when compared to the Jenu Kuruba and the Soliga tribal households taken for the study. This may be substantiated with the fact that from 11 Betta/Kadu Kuruba households there are 15 members (nine males and six females) who studied upto primary level of education, one female in upper primary level and five males who studied upto secondary level. The total literates among the Better/Kadu Kuruba are 21 (14 males and 7 females). There are only 12 members (five males and seven females) who are illiterates. Among the five Jenu Kuruba households, there are 12 members (five males and seven females) who studied only upto primary level. None of the persons from this community studied upto upper primary and secondary levels. There are 9 members (3 males and six females) who are illiterates. Among the four

Table 2.4 Tribals Employed in Bandipur National Park, No. of Households, Sex-wise and Tribe-wise Literates and Illiterates

Sl No	*Tribe*	*No of House holds*	*Primary*			*Upper primary*			*Secondary*		
			M	*F*	*T*	*M*	*F*	*T*	*M*	*F*	*T*
1.	Betta/ Kadu Kuruba	11	9 (22.50)	6 (15.00)	15 (37.50)	-	1 (2.50)	1 (2.50)	5 (12.50)	-	5 (12.50)
2.	Jenu Kuruba	5	5 (22.73)	7 (31.82)	12 (54.55)	-	-	-	-	-	-
3.	Soliga	4	2 (14.29)	-	2 (14.29)	-	-	-	1 (7.14)	-	1 (7.14)
	Total	20	16 (21.05)	13 (17.11)	29 (38.16)	-	1 (1.32)	1 (1.32)	1 (1.32)		6 (7.89)

(Contd.)

(Contd. Table 2. 4)

Sl No	*Tribe*	*No of House holds*	*Total literates*			*Total illiterate*			*No . of persons employed*
			M	*F*	*T*	*M*	*F*	*T*	
1.	**Betta/ Kadu Kuruba**	11	14 (35.00)	7 (17.50)	21 (52.50)	5 (12.50)	7 (17.50)	12 (30.00)	12
2.	**Jenu Kuruba**	5	5 (22.73)	7 (31.82)	12 (54.55)	3 (13.64)	6 (27.27)	9 (40.91)	5
3.	**Soliga**	4	3 (21.43)	-	3 (21.43)	6 (42.86)	4 (28.57)	10 (71.43)	4
	Total	20	22 (28.95)	14 (18.42)	36 (47.37)	14 (18.42)	17 (22.37)	31 (40.79)	21

Figures in the brackets are percentages (7.89)

Soliga households there are only two males who studied upto primary level and only one male upto secondary level. There are ten individuals (six males and four females) who are illiterates. (see Table: 2.4)

Type of Employment Among the Tribals in Bandipur National Park

Tribals in Bandipur National Park are given employment in low cadre jobs, a few among them being permanent and most of them being appointed on daily wages. From the 20 households who have one or two persons employed from each household in the National Park. 11 households are from Betta / Kadu Kuruba tribal community, five households are from Jenu Kuruba and four households from Soliga Tribal Community. There are 12 persons employed from 11 Belta / Kadu Kuruba households. Of the 12 persons, one person is working as watcher, six members are working as anti-poaching watchers, one person as an elephant rider (mahoth), two persons as forest guards and another two persons as drivers – one in Bandipur National Park and the other person in a tourist resort. There are five Jenu Kuruba men from five households working in Bandipur National Park. Of the five members two persons are employed as watchers and one member each is employed as an elephant rider, forest guard and as a gardener. There are four Soliga men from four households employed in the Park. Of the four persons three numbers are employed as watchers and one person as anti-poaching watcher (See Table 2.5). The daily wage labourers are also employed for forest operations such as formation of view lines, fire lines operations, making water holes, making soil conservation and water conservation works.

Villagewise and tribewise employees in Bandipur National Park (see table: 2.6) reveal that out of the 12 Betta/Kadu Kuruba men employed in the National Park eight men are from Melakamanahalli tribal colony while the remaining four members are from Karemalai village; out of the five Jenu Kuruba men employed, two members are from Melakamanahalli Tribal Colony, two members from Karemalai and one person is from Nuvvulagundi colony; and all the four persons from Soliga tribal community who are employed in the park are from Karemalai village.

Table 2.5 Type of Employment Among the Tribals in Bandipur National Park

Sl. No.	*Tribe*	*No. of House holds*	*No. of persons employed in different capacities in Bandipur National Park*						
			Watchers	*Anti poaching watchers*	*Elephant rider*	*Forest guard*	*Driver*	*Gardner*	*Total*
1.	Belta/ Kadu Kuruba	11	1	6	1	2	2	-	12
2.	Jenu Kuruba	5	2	-	1	1	-	1	5
3.	Soliga	4	3	1	-	-	-	-	4
	Total	20	6	7	2	3	3	1	21

Table 2.6 Village-wise and Tribe-wise Employees in Bandipur National Park

Sl. No.	Tribe	No. of employees from Melakamanahalli Tribal Colony	No. of employees from Karemalai	No. of employees from Nuvvulagundi Colony	Total no. of persons employed
1.	Betta/Kadu Kuruba	8	4	-	12
2.	Jenu Kuruba	2	2	1	5
3.	Soliga	-	4	-	4
	Total	10	10	1	21

The tribewise annual income range per employee in Bandipur National Park may give us an idea of economic stratification among the tribals. From Table 2.7, it is observed that none of the employee / worker fall within the annual income range of Rs. 10,000/-. In the annual income range of Rs. 10,001/- to Rs. 20,000/- only one Betta / Kadu Kuruba man is identified. However, in the annual income range of Rs. 20,001/- to Rs. 30,000/- as many as seven Betta/Kadu Kuruba men, some three Jenu Kuruba men and two Soliga men come under this income range. Only one employee from Betta / Kadu Kumba community and two employees from Soliga community come under the income range of Rs. 30,001/- to Rs. 40,000/-.In the income range of Rs. 40,001/- to Rs. 50,000/- only one Jenu Kumruba employee has been identified, and in the income range of Rs. 70,001/- to Rs. 80,000/- some three employees from Betta / Kadu Kuruba community are found. Only one Jenu Kuruba employees income falls in the income range of Rs. 80,001/- to Rs. 90,000/-. From the above mentioned information on literacy and income through employment in Bandipur National Park, we understand that the Betta/Kadu Kuruba are educationally and economically better off when compared to the Jenu Kuruba and Soliga tribal communities in the area of study.

The persons who are employed as watchers, anti-poaching watchers, fire watchers – be it from a tribal or a non-tribal community, they are paid Rs. 68/- per day. The persons who are employed on daily wage get employment for three to four months in a year in the National Park. But it is informed by some, that the daily wage employees were given Rs. 50/- per day to work in the park due to paucity of funds and secondly to generate employment for more number of unemployed youth in the National Park. But the employees who are engaged as Forest Guard are employed on permanent basis and get a monthly income of Rs. 6,000/- to Rs. 8,000/- depending upon one's basic pay and other allowances.

Table 2.7 Tribe-wise Annual Income Range Per Employee in Bandipur National Park

Sl. No.	*Annual Income Range per employee (in Rs.)*	*No. of Betta/Kadu Kuruba persons employed*	*No. of Jenu Kuruba persons employed*	*No. of Soliga persons employed*	*Total no. of persons employed*
1.	Upto Rs. 10,000	-	-	-	
2.	Rs. 10,001 to Rs. 20,000	1	-	-	1
3.	Rs. 20,001 to Rs. 30,000	7	3	2	12
4.	Rs. 30,001 to Rs. 40,000	1	-	2	3
5.	Rs. 40,001 to Rs. 50,000	-	1	-	1
6.	Rs. 50,001 to Rs. 60,000	-	-	-	-
7.	Rs. 60,001 to Rs. 70,000	-	-	-	-
8.	Rs. 70,001 to Rs. 80,000	3	-	-	3
9.	Rs. 80,001 to Rs. 90,000	-	1	-	1
	Total	12	5	4	21

There was a proposal for recruitment of forest watchers from the tribals of Bandipura and Gundulpet area, but it was later cancelled/ withheld due to some political reasons, the details of the same is described below.

About 24 tribal youth have appeared for written test, interview and physical fitness and in sports for the posts of permanent Forest Watchers. About 12 candidates were selected for the posts with starting basic pay of Rs. 2750/-. Just before they were to be recruited in the Forest Department, a court case was filed against their recruitment by non-tribals working in Forest Department on daily wages under the guidance of a very powerful political leader who belong to Kuruba Caste (a non-tribal) as his candidates were not selected. However, it is further informed that the case may go in favour of the tribals very soon and they are likely to be recruited in the Forest Department in Bandipura and Gundulpet area.

In addition to the employment in Bandipur National Park, there are a few tribals employed in Hotels and Resorts around

Bandipur National Park as waiters and sweepers. There are three resorts very near to Melakamanahalli tribal colony. They are M.C. Resorts, Nilgiri Resorts and Jungle Resorts. Yet, there is no much impact of tourism on tribals living in Melakamanahalli tribal colony. It is informed that only two persons from Betta/Kadu Kuruba tribal community are employed in these resorts. There are ten members employed occasionally as trekking guides. They are paid Rs. 150/- per day and this employment is seasonal.

Risk Factors in Sustainable Development of Ecotourism

For sustainable development we may have to overcome certain hurdles and risks which may be ecological, administrative, lack of communication facilities and education, attitudes of officials, conflicts between man and animals, frequent changes in development programmes, fire damages etc. (see Table 2.8).

Table 2.8 Risk Factors in Sustainable Development on Ecotourism (as informed by Scheduled Tribes Employees Working in Bandipur National Park)

Sl. No.	*Risk Factors*	*No. of ST Employees*
1.	Ecological degradation	14
2.	Top down approach	9
3.	Development programmes not related to local needs and culture	10
4.	Benefits not distributed equally	17
5.	Poaching	-
6.	Lack of communication facilities	3
7.	Lack of education	18
8.	Different attitudes of officials towards tribal	4
9.	Man and animal conflict	-
10.	Frequent changes in development programmes	1
11.	Fire damage	1

About 20 informants have been interviewed to know from them about the probable risk factors in sustainable development on eco-tourism. Of the 20 informants about 14 informants expressed that ecological degradation is one of the risk factors in sustainable development on eco-tourism. About 9 informants conveyed that top-down approach of the government as one of the risk factors while 10 respondents are of the opinion that the development programmes being implemented by the government are not related to local needs and culture of the people. As many as 17 respondents feel that the benefits are not being distributed equally as one of the risk factors, while only three informants say that lack of communication facilities as one of the risk factors. As many as 18 respondents conveyed that lack of education could be one of the risk factors responsible in sustainable development on eco-tourism but some four informants are of the opinion that different attitudes of the officials towards tribal as one of the risk factors. Only one informant each is of the view that frequent changes in development programmes and lastly the fire damage as one of the important risk factors responsible for sustainable development on eco-tourism.

Suggestion for Eco-tourism and Sustainable Development by Scheduled Tribes Employees

When we asked suggestions for improvement of eco-tourism and sustainable development from schedule tribes employees working in Bandipur National Park, about half of the informants conveyed that they have no idea to give any suggestions for eco-tourism and sustainable development. About five informants suggested that people's participation is necessary for eco-tourism

Table 2.9 Suggestions for Eco-tourism and Sustainable Development by Scheduled Tribes Employees Working in Bandipur National Park

Sl. No.	*Suggestions for Eco- Tourism and sustainable development*	*No. of ST Employees*
1.	Peoples' Participation	5
2.	Training to be given in agricultural operations	1
3.	Education	3
4.	Employment	1
5.	No idea	10
	Total	20

and sustainable development while three informants suggested for more education. Only one informant has suggested to provide training in agricultural operations as they were ones food gatherers while another respondent suggested to generate employment for promotion of eco-tourism and sustainable development (see Table 2.9).

For Eco-tourism and sustainable development in biosphere reserves it is imperative to follow some conservation measure to preserve the bio-diversity existing in the biosphere reserves, lest there is possibility of depletion and disappearance of certain species of flora and fauna. The following are the conservation measures for preservation of biospheres.

1. Eco-tourism Supplementing development while imparting enjoyment
2. Fencing for the sanctuary : Protection for people and animals
3. Nature education : Spreading awareness about conservation
4. Trekking : Exposure to wonders of nature
5. Veterinary care: Preventing spread of diseases
6. Patrols: Enforcing law and order
7. Resettlement of tribals : Providing livelihood for the people of the forest
8. Aforestation : Planting trees for the future
9. Fire Fighting : Prevention and control of forest fire
10. Water holes : Combating drought for the animals.

The Wildlife (Protection) Act 1972: The brief summary of Wildlife (Protection) Act 1972 as enacted by the Parliament in the 23rd year of Republic of India is as follows. "No person shall interfere, conduct any activities which touches upon the life of aquatic, terrestrial, aerian, flora, fauna and eco-system except with express sanction of the competent authority empowered under this act."

"This act is in force throughout the territory of India. Any contravention of the provisions of this act attracts prosecution and penalty.

The act has been made applicable in Karnataka State with effect from 1st July 1973, vide G.S.R. BSSCE, 1st July 1973 No. 53 of 1972.

Tourists

Smith (1977) defines the tourist as "temporary leisured person who voluntarily visits a place away from home for the purpose of experiencing a change".

Valene Smith (1977) classified seven types of tourists. These are:

1. Explorer
2. Elite tourists
3. Off-beat tourists
4. Unusual tourists
5. Incipient mass tourists
6. Mass tourists
7. Charter tourists

1. Explorers

This type of tourists are very limited and they are active participants and observe among the local people.

2. Elite Tourists

This type of tourists are few in number, rarely seen, but with pre-arranged service facilities.

3. Off-beat Tourists

This type of tourists are uncommon but they seek to get away from the tourist crowds.

4. Unusual Tourists

These tourists are occasional in number. They travel in an organized tour and they travel on one day package tour to visit some natives.

5. Incipient Mass Tourists

This type of tourists seek western amenities and comforts.

6. Mass Tourists

These tourists expect trained multilingual hotel and tourists staffs to fulfill their needs.

7. Charter Tourists

These tourists have minimal involvement with the local people and culture.

Nature of Composition of Tourists

The nature of composition of tourists can be stratified into family, party / group and alone. The following Table 2.10 depicts the nature of composition of tourists. Who visited Bandipur National Park.

Table 2.10 Nature of Composition of Tourists

Sl.No.	*Composition*	*No. of Tourists*	*Percentage*
1.	Alone	6	6
2.	Family	29	29
3.	Party / Group	65	65
	Total	100	100

This table reveals that 65 per cent of the tourists travelled in a group / party while 29 per cent of the tourists travelled with their families. The remain 6 per cent of the tourists reported to have been traveling alone.

State-wise profile of the tourists

The following table 2.11 depicts the state- wise profile of the tourists coming to Bandipur National Park.

Table 2.11 State-wise Profile of the Tourists

Sl. No.	*Name of the State*	*No. of Tourists*	*Percentage*
1.	Karnataka	41	41
2.	Kerala	30	30
3.	Tamil Nadu	8	8
4.	Maharashtra	1	1
5.	Himachal Pradesh	3	3
6.	Andaman and Nicobar Islanders	2	2
7.	West Bengal	1	1
8.	Rajasthan	1	1
9.	Uttar Pradesh	1	1
10.	Jammu and Kashmir	1	1
11.	Foreign Countries	11	100
	Total	100	100

Among the tourists coming to Bandipur, most of the tourists (41 per cent) were from Karnataka and 30 per cent of the tourists were from Kerala and only 11 per cent of the tourists from the abroad. A very few tourists visited this place from Himachal Pradesh (3 per cent), Andaman and Nicobar Islands (2 per cent), West Bengal (1 per cent), Rajasthan (1 per cent), Uttar Pradesh (1 per cent) and Jammu and Kashmir (1 per cent).

Table 2.12 Education-wise Distribution of the Tourists

Sl. No.	*Educational Level of the Tourists*	*No. of Tourists*	*Percentage*
1.	Secondary Education	4	4
2.	PUC (+2)	8	8
3.	Diploma in Computers	6	6
4.	Graduates	56	56
5.	Post Graduate	24	24
6.	Ph. D. holders	2	2
	Total	100	100

To know the educational background of the tourists, they are classified into six groups. The above Table: 2.12 reveals the education-wise distribution of the tourists.

This table shows that 56 per cent of the tourists are graduates and 24 per cent of the tourists are post-graduates while 2 per cent of the tourists are Ph.D. holders. A few tourists completed secondary education (4 per cent, PUC (8 per cent) and Diploma in Computer (6 per cent).

Occupation-wise Distribution of Tourists

This Table 2.13 shows the occupation-wise distribution of the tourists.

Table 2.13 Occupation-wise Distribution of the Tourists

Sl.No.	*Occupation of the Tourists*	*No. of Tourists*	*Percentage*
1.	Employees / Salaried service	78	78
2.	Business	22	22
	Total	100	100

This Table 2.13 reveals that the maximum number of tourists constituting 78 per cent had come from service or salaried class and 22 per cent of the tourists had come from business category.

Religion of the Tourists

To know the religion of the tourists, religious groups can be classified as Hindus, Christians, Muslims and Buddhists.

Table 2.14 Religion of the Tourists

SL. No.	Religious Group	No. of Tourists	Percentage
1.	Hindus	68	68
2.	Muslims	16	16
3.	Christians	15	15
4.	Buddhists	1	1
	Total	100	100

This Table 2.14 shows that most of the tourists (68 per cent) belong to the Hinduism, 16 per cent of the tourists belong to the Islam religion while 15 per cent of the tourists belong to the Christianity and one per cent of the tourists belong to the Buddhism.

Purpose of Visit

The following Table 2.15 reveals that the tourists have different purposes of their visit. Bandipur National Park has remained the main attraction for both domestic and international tourists.

Table 2.15 Purpose of Visit

Sl.No.	Purpose	Number of Tourists	Percentage
1.	Natural Beauty	84	84
2.	Adventure	16	16
	Total	100	100

Almost 84 per cent of the tourists responded that they came to Bandipur National Park to see its natural beauty i.e. forests, greenery and animals, etc., while only 16 per cent of the tourists visited for adventure.

Sources of Information about the Places Visited

To find out how tourists are motivated to visit this tourist spot, tourists were interviewed and the following information has been drawn (see Table 2.16).

Table 2.16 Sources of Information about the Place Visited

Sl. No.	*Sources*	*No. of Tourists*	*Percentage*
1.	Books and Journals	35	35
2.	Friends	45	45
3.	Family Members	13	13
4.	Newspapers	5	5
5.	Tradition	2	2
	Total	100	100

Frequency of Tour

It is one of the parameters of the study. Tourists may visit places yearly, seasonally, half yearly and occasionally which may depend on their enthusiasm, love for nature or to spend their leisurely time.

Table 2.17 Frequency of Tour

Sl.No.	*Frequency of Tour*	*No. of Tourists*	*Percentage*
1.	Yearly	32	32
2.	Seasonally	48	48
3.	Half yearly	12	12
4.	Occasional	4	4
5.	No answer	4	4
	Total	100	100

This Table 2.17 shows that 48 per cent of the tourists travelled seasonally and 32 per cent of the tourists travelled yearly. Only 12 per cent of the tourists reported to have been visiting half yearly and 4 per cent of the tourists travelled occasionally.

Mode of Transport

In order to visit the places of tourist importance, tourists may avail different means of transport such as bus, car, van, etc, (See: Table 2.18).

It appears from the Table 2.18 that buses and cars are the main important modes of transport used by the tourists to reach this spot about 61 per cent of the tourists reached the place by car and 30 per cent of the tourists reached this tourists spot by bus. The remaining 6 per cent of the tourists reached Bandipur by van.

Table 2.18 Mode of Transport

Sl.No.	*Mode of Transportation*	*No. of Tourists*	*Percentage*
1.	Bus	30	30
2.	Car	61	61
3.	Van	6	6
4.	Motor Bike	3	3
	Table	100	100

Number of Tourists visited Bandipur National Park

This table: 18 depicts the details of tourists who have visited Bandipur National Park during the year (2003-2004)

Table 2.19 Details of Tourists who have visited Bandipur National Park from 2003-2004

Sl. No.	*Month*	*Tourists*		*Total*
		Indians	*Foreigners*	
1.	April	6883	70	6953
2.	May	9690	27	9717
3.	June	4351	46	4397
4.	July	3440	32	3472
5.	August	3925	62	3987
6.	September	3194	15	3209
7.	October	3675	106	3781
8.	November	3989	110	4099
9.	December	3332	91	3423
10.	January	2974	167	3141
11.	February	1649	71	1720
12.	March	958	50	1008
	Total	48060	847	48907

The Table 2.19 shows that the total number of tourists visited Bandipur National Park was 48907, of which 48,060 tourists are domestic tourists and 847 tourists are foreign tourists. This table also shows that the inflow of tourists is more in the months of April and May.

Problems of the Tourists

Tourists face problems of different nature like food, accommodation, cleanliness, etc.

Table 2.20 Problems of the Tourists

Sl. No.	*Problems of the tourists*	*Number of tourists*	*Percentage*
1.	Food	54	54
2.	Accommodation	16	16
3.	Cleanliness and hygiene	12	12
4.	Transport	2	2
5.	No problems	16	16
	Total	100	100

The food and drink that are available to tourists when they are away from home is very important to them.

It appears from this Table 2.20 that most of the tourists (54 per cent) are not satisfied with food available in Bandipur National Park. About 16 per cent of the tourists are not satisfied with the accommodation available at Bandipur National Park. Another important aspect of tourist attraction is the shopping facilities such as shops of handicrafts, works of art, decorated garments etc. in the tourist spot. The tourists reported that such type of shops are not available in this tourist spot. They suggested that such shops may be opened to cater the needs of the tourists.

Attitude of the Forest Officials about Tourists

The attitude of the forest officials about the tourists visiting the Bandipur National Park is mixed. It is reported that some tourists come to enjoy nature and spend their leisure times whereas some tourists visit the National Park for enjoying alcoholic drinks. What so ever be the purpose of tourists visits, there is no harm to the bio-diversity of the Bandipur National Park by the tourists.

While the tourists are in the premises of the National Park they are required to follow certain restrictions as mentioned below:

1. No fire arms are allowed to be carried inside the park.
2. Pets, transistors and tape recorders are not permitted to be taken inside the park.
3. Smoking is strictly prohibited especially during the summers.
4. Cooking in cottages and room is strictly prohibited.
5. Fast driving and blowing of horns of vehicles is strictly prohibited in the complex and inside the park.
6. Tourists are not allowed to move out of the campus on foot, because man on foot is a greater disturbing element than on a moving vehicle.
7. Shouting or teasing or chasing animals is discouraged so that the animals do not get disturbed.
8. Organizing camp fire at or near the campus is prohibited.

Suggestions

Participatory Development

Under participatory development strategy, traditional tribal huts may be constructed by the tribals themselves with all amenities in the tribal villages/colonies outside the National Park and give them to the tourists, on rent. For construction of tribal huts, financial assistance to the tribals may be extended and the loan amount may be recovered in equal easy installments. Tribal huts may attract the tourists for accommodation and also for their unique culture. Establishment of traditional tribal huts for accommodation to tourists would help in sustainable development of the tribals.

Encouragement of Local Crafts

The Betta/Kadu Kuruba women are defted with the craft of making basketry items. They can as well be encouraged to make lamp shades, hats, bags etc. with bamboo splits with intrinsic designs and attractive colours and sell them to the tourists through the management of the Bandipur National Park. The income which they get from the sale of these items may support towards their sustainable development.

Tribals and Sustainable Development in the Rehabilitated Village

Environment and development are correlated. Environmental issues and developmental issues go hand in hand.

Social scientists have explored the different shades, meaning associated with the concept of development. For economists, development is an increase in per capita income, for administrators it is achieving the targets of social planning and for anthropologists it is the enhancement of quality of life or satisfaction of basic needs (Mathur 1989, Dube 1988).

"Sustainable Development (SD) is development that meets the needs of the present without compromising the ability of future generations to meet their own needs" (WCED, 1987, Brundtland report). And sustainable 'developments' strategy includes the sense of sustainable environmental resources management system (Pottier 1993:4). Sustainable development is likely to achieve lasting satisfaction of human needs and improvement of the quality of human life (Allen, 1980).

Dependence on the Resources

Traditionally the tribal economy was a sustenance economy, their dependence on the environment around them was total. Earlier the tribals got 80 per cent of their food from the forest. At present the tribals get 50 per cent of their food from the forest due to deforestation (Fernandes, Menon and Viegas 1988).

There are two important tribes, Jenu Kuruba and Betta Kuruba living in the rehabilitated village, Melakamanahalli Tribal Colony. Traditionally they lived in forests and their life is closely interrelated with the forest. These tribes primarily depend on the non-timber forest produce for their subsistence. They collect food from the forest. They also use the timber to construct their houses and collect fuelwood from the forest. Jenu Kuruba collect honey and other NTPS from the forest. The Jenu Kuruba, a P.T.G. of Karnataka, is in transitional stage from food gathering and hunting to forest economy.

Local tribals exploit the natural species and other resources in sustainable way. "The conservation of the resource was ensured through restrictions on using economically useful species while such restrictions existed also in other communities. Specific to tribal communities was their cohesion and equity and the consequent possibility of enforcing norms meant to ensure ecological balance" (Fernandes, 1995:36).

Local tribals put restrictions. Jenu Kuruba and Betta Kurubas forbade the cutting or hunting of the species which are affiliated with the totemism. Moreover, they forbade the killing of pregnant animals. In recent times, they forbade the killing of peacock due to the impact of sanskritisation process.

Local tribals can not cut the trees till the trees are old. While digging the roots and tubers, they leave a portion of tuber in the underground. Again this portion of the roof and tuber sprout and regenerates. Other restrictions were put on the use of natural species essential for survival, by declaring them 'sacred', as such not to be destroyed. In addition to the collection of non-timber forest produce, the tribals inhabiting around the National Park also collect certain roots, tubers and leafy vegetables from the reserve forests from the months of February to May every year. The roots and tubers collected by the tribals are Melugehensu, Nargensu and Moplagensu to mention a few. It is informed that collection of roots and tubers has come down. The leafy vegetables collected by them are *garikesappu, keeresoppu, kadusuge soppu, vamagele soppu, gaddimoole soppu, madresoppu, thatthe soppu (kangali ekeri), sebuele and thavesoppu, mulgire soppu and vongane soppu, madleki (ekri)* is collected during fire season and it is useful for sugar patients. The tribals perceive that the collection of tree mass does not affect the growth of the trees in the forest, in fact the growth of the tree will be more, as nutrients from the tree surface are absorbed by the lichens (tree mass).

They also believe that if amla fruits are not plucked in the right season the trees will be infected with certain diseases. From every amla tree about four to five bags of amla fruits were collected from the Reserve Forests, but now plucking of amla fruits is prohibited.

Magleberu (a root) is also collected during December and January. It has medicinal value and it is also used in making soft drinks (*sharbat*), and contains vitamin C. *Parekhe / eechalu* branches are also collected from forests which are used for broom sticks. They are collected in all seasons.

The Situation Today

At present the situation has changed in the tribal areas. The symbiotic relationship between the tribals and forests is breaking down and now tribals are in a transition to destructive dependence. According to Agarwal and Narain (1985) estimate that India has over three million head loaders to whom the sale of fuel wood is the main mode of survival. This causes deforestation. As a result the tribals are trapped into the various vicious circles of poverty, indebtedness land alienation, food insecurity, malnutrition etc. Further, their community has been weakened and social control mechanism destroyed (D.K. Behura, 1996).

Most of the primitive tribal groups in the country are marginalized. Their environment is encroached upon by the immigrants, industries, mine operations, animals sanctuaries, National parks and even by the government.

Main Constraints and Obstacles to the Sustainable Development

Anthropologists and other social scientists delineated the main constraints and obstacles to the sustainable development. These are :

1. Poverty.
2. Inadequate Development Planning.
3. Issues in rehabilitation.
4. Frequent changes in policies and programmes.
5. Top-down approach in planning.
6. Limited peoples participation in planning, monitoring and evaluation.
7. Wasted human resources.
8. Lack of financial resources.
9. Attitudes that did not favour sustainability.
10. Corruption.
11. Developmental benefits are not distributed equally to all member of the community.
12. Environmental degradation.

Ethnic Composition in Melakamanahalli Tribal Colony

The Melakamanahalli Tribal Colony is inhabited by two tribal communities – Jenu Kuruba and Betta / Kadu Kuruba.

The total households in the village is 48 with a population of 172 having 91 males and 81 females. Tribewise, Betta Kuruba constitute the highest percentage 63.37 per cent and the Jenu Kuruba constitute only 36.63 per cent to the total population in the village.

Table 2.21 Ethnic Composition in Melakamanahalli Tribal Colony

Sl. No.	Tribe	No. of House holds	Population			Percentage of the total population
1.	Betta /Kadu Kuruba	30	58	51	109	63.37
2.	Jenu Kuruba	18	33	30	63	36.63
	Total	48	91	81	172	100.00

Local tribals, officials are interviewed to find out the reasons for risk factors in sustainable development. The main risk factors are mentioned below.

Poverty

Poverty is the major economic problem among the tribals. According to Planning Commission (1993-94), 51.92 per cent in rural and 41.40 per cent in urban areas S.Ts were still living below the poverty line. Food insecurity, indebtedness, illiteracy and malnutrition are linked with the problem of poverty.

Table 2.22 Tribe wise Annual Income Range per Household in Melakamahalli Tribal Colony

Sl. No.	Annual Income per household (in Rs.)	No. of Betta/Kadu Kuruba Households.	No. of Jenu Kuruba Households	Total No. of Households
1.	Upto Rs. 10,000	13	15	28
2.	10,001 - 20,000	6	1	7
3.	20,001 – 30,000	4	-	4
4.	30,001 – 40,000	2	1	3
5.	40,001 – 50,000	3	-	3
6.	50,001 – 60,000	-	-	-
7.	60,001 – 70,000	-	-	-
8.	70,001 – 80,000	1	1	2
9.	80,001 – 90,000	1	-	1
	TOTAL	**30**	**18**	**48**

According to annual income, majority of the households of Betta Kuruba (13 households) and 15 Jenu Kuruba households are having annual income up to only Rs. 10,000/- as shown in Table 2.22.

Non Timber Forest Produce and Tribal Economy

Non-timber Forest produce (NTFP) is a precious forest produce. NTFP provides livelihood sustenance to the local tribals living in the Melakamanahalli.

The local tribals collect forest products such as fuel wood, fruits, roots, leaves etc., for self consumption. The local tribals collect the following NTFP items.

1. Tree mass
2. Honey
3. Gum
4. Jenu Mena
5. Nalli Kaya

The following NTFP items are available in the following seasons only.

Sl. No.	*Name of NTFP*	*Season*
1.	Tree Mass	All seasons
2.	Amla	Dec – January
3.	Gum	All seasons
4.	Honey	May – July
5.	Tamarind	Jan – Feb
6.	Magaliberu (Root)	Dec – January
7.	Sheekai	Jan – Feb

Particulars of the price list of the NTFP

Sl. No.	*Item*	*Trader*	*LAMPS*
1.	Tamarind	Rs. 60/- (1 bag of , 50-60 kg)	Rs. 120/- per bag
2.	Honey	Rs. 30-40/- per kg	Rs. 60/- per bag
3.	Tree Mass	Rs. 30/- per bag	Rs. 60-70/- per bag
4.	Amla	Rs. 20-30/- per bag	Rs. 50/- per bag
5.	Sheekai	Rs. 6-10/- per bag	Rs. 20/- per bag
6.	Gum	Rs. 45/- per bag	Rs. 40/- per bag

The forest officials claim that the local tribal people go to the core area of the National Park for collection of non-timber forest produce/MPSP as mentioned above. In addition to the collection of NTFP they also collect stag horns which are very remunerative. A kilogram of stag horns may be sold to the local traders at the rate of Rs. 65/- to Rs. 70/-. A pair of stay horns may weigh about two to three kgs and may earn about Rs. 150/- to Rs. 200/-. In addition to that they (the tribals) go for small games by traping hares and rabbits and also a variety of rare birds. It is further informed that the tribals also catch snakes such as cobra and remove its skin which has good market value. Hence, the forest officials at times restrict the entry of the tribals with into the wildlife sanctuary as they are clandestinely involved in disturbing the biodiversity. If a lot of pressure is exerted by the forest officials for the entry of the tribals into the Wildlife Sanctuary, they may resort to putting of fire in the forests. They (the forest officials) say that they (tribals) are taking revenge by putting fire in the National Park for not allowing them to do such clandestine acts. The local tribals on the contrary informed that they are being harassed by some forest officials.

Their main collection of NTFS is 'Tree mass'. They sell these products to the local traders and LAMPS.

LAMPS: (Large size Multipurpose Cooperative Societies)

The major objective of Multi Purpose Cooperative Societies (LAMPS) is to help tribals to ameliorate their socio-economic condition by providing credit and other services for increasing production, employment, income and marketing of agricultural and forest produces.

It is informed that LAMPS have failed to give loans to all the tribals living in the Melakamanahalli colony due to financial constraints.

Exploitation of Tribals by Non-Tribals

It is informed by the Bandipur National Park's forest officials that liquor packets were sold in the tribal villages by non-tribals from neighbouring villages through tribal women. The forest officials intervened and caught hold of the non-tribal woman and the tribal woman who were involved in illicitly selling of liquor. Since then, sale of liquor in villages around the National Park has been controlled by the forest officials. They have been trapped into vicious circles of poverty and indebtedness.

The tribals take loans from private traders and moneylenders and fail to repay the loans with interest, with the result tribals are forced to work as labourers in the trader's/moneylender's cultivable land till the loan is cleared.

Constraints in Education

Education is a harmonious development of the individual in the context of the community to which he belongs. There is always interaction between the environment and the individual. The personality of the individual is moulded to a large extent by the culture in which he is born and brought up. Thus education is related to culture. Since education has an intrinsic relation with the culture, the need for an anthropological approach to the education, particularly in tribal areas, is a must (Ambasht, 1994).

Despite many developmental and educational programmes launched for the benefit of the tribal communities, they still remain backward both educationally and economically. Education is essential to teach the tribals improved methods of agriculture and other economic pursuits and to educate them not merely to retain the value of their own tribal culture but to take their due place in the social, cultural and economic life of modern India.

According to 1991 census, the literacy percentage of Scheduled Tribe population is 29.60.

Educationally, the village is relatively backward. Though majority of the literates being (113 persons), even then the number of persons who have primary education has been good (95 persons). Only 11 persons have secondary education. The number of females among them has been much less (29 persons) than the males (16 persons). Further, the number of literates are more among the Betta Kuruba (72 persons) than the Jenu Kuruba (41 persons).

Constraints in tribal education can be classified as follows.

1. Economic constraints
2. Social and cultural constraints
3. Educational constraints.

Table 2.23 Literacy Rate in Melakamanahalli Tribal Colony

Tribe	*No.of House holds*	*Primary*			*Upper Primary*			*Secondary*		
		M	*F*	*T*	*M*	*F*	*T*	*M*	*F*	*T*
Betta Kuruba	30	29 (29.29)	26 (26.26)	55 (55.56)	4 (4.04)	3 (3.03)	7 (7.07)	9 (9.09)	1 (1.01)	10 (10.10)
Jenu Kuruba	18	20 (33.90)	20 (33.90)	40 (67.80)	-	-	-	1 (1.69)	-	1 (1.69)
	Total 48	49 (30.01)	46 (29.11)	95 (60.13)	4 (2.53)	3 (1.90)	7 (4.43)	10 (6.33)	1 (0.63)	11 (6.96)

(Contd.)

(Contd. Table 2.23)

Tribe	*No. of House holds*	*Total literates*			*Illiterates*		
		M	*F*	*T*	*M*	*F*	*T*
Betta Kusuba	30	42 (42.42)	30 (30.30)	72 (72.73)	7 (7.07)	20 (20.20)	27 (27.27)
Jenu Kuruba	18	21 (35.59)	20 (33.90)	41 (69.49)	9 (15.25)	9 (15.25)	18 (30.51)
	Total 48	63 (39.87)	50 (31.65)	113 (71.52)	16 (10.13)	29 (18.35)	45 (28.48)

Note: (Figures in the parenthesis are percentages).

Economic Constraints

The children belonging to Scheduled Tribes are considered to be economic assets to the family because sending a "grown-up boy or girl to school is essentially a matter of economics and entails dislocation of traditional pattern of division of labour. Girls give every kind of help to their mothers at home. During agricultural seasons, boys work in the fields with their parents. At other seasons, they are busy collecting minor forest produce and fire wood, grazing goats and cattle, watching crops, bring water, hunting and fishing" (Elwin, 1966). The local tribals are not interested to send their children to high schools because children's services are utilized in their economic activities.

Social Constraints

Further the parents think that the child will be loss to the family if he/she gets educated. Tribals consider that the girls are not supposed to be the paternal property. After their marriage, they live in their in-laws house. Hence, the parents of tribal girls are little interested in their studies.

Generally tribal children go to schools after attaining age of 7 to 8 years. The girls attain puberty before completing primary education. In such cases, the parents of such girls withdraw their daughters.

Constraints of the Educational System

One of the main constraints in education among the local tribal communities is the curriculum which has to be carefully evolved. It has to take into consideration the socio-cultural milieu of the Scheduled Tribes. Presently the general contents of education have been extended to the tribal areas which in many cases are not relevant particularly at the primary stages.

"So far there is no clear educational policy for the tribal areas has been evolved. In some states the schools in tribal areas are under the control of Education Department and in some under the Tribal Welfare Department. Lack of administration policy regarding the schools in tribal areas adversely affect the education of the tribals" (Verma, 2002).

Action Points

1. All tribal schools should be of the residential type with adequate hostels. In Melakamanahalli Tribal Colony, the school can be converted into Ashram School.
2. Schemes of non-formal education should be strengthened to cover the drop-outs.
3. All the teachers posted in the tribal areas should be given orientation training in tribal life and culture.
4. The teachers should be selected from the tribals themselves.

Rehabilitation Programmes

In the wake of development programmes, dams, mines, power plants, industries, parks and sanctuaries induce varying magnitudes of displacement of tribal people from their traditional habitat. Displacement is followed by some form of voluntary or involuntary resettlement.

Scale of Displacement

Since Independence though millions of people have been displaced by various planned development schemes, no reliable data exists on the extent of displacement and rehabilitation. The tribals before coming to Melakamanahali tribal colony, they were earlier living in Bandipur core area which is about one kilometers from the existing administrative zone. Just in front of the Bandipur administrative zone a small colony was established in the year 1983 and about seven families were rehabilitated in the colony but no financial assistance was given to them though they were assured of it by the Forest Department. Huts and sheds were constructed by the tribals themselves with their own financial resources. In the year 1988 the uprooted tribals from the National Park were given constructed houses and lands free of cost at the outskirts of Melakamanahalli village adjoining the Bandipur National Park. Soon after they were allotted lands and houses, about 13 families shifted voluntarily to Melakamanahalli tribal colony in the year 1988 while the remaining families were forced to vacate the core area and of the National Park and ultimately shifted to the tribal colony in the year 1993. In the same year a total of 97 families where rehabilitated from the core area – 61 families to Karemele Colony and 36 families to Melakamanahalli tribal colony.

At present there are 11 Jenu Kuruba and 26 Betta Kuruba households in the Melakamanahalli tribal colony.

When the first news of dislocation reached the local tribals, the people were unhappy. Local forest officials approached the tribals leaders, elites, etc., for rehabilitation.

Table 2.24 Approaches followed by Forest Officials for Rehabilitation (As informed by Heads of the Households in Melakamanahalli) Tribal Colony

Sl.No.	*Approaches made to*	*No. of Betta Kuruba households*	*No. of Jenu Kuruba Households*	*Total No. of Households*
1.	Local tribal leaders	16	12	28
2.	Local tribal leaders and educated tribal youth.	9	5	14
3.	Local tribal leaders, educated tribal youth and tribal elite	2	-	2
4.	Local tribal leaders and NGOs	1	-	1
5.	Local tribal leaders and tribal elite	1	-	1
6.	Tribal elite	1	-	1
7.	Local tribal leaders, educated tribal youth and NGO	-	1	1
	TOTAL	30	18	48

This Table 2.24 depicts that most of heads of the households (28) informed that the forest officials approached the local tribal leaders and 14 of the heads of the households informed that forest officials approached the local tribal leaders and educated tribal youth for rehabilitation.

Resettlement and Rehabilitation Policy (R & R Policy)

Despite large scale displacement of people by various development projects since Independence, the country lacks a comprehensive resettlement and rehabilitation (R & R) Policy. In 1993 Ministry of Rural Development drafted a national rehabilitation policy. Thus, due to lack of a detail and comprehensive R and R policy, the process of resettlement and rehabilitation of uprooted people has been minimal and not very successful (Morse and Berger 1992: 17). Resettlement is a state issue, but only a few state Govts. have come out with a comprehensive R and R policy to resettle project affected people". The Govt. of Karnataka (GOK) did not have an official resettlement and rehabilitation (R and R) policy for project affected persons" (Parasuraman, 1996: 1530).

Consequences of Rehabilitation

The people displaced by development project must move elsewhere (Mathur, 1995). "It affects entire communities. It evicts the literate, the weak and strong, skilled and unskilled, the poor and wealthy, healthy and crippled alike. It disrupts long established social networks" (Partridge, 1989).

According to Cernea and other anthropologists, involuntary resettlement leads to increased stress both psychological and social, cultural and also heightens morbidity and mortality. One researcher described the effects of evacuations on indigenous peoples in Malaysia as follows:

"For many – particularly those from isolated tribal cultures – the move proves disastrous. With their lands, their sacred shrines, the historic monuments, their homes and the villages drowned beneath the reservoirs, their whose life falls apart. Suffice it to say that many displaced tribals simply drift towards the nearest city, there to join the burgeoning number of slum dwellers" (Colchester, Marcus 1988).

Loss of Traditional Rights by Tribals over Sacred Shrine

The tribal communities namely the Jenu Kuruba, Betta/Kadu Kuruba and Soliga were once living in Bandipur forest reserves. They used to worship the diety Thavaragetta Madappa since time immemorial. The shrine of the deity is in Bandipur. All the tribals were either evacuated voluntarily or involuntarily from Bandipur after it was declared as a National Park. Traditionally the local tribals celebrate festival of Thavaragetta Madappa every year on Mahasivarathri in the Bandipur. Even the people from non-tribal communities such as Lingayats, Vokkaligas and other communities living near the National Park come and offer their abeyance to the diety. Traditionally, the tribals were the custodians of the shrine.

But with the passage of time and after the tribals were rehabilitated, the Lingayat community people living in Mangala, Hangala and Jekkali villages taken over Thavaragetta Midappa shrine from the hands of the local tribal leaders and reconstructed the shrine with installation of Shiva Linga (phallic symbol of Lord Shiva) and His Vahana sacred bull the Nandi in the shrine in the year 2001. After taking over the shrine from the tribal people, the non-tribal leaders from the neighbouring villages renamed the shrine as Thavaragatta Mahadeshwara and removed the old priest Sri Kungalappa a Lingayat of Shivapura village and appointed a new priest of their choice to the shrine.

The non-tribal leaders who reconstructed the shrine imposed restrictions on the tribals not to take alcoholic drinks and behave indifferently with the people/devotees coming to the shrine. There was a tussle between the tribal leaders and the non-tribal leaders on imposition of certain restrictions on the tribals and this resulted in partial boycotting of the Mela on Mahasivarathri day by the tribals. It is further reported that their tribal deity Thavaragetta Madappa has been removed from the shrine and only the Shivalinga and the Nandi exist at present in the shrine. Our observations on attending the Mela revealed that more number of non-tribals attended the Mela than the tribals (where the former represented in small number). On the next day of Mahasivarathri a Mela and communal feast was arranged by the Forest Department of Bandipur National Park and the non-tribals from the neighbouring villages. Strict vigilance was also observed by the forest department to control any untoward incidents during the Mela. Transport was also arranged by the forest department to the devotees coming from neighbouring villages to attend the Mela. The Mela went on peacefully without any untoward incident and it was concluded in the afternoon by about 3.00 P.M. Some of the tribals participated in their traditional dance forms in front of the shrine with accompaniment of pipe and percussion musical instruments played by the tribals themselves.

Taking over the shrine from the hands of the tribals by the non-tribal leaders may speak of psychological stress.

Cernea (1999) has identified eight dimensions of impoverishment risk factors in rehabilitation.

Table 2.25 Tribe-wise land holding Range among the households of Melakamanahalli Tribal Colony

Sl.No.	Land Holding Range (in acres)	Betta /Kadu Kuruba		Jenu Kuruba	
		No. of Households	Percentage to the total No. of HHs.	No. of HHs	Percentage to the Total No. of HHs
1.	Upto 1.00 acre	1	5.88	-	
2.	1.01 to 1.25 acres	1	5.88	1	11.11
3.	1.26 to 1.50 acres	-	-	1	11.11
4.	1.51 to 1.75 acres	-	-	-	-
5.	1.76 to 2.00 acres	7	41.18	4	44.45
6.	2.01 to 2.25 acres	1	5.88	-	
7.	2.26 to 2.5 acres	-	-	-	-
8.	2.51 to 2.75 acres	7	41.18	3	33.33
	Total	17	100.00	9	100.00

1. Landlessness
2. Joblessness
3. Homelessness
4. Marginalisation
5. Food insecurity
6. Increased morbidity and mortality
7. Loss of access to common property
8. Social disarticulation

In recent years anthropological research on these impoverishment risks has acquired a new prominence. There are only four major risk factors observed in the Melakamanahalli tribal colony. These are landlessness, joblessness, marginalisation and food insecurity.

In tribal areas, key parts of the local religious beliefs and customs are closely associated with the forest land.

After rehabilitation, the local tribals were given land by the government.

Introducing Agriculture among the Jenu Kuruba and Betta Kuruba

The cultivable land to the extent of 54.25 acres was given to 26 households in Melakamanahalli Tribal Colony.

This Table 2. 25 depicts that 10 households had not been provided with land by the government. Out of 54.25 acres of land, 36.00 acres of land was given to 17 Betta / Kadu Kuruba households and 18.25 acres of land was given to nine Jenu Kuruba households. The extent of land given to them varied from one household to another ranging from 1.00 acre to 2.50 acres.

Tribal Welfare Department has done leveling of lands for cultivation in the rehabilitated village. In the year 2003 about 26 pairs of bullocks were given to 26 households. This Department provided food items for three months for doing cultivation, and for digging of bore wells. But later, the bullocks were sold to the non-tribals as they were not able to utilize them for ploughing. It is informed that some bullocks died due to foot and mouth diseases. At present, only three households have plough bullocks.

In the year 2002, the Forest Department had desiminated technical knowledge of agricultural operations. They were also given a few agricultural implements such as spade (*elkottu*), hoe (*gujili*), knife (*katti*), metal basket (*thatte*), wooden plough, *pikasi*, are, sickle (*kodugalu*). The main reasons for failure of agriculture as informed by the respondents are that:

They are not properly trained by the development authorities. Once they were hunters and gatherers and it takes some more time to get acclimatized to acquire the skills of agriculture. Further it is observed that they seem to be lazy. The world view of the local tribals is that they always look forward for temporary benefits rather than long term benefits. Moreover, they are more inclined towards collection of non-timber forest produce.

Presently, only one household from Jenu Kuruba and two households from Betta / Kadu Kuruba are doing agriculture. They are growing ragi and jola in their cultivable lands. The rest of the households kept their lands barren with a fear of being raided by elephants as the solar fencing to their cultivable land went out of order and secondly the elephant proof trenches seem to be not fool proof.

Joblessness

In tribal areas, joblessness can also be seen in terms of loss of income-earning opportunities. At new rehabilitation sites, employment availability becomes very scarce, which leads to joblessness. The present study shows that the percentage of wage labourers has increased in the rehabilitated village. The average number of days in a year a displaced family gets work has also reduced. All these facts confirm that joblessness had added to the impoverishment.

The Table 2.26 depicts that 11 Betta Kuruba members and only two Jenu Kuruba members got employment opportunities in Forest Department. Further this table shows that most of the Jenu Kuruba members (17 members) depend on collection of minor forest produce.

It is interesting to note from the above table that the number of agricultural labourers has increased among the Betta Kuruba (24 persons) and Jenu Kuruba (20 persons) after rehabilitation.

This Table 2.27 shows that 9 Betta Kuruba households and only two Jenu Kuruba households got regular employment. Out of 48 households, 21 Betta Kuruba households and 16 Jenu Kuruba households did not get regular employment.

Table 2.26 Sex-wise and Tribe-wise Occupational Pattern Rehabilitated Village

Sl. No.	Occupation	Betta Kuruba			Jenu Kuruba		
		M	F	T	M	F	T
1.	Employment in Forest Department	11	-	11	2		2
2.	Agriculture	2	1	3	1	1	2
3.	Collection of NTFP	4	-	4	10	7	17
4.	Other salaried persons	2	-	2	1	-	1
5	Pension	1	1	2	-	-	-
6.	Forest labour	13	7	20	10	5	15
7.	Agricultural labour	12	12	24	11	9	20
8.	Social work	1	-	1	-	-	-
	Total	46	21	67	35	22	57

Table 2.27 Tribe-wise Details of Employment

Sl. No.	Particulars	Betta Kuruba	Jenu Kuruba	Total No
1.	No. of household heads who got employment	9	2	11
2.	No. of individuals who got employment	10	2	12
3.	No. of house holds who did not get regular employment	21	16	37
	Total No. of households	30	18	48

Housing

After rehabilitation, housing facilities were provided to 36 families living in Melakamanahalli tribal colony. The local tribals are not facing the risk factor of homelessness.

Marginalization

Marginalization is an outcome of joblessness and is an indication that the loss of productive assets, and the loss of livelihood have resulted in downward mobility. Though marginalization is looked through the perspective of loss of livelihood, it is necessary to give attention to the marginalization of tribal women. Rehabilitation and displacement adversely affected their economic freedom and status in the family as well as in their community. Before rehabilitation, women of Betta Kuruba were engaged in basket making. They used to sell basketry items in the nearby markets. Thus the tribal women in the traditional village could generate sum income. They never depended on their husbands. But in the rehabilitation colony such incomes by the Betta Kuruba women were virtually absent. This results in the marginalization of tribal women.

Food Insecurity

Food insecurity is caused by deforestation and loss of traditional rights over the local flora and fauna. As per National Park Regulations, local tribals are deprived of access to non-timber forest produce. It is said that they are not allowed freely to collect NTFP inside the National Park. These losses affect food acquisitional / collection and availability of food. This results in food insecurity. Under ICDS Programme, Anganwadi was introduced in the year 2004 at Melakamanahalli tribal colony. About 48 children of the age group of three years to six years come to this center. The week long menu is mentioned below:

65 grams of Chitranna on Monday
65 grams ICDS of Karnataka Energy food on Tuesday
65 grams of Chitranna on Wednesday
Pongal on Thursday
Chitranna on Friday
Energy food on Saturday
Energy food on Sunday

The Nutritive value of 100 grams of Energy Rich food of ICDS has 15 grams of protein, 360 kilo calaries, vitamins and minerals.

Loss of Access to Common Property

Another impoverishment risk factor is the loss of access to common property, particularly forest and village common lands.

These resources are not owned by families but customarily they are owned at community level. After rehabilitation, they were deprived of these traditional rights inside the National Park.

Environmental Degradation

On enquiry about existence of valuable wood like sandalwood and rose wood in the National Park, it is informed that sandalwood is not totally extinct as sandalwood and rosewood trees are there in the National Park in infant stage. Big sandalwood trees are cut and smuggled from Bandipur National Park by the poachers from neighbouring states, as three sandal wood factories are located in the state of Kerala. Cutting of rosewood trees is also done illegally by some poachers from neighbouring states but not by the people of Karnataka. Roots and tubers which are being collected by the tribals are on the decline.

Facilities Extended to Melakamanahalli Tribal Colony

After rehabilitation from Bandipur, the tribals in Melakamanahalli tribal colony were provided with certain infrastructural facilities as well as other facilities for their sustainable development. Solar fencing was provided in the year 2001-2002 to the village by Social Welfare Department with a condition that a few tribal youth will be imparted training for maintenance of solar fencing. But as far as the tribals knowledge is concerned none of them were imparted with training for maintenance of solar fencing. Since the solar fencing went out of order, due to lack of maintenance, it is reported that elephants from the Park area come to the village and spoil the cultivated crops. About four solar street lamps were provided for the tribal colony by the Village Panchayat free of cost. However, it is reported that they are not functioning properly as no youth are provided with training for maintenance of these solar street lamps.

Tribal Welfare Department has done leveling of lands for cultivation in the tribal villages. The forest department provided temporary employment to the tribals three to four months in a year for construction of check dams, farm ponds, repairing of school quarters and community hall (Samudaya Bhawan) as fire watchers, anti-poaching watchers etc. The local tribals were given three to four poultry birds (chickens) of Giriraja variety in the year 2001-2002 to all the households.

Hastravale - smokeless choolas were given to all the households in the years 1999 to 2002. However, these smokeless choolas are not in use by the tribals, as they do not suit their requirement.

Under Self Help Group formation – Mahila Sahaya Sangha, was established in the year 2001 for promotion of small savings. Under this scheme about 25 women have enrolled as members. In this scheme if the tribals have 20 per cent investment, the remaining 75 percent is given by Cauvery Grameena Bank. About Rs. 20,000/- fund was raised and accumulated and was deposited in Cauvery Grameena Bank (CGB). Under this scheme each woman saves Rs.10/- per week. The accumulated fund is proposed to be utilized for purchase of milch cattle and purchase of general provisions.

Fruit bearing seedlings of coconut, mango, papaya, drum sticks and lemon were also given on an average of two seedlings of each variety in the year 1986-87.

About 12 bore wells were given under Ganga Kalyana Yojana by S.T. and S.C. Corporation in the year 2000 for irrigation and four hand pumps for drinking water purpose in the year 2001 and 2002 by the Forest Department. But no motor pump sets were given for the bore wells sunk for irrigation of land.

Immunization to local cattle is being administered every year to the cattle living in the tribal colony and health camps were also organized in the year 2002 by the Forest Department.

Non-Government Organisations NGO

There are a few N.G.Os near to the Bandipur National Park which have taken development programmes for physical and intellectual well being of the children and to elevate socio-economic status of the people. The World Vision and Dudi Samstha are the two NGOs working for the well being of the people around the National Park.

World Vision of India: World Vision of India is an NGO located at Gundlupet in Chamarajanagar district in Karnataka. This institute has launched Area Development Programme (ADP) to empower children, families and communities for transformational development. The ADP is implemented in 38 villages in Gundlupet covering 2762 families comprising a population of 21389. The programme caters to meet the basic needs of the people and child – focused in all development initiatives.

In Melakamanahalli tribal colony the World Vision of India started providing medical aid since 1997. In the year 1998 Village Development Committee was introduced. There are about 12 members from Melakamanahalli tribal colony. The duty of the members is to inform about the health situation in the village. If there are any health problems informed by the members, the World Vision members would come to the village and take the patient to a hospital. The World Vision offers financial assistance to the extent of Rs. 8,500/- and the remaining shall have to be borne by the patient. This medical facility was abandoned about three years ago. The members of the village appeal to the organization to extend this facility to the poor tribals.

The organization also distributes medicines to the needy persons. For instance, iron tablets are given to pregnant women and children who are aneamic, and also tablets for fever etc.

A youth belonging to Jenu Kuruba in the tribal colony (who studied upto SSLC) used to teach the children of the village from 6.00 pm to 8.00 pm. In return he was given Rs. 400/- per month from by World Vision. This kind of employment to the tribal youth was abandoned about seven months ago. He used to teach children of class I to class V.

The World Vision of India used to give free uniform; text books and note books to the children of the tribal colony. Two sets of uniform cloth were given per child with a condition that the stitching charges were to be borne by the child's parents. This organization also constructed a tank for the cattle in the year 2002. The tribals have a positive attitude towards this voluntary organization.

It is informed that "The Anandajyothi Women Self Help Group" organized and trained by World Vision in the tribal colony have realized that liquor that was sold in the village was injurious to health and fatal for their families and overall development. They discussed with the members of the village and removed the liquor shop. They warned the seller and reported to the concerned taluk authorities to assist them in the development programmes by cancelling the permit to sell liquor in the village. The removal of liquor shop improved their living condition to some extent, and helped to live peacefully and happily.

Dudi Samstha

This is another NGO at Gundlupet in Chamarajanagar district of Karnataka state. This organization was established in the year 1980 and conducted census and promoted cultural programmes. The tribals inhabiting around the National Park had a good opinion about this organization at the initial stage as they also provided medical care. But of late, they have a negative attitude about this organization as it misappropriated the funds given by various donors. It is informed that they also indulged in local politics and misappropriate the funds they received.

It is informed by Forest Range Officer of Bandipur that under Project Tiger a sum of Rs. 55 lakhs has been granted for distribution / issue of L.P. gas connection in and around Bandipur National Park. The beneficiaries will be given one gas stove free of cost for every L.P. gas connection. However, the consumer / beneficiary has to pay Rs. 1290/- for each connection of LPG towards registration, cost of cylinder and regulator. On issue of about 11,000 gas connections in the rural areas around Bandipur National Park the forest department would be earning commission of Rs. 15,000/- per month. It is observed that most of the beneficiaries / consumers are non-tribals but not the tribals inhabiting around Bandipur National Park as the tribals, cannot afford to take L.P. gas connections due to their state of poverty. It is informed that the Indian Oil Corporation (IOC) is ready to give any number of L.P. gas connections in the villages around Bandipur National Park which would reduce the pressure of the people living around the National Park for fuel wood.

The Eco-development programme implemented in the last ten years in Melakamanahalli tribal colony in brief are:

1. Providing solar fencing
2. Providing solar lights
3. Supply of smokeless choolas

4. Making farm ponds
5. Construction of check dam
6. Supply of fruit yielding seedlings
7. Providing poultry birds (chicken)
8. Organizing health camps
9. Arrange driving licence to tribal youth
10. Providing L.P. gas connections.

It may be brought into relief that after rehabilitation, awareness in modern politics has increased among the tribals of Melakamanahalli tribal colony. It is substantiated by the fact that a Kadu Kuruba woman from this village has been elected as a member of the statutory gram panchayat of Hangala village in the year 2005.

Strategies for Sustainable Development and Sustainable Rehabilitation

1. The natural resources of any kind should be exploited to the extent that ecological imbalance is not caused.
2. Measures should be undertaken to ensure the renewable of natural resources for future generations.
3. Besides physical rehabilitation, 'Cultural rehabilitation' should also be taken into consideration.
4. Suitable income generating schemes should be introduced among the local tribals.
5. Rights and interests of the local tribals should be protected.
6. There should be emphasis on 'equity principle' while implementing the development programmes.
7. Local people should participate in planning, monitoring and evaluation.
8. There should be better co-ordination between the forest department, Tribal Welfare Department and NGOs.
9. The Gram Panchayat has to play a vital role in tribal development programmes.
10. Wage labour rate should be given as per Government rates.
11. Forest protection committees should be formed.
12. Empowerment should be given to the local tribals.
13. More employment opportunities should be given to the local tribal women.

Tribal Situation in the Traditional Village

For comparison with a rehabilitated village – Melakamanahalli tribal colony, a traditional village namely Chennaikattai Colony was taken for the study. Chennaikattai colony comes under Mangala Gram Panchayat and Gundulpet taluk of Chamarajanagar district in Karnataka State. It is about 3.5 kms from Bandipur National Park's administrative zone, 21.5 kms. from Gundulpet and 5.00 kms from Mangala Gram Panchayat village. This village is a mono ethnic village inhabited by the Soligas.

Brief history on Migration of Soligas to Chennaikottai Colony

The Soliga who came to Chennaikattai Colony, were once living in Bandipur National Park area near the Police Station. Shri Karia who is the headman of the area first shifted voluntarily to Chennaikattai in the year 1984 and brought along with him 14 families in the same year and the rest of the families came to this village in the year 1988. It is informed that the Forest Department has not provided any facilities to this village. Whatever they got i.e., land for cultivation and houses for living were obtained through Block Development Office at Gundlupet under Tribal Development Programme. This village has not been covered under any eco-development activities like installation of solar fencing, solar street lamps, formation of elephant proof trenches etc.

There are 32 households in Chennaikattai and all of them belong to the Soliga tribal community and their total population is 93 of which 47 are males and 46 are female See Table 2.28).

The data on literates and illiterates reveal that there are 31 literates (33.33 per cent) out of which 14 are males and 17 are females. Among the literates 23 persons (24.73 per cent) (13 males and 10 females) studied upto primary level and five females (5.38 per cent) studies upto upper primary level. Only three persons (3.23 per cent) (one male and two females) studied upto secondary level. There are as many as 54 persons (58.06 per cent) as illiterates of which 28 are males and 28 are females. From Table 2.29 we understand that among the Soligas in this village there are more number of illiterates than literates, which may speak of their backwardness in formal education.

Table 2.28 Ethnic Composition in Chennaikattai Village

Sl. No.	Tribe	No. of Households	Population		
			Male	Female	Total
1.	Soliga	32	47	46	93
	Total	32	47	46	93

Table 2.29: Literates and Illiterates among Soligas of Chennaikattai Village

Sl No	Tribe	No of House holds	Primary			Upper primary			Secondary		
			M	F	T	M	F	T	M	F	T
1.	Soliga	32	13 (13.98)	10 (10.75)	23 (24.73)	-	5 (5. 38)	5 (5.38)	1 (1.0.8)	2 (2.15)	3 (3.23)
	Total	32	13 (13.98)	10 (10.75)	23 (24.73)	-	5 (5. 38)	5 (5.38)	1 (1.08)	2 (2.15)	3 (3.23)

(Contd.)

Sl No	Tribe	No of House holds	Total literates			Total illiterates		
			M	F	T	M	F	T
1.	Soliga	32	14 (15.05)	17 (18.28)	31 (33.33)	28 (30.11)	26 (27.96)	54 (58.06)
	Total	32	14 (15.05)	17 (18.28)	31 (33.33)	28 (30.11)	26 (27.96)	54 (58.06)

Figures in the brackets are percentages to the total population

Occupational Pattern in Chennaikattai Colony

The Soliga inhabiting Chennaikattai Colony are employed in different pursuits, such as employment in forest department, collection of non-timber forest produce, agriculture, forest labour, agricultural labour, employment in Anganwadi centre, labourers in coffee plantation in Kerala and priestly service (see table 2.30).

It is observed that only three male members are employed in the forest department as forest watchers and fire watchers on daily wages. They get employment for about three to four months in a year. They are paid Rs.50/- per day. Earlier they were getting Rs.68/- per day. The decrease in payment of daily wages is attributed to the decrease in sanctioning of funds to the forest department and secondly to provide employment to more number of persons as informed by the forest officials.

Table 2.30 Sex-wise Occupational Pattern among the Soliga of Cheenaikattai Village

Sl. No.	*Occupation*	*No. of persons employed*		
		No. of Males	*No. of Females*	*Total*
1.	Employment in forest department	3 (3)	-	3 (3)
2.	Collection of Non Timber Forest Produce	22 (21)	11 (10)	33 (23)
3.	Agriculture	3 (3)	2 (2)	5 (3)
4.	Forest Labour	8 (8)	5 (5)	13 (9)
5.	Agricultural Labour	18 (17)	15 (14)	33 (17)
6.	Employment in Anganwadi Centre	-	2 (2)	2 (2)
7.	Labour in Coffee Plantation in Kerala	1 (1)	-	1 (1)
8.	Priestly service	2 (2)	-	2 (2)

Figures in the brackets are the number of households

As many as 33 persons (22 males and 11 females) from 23 households are engaged in collection of non-timber forest produce. They collect gum, tree mass (*pasa*), honey (*jenu*), goose berry / amla (*nellikai*), tamarind (*hulsehannu*), soap nuts, (*antuvalakkai*), sheekakai from the reserve forest and sell these produce to Large Size Multipurpose Cooperative Society Limited (LAMPS) at Gundulpet at the prices fixed by them as detailed below:

Gum Rs. 40/- per kg.

Tree Mass (*pasa*) Rs. 55/- per kg.

Honey (*Jenu*) Rs. 60/- per litre

Goose berry (*Nellikai*) Rs. 300/- per 100 kgs
Tamarind (*Hulsehannu*) Rs. 60/- per moota (about 50 kgs)
Sheekakai Rs. 20/- per kg.
Soapnut (*Antuvalakai*) Rs. 60/- per kg.

They also collect non-timber forest produce such as *arlekai*, *magaliberu*, and *vongekai* and sell them to the local traders at Mangala, Hangala, Jekkali and Gundulpet.

Collection of non-timber forest produce is prohibited in the Reserve Forests. However the forest officials allow tribal inhabiting around the National Park to collect these produce. If the tribals are involved in clandestine activities like smuggling of products pertaining to wildlife, it is informed that they are booked as per the Wildlife Protection Acts.

Amala is collected during the months of December and January; Tree mass is collected in all the three seasons; honey during the months of January, February and March; tamarind during the months of January, February and March; soapnuts during the months of December and January; and Sheekakai also during December and January.

Impression of Forest Officials on Collection of NPFP by Tribals

According to some forest officials in the National Park the tribals trap birds such as woodpeckers and patridges with snares, he stage horns are also collected from the Park along with non-timber forest produce. They sell the stage horns to the traders at the rate of Rs. 80/- per kilogram. On collection of lichens (tree mass) *pasa* by the tribals, it is informed that not much damage is caused to the trees bearing lichens, but the illegal acts of traping birds and animals by the tribals in a way disturbs the biodiversity of the Bandipur National Park.

In Chennaikattai Colony the Soligas hold agricultural land to the extent of 27.00 acres by eleven households with different land holding ranges. There are seven households who hold land in the range of 1.51 acres to 2.00 acres; three households in the land holding range of 2.51 acres to 3.00 acres and only one household has land in 3.51 acres to 4.00 acres range (see Table 2.31). Though there is about 27.00 acres of land possessed by 11 Soliga households, only three households are engaged in agriculture involving three men and two women. Their lack of interest for agriculture may be attributed to frequent crop raids of the elephants on the crops grown by them as they are not provided with solar fencing and elephant poor trenches around their cultivable lands. The three households reported to have grown ragi and jawar in their cultivable lands in the year 2004-2005.

Table 2.31 Landholding Range among the Soliga of Chennaikattai Village

Sl. No	*Land holding Range in acres*	*No. of Households*
1.	Upto 1.00 acre	-
2.	1.01 to 1.50 acres	-
3.	1.51 to 2.00 acres	7
4.	2.01 to 2.50 acres	-
5.	2.51 to 3.00 acres	3
6.	3.01 to 3.50 acres	-
7.	3.51 to 4.00 acres	1
	Total	11

It is informed that they use seeds of high yielding variety for *jola, ragi, alasanda, toori,* chillies and onions in addition to traditional variety of seeds for crop such as *ragi* and *nadijola*. They engage tractor from Mangala village for ploughing and pay Rs. 50/- per hour. It is informed that they use chemical fertilizer – urea only, for all the crops that are grown by them. On an average they get two quintals of ragi per acre during lien period and six quintals if there is good rainfall. Similarly on an average they get four quintals of jola per acre during lien period and about eleven quintals per acre if there is good rainfall. Reportedly, the Soliga in Chennaikattai colony do not use any pesticides or insecticides for the crops raised by them. They use organic manure (hosure gobra) in their cultivable lands.

The Soliga of Chennaikattai Colony use simple agricultural implements during their agricultural operations. The implements used by them are *mamte, kudili, pikasi, hara* (spade), *katte* (knife) and sickle (*kodugulu*). For improvement in agriculture they need to use bullocks, *kabbadi*, *negulu* (plough) and borewells for irrigation and solar fencing for protection of crops from elephant raids, and also acquire agricultural skills from the non-tribals inhabiting around the National Park. Reportedly, two members of this village have disposed of some portion of their agricultural lands to a non-tribal entrepreneur living in Bangalore for a good price. These two members after receiving payment on selling their lands had spent some portion of the amount to clear their loans and the remaining amount they have deposited in a bank as a fixed deposit. The increase in cost of land around Bandipur National Park may be attributed to the impact of tourism.

It is informed that about 13 members (8 males and 5 females) from nine households go for forest labour for works such as fencing for the sanctuary, planting trees for the future (aforestation works), conservation of water holes for combating drought for the animals in the reserves forests. They get employment on daily wage basis for about two to three months in a year at the rate of Rs. 50/- per day. The extent of backwardness at the economic level may be attributed to lack of education, food insecurity, joblessness and marginalisation as viewed in Melakamanahalli Tribal Colony.

As many as 33 individuals (18 males and 15 females) from 17 households go for agricultural labour to the neighbouring village Mangala; in the agricultural lands belonging to Lingayats, Adi Karnataka, Medar, Vadru, Shetru, and others. The agriculturists in Mangala village grow crops such as ragi, jawar, onions, beans, tomatos, chillies, sunflower and *uchchallu, thuguribela* and groundnut (*kadlekai*). The Soliga from Chennaikattai Colony are employed for agricultural operations such as ploughing, weeding and harvesting of the above mentioned crops. They are paid Rs. 50/- per day and a meal in the afternoon or four kgs of ragi for one day's labour. They get agricultural labour work in Mangala in the months of June, July, August and September. Their employment as agricultural labourers by the non-tribal communities in Mangala village will in a way help them to acquire knowledge in agriculture practices as they were earlier engaged in shifting cultivation and in collection of non-timber forest produce from the Reserve forests.

Only two women from two households in the village are employed in Anganwadi center as helper and as teacher and they are paid Rs. 300/- and Rs. 1000/- per month respectively. Only one male member from one household is engaged as labourer in coffee plantations in Kerala. He gets employment as a labourer for about three months and earn about Rs. 1500/- per month. Only two persons from two households are engaged in priestly service.

Inspite of their involvement in different pursuits, the Soliga inhabiting Chennaikattai live in poverty. It is observed from Table 2.32 that one household do not have any income as they are in old age and depend upon their grown up sons. Majority of the households i.e., as many as 24 households' annual income come under the income range of upto Rs. 10,000/- and some six households annual income come under the income range of Rs. 10,001/- to Rs. 20,000/-. Only one household's annual income falls under the income range of Rs. 30,001/- to Rs. 40,000/-

Table 2.32 Annual Income Range per Household among the Soligas of Chennaikattai Village

Sl. No	*Annual Income Range per household (in Rs)*	*No. of Households*	*Percentage to the total number of households*
1.	No income	1	3.13
2.	Upto Rs. 10,000	24	75.00
3.	Rs. 10,001 to Rs. 20,000	6	18.75
4.	Rs. 20,001 to Rs. 30,000	-	-
5.	Rs. 30,001 to Rs. 40,000	1	3.12
	Total	32	100.00

Methods Followed for Conservation of Forest Resources by the Tribals in Chennaikattai Colony

Cultures of different tribal communities play an important role in conservation of forests and their resources and bio-diversity to some extent. The Soliga inhabiting in Chennaikattai Colony adjoining the National Park observe / follow some methods for conservation of forests and their resources, the details of which are brought into relief in the following paragraphs (See Table 2. 33).

It is informed by the Soligas that they do not cut plants associated with clans as it is considered taboo. So is the case with the animals associated with clans which is prohibited killing them. They also do not cut the sacred groves under which certain deities are worshipped. Some of them observe certain techniques for conservation of forests. For instance, whenever they want to cut a particular tree they cut the trunk of the tree in a conical shape for regeneration which speaks of their indigenous knowledge. Killing of pregnant animals is considered to be a very sinful act, hence the Soliga do not kill pregnant animals. Similarly, for conservation of forest treasure they avoid cutting valuable trees. The Soliga acquired traditional knowledge from their elders from generation to generation of resources-roots and tubers. On identifying root or tuber, they first make a trench of about 6 inches to one foot deep around the existing root/tuber and remove the major edible part and cover it again with soil. They shall ensure that the left over root or taber has good root system and vegetative part for regeneration. Some of the Soliga also have knowledge of collecting medicinal plants, roots, tubers etc., without affecting the conservation of such medicinal plants. The above mentioned methods for conservation of forest resources also helps them for their sustainable development.

Table 2.33 Methods followed for Conservation of Forest Resource by Soligas in Chennaikattai Village

Sl. No.	*Method followed for conservation of forest resource*	*No. of HHS*	*Percentage*
1.	Not cutting of plants associated with clans	16	50.00
2.	Not killing of animals associated with clans	14	43.75
3.	Not cutting sacred groves	32	100.00
4.	Techniques observed for conservation of forests	9	28.13
5.	Not killing of pregnant animals	32	100.00
6.	Not cutting valuable trees	26	81.25
7.	Soil conservation	1	3.13
8.	Traditional knowledge used for regeneration of resources - roots and tubers	10	31.25
9.	Knowledge of collecting medicinal plants, roots, tubers etc.	10	31.25
10.	Traditional knowledge in soil conservation, cropping pattern, selection of seeds, practice of traditional methods in agriculture	1	3.13

Risk Factors in Sustainable Development of Tribals Around the National Park

For any kind of sustainable development one has to overcome certain hurdles and risks which may be ecological, administrative, lack of communication facilities, lack of education, attitudes of officials, conflicts between man and animals, frequent changes in development programmes, fire damage etc.

On enquiry about the risk factors that we may come across in sustainable development of tribals, it is informed by the Soliga of Chennaikattai Colony as detailed below (See Table 2.34).

Table 2.34 Risk Factors in Sustainable Development of Tribals (as informed by Soligas of Chennaikattai)

Sl. No.	*Risk factors*	*No. of households reported*	*Percentage to the total no. of households*
1.	Ecological degradation	11	34.38
2.	Top down approach	16	50.00
3.	Development programmes not related to local needs and culture	22	68.75
4.	Benefits not distributed equally	26	81.25
5.	Poaching	-	-
6.	Lack of communication facilities	11	34.38
7.	Lack of education	17	53.13
8.	Different attitudes of officials towards tribals	21	65.63
9.	Man and animal conflict	1	3.13
10.	Frequent changes in development programmes,	2	6.25
11.	Fire damage	4	12.50

Out of the 32 Soliga households inhabiting Chennaikattai Colony about 11 households corresponding to 34.38 per cent informed that ecological degradation is one of the risk factors in sustainable development due to exploitation of forest resources by the people living around the National Park. Another factor is the top down approach of the planning. About 16 households (50.00 per cent) informed that the top down approach of the planning is one of the risk factors. A good number of households i.e., about 22 households corresponding to 68.75 per cent informed that the development programmes are not related to local needs and culture of the people. As many as 26 households corresponding to 81.25 per cent of households taken for the study informed that the benefits to be provided by the government agencies are not distributed equally. About 11 households (34.33 per cent) reported that they lack proper communication facilities and a good number of households, 17 households (53.13 per cent) informed that lack of education among the tribals is one of the risk factors. As many as 21 households corresponding to 65.63 per cent say that negative attitudes of officials towards tribals is one of the risk factors towards tribal development. Only one household informed that conflict between man and animal as one of the risk factors, and two households believe that frequent changes in development programmes may turn out to be risk factors for sustainable development. About four households (12.50 per cent) reported that fire damage as an important factor for consideration of forests as well as for sustainable development of tribals.

It is informed that one person was attacked by a bear (*karidi*) five years ago while he was working as forest labourer in Bandipur National Park. He was immediately taken to government hospital by the concerned Forest Range Officer and the expenditure incurred towards his medical treatment was borne by the government. He was hospitalized for about 15 days and after his discharge from the hospital he was given Rs. 100/-.

Other Facilities Extended to Chennaikattai Colony

About 30 households were given houses free of cost by Block Development Office under Tribal Development Programme. Pisciculture training was given to about six members in the village. But the training was not of much use as they do not do pisciculture.

Under DWACRA about 10 Soliga women formed a group (Sthree Sakthi) in the year 2002 and each woman deposited Rs. 10/- per week and accumulated fund of Rs. 10,000/-. The group has taken loan of Rs. 5,000/- and now they are unable to contribute their membership and repay the loan taken by them due to poverty.

The Soliga of Chennaikattai Colony have a negative attitude towards Dudi Samstha (a non-government organisation). Each household at this village has given Rs. 770/- to the Samstha. About Rs. 500/- was taken as loan by all the bonafide members of the Samstha. Reportedly, there is no communication from this organisation. The remaining Rs. 220/- of each bonafide member is lying with the Dudi Samstha and has left a negative attitude among the members of this village.

Summary and Conclusion

Tourism is the temporary movement of people to places outside their normal places of work and residence. Anthropological analysis of the impacts of tourism have increased rapidly in the past decade. Tourism affects culture changes and central to its anthropological study is the impact between the hosts and guests, which may be positive and negative. The present study is on eco-tourism and sustainable development: a case study of Bandipur National Park, which is a part of the Nilgiri Biosphere Reserve.

A Biosphere Reserve is a conservation area created to protect the biological and cultural diversity of the region. Moreover, it is a place where local tribal communities, government officials, N.G.O.s and environmental groups work collaboratively on the issues of conservation and development.

The main objectives of Biosphere Reserves are (1) to conserve the diversity and integrity of flora and fauna within the natural ecosystem, (2) to protect genetic diversity of species, (3) to provide areas for ecological research and monitoring, (4) to provide facilities for education and training (5) to ensure sustainable use of natural resources through traditional methods for improvement of economic living of local people.

Bandipur National Park is one of the twelve tourist areas of Nilgiri Biosphere Reserve. The Park attracts many tourists from different parts of the country and also abroad. The forest department has given attention for development of tourism with infrastructural facilities to tourists such as comfortable accommodations, local transport and food etc. Forest department employed local tribal people as forest guards, fire watchers, guides and also workers at guest houses, resorts and cottages. The Bandipur National Park occupies a special place in the country's efforts towards natural conservation. The entire area of the National Park is a protected forest area designated as Tiger Reserve in 1973. In 1974 intention was declared under the Wild Life Protection Act to notify it as a National Park. There are very few studies done on impact of eco-tourism on tribal communities and this is one of the reasons for taking up the study.

The main objectives of the present study are:

1. To study the dynamics of development of National Park and tourism in the area.
2. To project positive and negative impacts of ecotourism on local tribal communities and to suggest the ways and means to minimize the negative impacts and to make the positive impacts more meaningful.
3. To draw perceptions of the tourists towards the area and infrastructural facilities extended by the forest department for promotion of tourism in the area.
4. To study obstacles that are instrumental for conservation and sustainable development.
5. To study tribals and sustainable development in the rehabilitated village.
6. To study the tribal situation in the traditional village.
7. To explore the opportunities for achieving ecological sustainable development with the growth of tourism in the area.

The Bandipur National Park is a famous Wildlife Tourism Centre with an area of 880.00 square kilometers. It is a famous wildlife tourism center known for its rich flora and fauna and also for complex biotic pressures deleterious to its conservation and protection. The human habitation is confined to only northern region and to west for a short distance all along the boundary. Both these surroundings are thickly populated by agricultural communities. The landless people live on labour in agricultural fields and forests. The tribal communities namely Jenn Kuruba, Betta/Kadu Kuruba and Soliga who were once living in the Reserve Forests are now living in proximity to the National Park as they were rehabilitated and forced to settle at the allotted colonies after shifting from the protected area and other forest areas submerged in Kabini Reservoir. There are about 200 villages around the National Park with a population of about 1,60,000 individuals according to 1991 census. About 100 tribal families living in Bandipur were rehabilitated at Melakamanahalli tribal colony and Karemala outside the Park with the provision of housing and land for cultivation to each tribal family with an outlay of Rs.100 lakhs. This project was upto 1996-1997.

About 20 tribal households were taken for the study where in a member or two from each household are employed in the Bandipur National Park to draw the impact of tourism. Of the 20 tribal households, 11 households belong to Betta/Kadu Kuruba, five households to Jenu Kuruba and four households belong to Soliga tribal community. The tribals are employed as watchers, antipoaching watchers, elephant riders, forest guards, driver and gardener. The annual income of each employee varies depending upon his nature of work and substativeness. The income of an employee/worker ranges from Rs. 20,000/- to Rs. 90,000/- per annum. There was a proposal for recruitment of forest watchers from tribals of Bandipura and Gundulpet area, but it was later cancelled/ withheld due to some political reasons.

While assessing the risk factors in sustainable development of ecotourism, it is found that lack of education among tribals, benefits not been equally distributed by the government agencies, ecological degradation, development programmes not related to local needs and cultures and top-down approach in the planning are the major risk factors. Hence, it is suggested by the tribal respondents that people's participation in development programmes and education to all around the National Park would help in promotion of eco-tourism and sustainable development.

On analyzing the data on tourists, it is observed that majority of tourists come in party/group which is followed by family and alone, and most of the tourists visited the Bandipur National Park are from Karnataka and Kerala. The data on level of education of tourists reveals that most of them are graduates followed by post-graduates, senior secondary level and Diploma in computers. Among the tourists who came to the Park majority of them are employees followed by businessmen. From the data on religion of the tourists, it is observed that majority are Hindus, followed by Muslims and Christians. Most of the tourists came to the park to view the natural beauty and the rest for adventure. The tourists informed that they are not satisfied with the food available in the Bandipur National Park. Important aspect of tourist attraction is the shopping facilities such as shops of handicrafts, works of art, decorated garments etc.

Hence, it is suggested to provide good food, shopping facilities for purchase of decorated items, handicrafts, works of art, decorated garments etc. In this context it may be mentioned that the Betta/Kadu Kuruba women are defted with the craft of basketry made with split bamboo. As a supplementary to their income the women can as well make decorated baskets, lamp shades, and hats etc., and sell them to the tourists through the management of the Park.

For information on tribals and sustainable development in the rehabilitated village – Melakamanahalli tribal colony was taken for the study. The village is inhabited by the Jenu Kuruba and Betta/Kadu Kuruba. The later are numerically, economically and politically dominant tribe. The main constraints and obstacles to the sustainable development in Melakamanahalli tribal colony are poverty, education, economic constraints, social constraints, and constraints of educational system.

When the first news of dislocation reached local tribals, the people were unhappy. Local forest officials approached the tribal leaders, elites, educated tribal youth and other for rehabilitation.

Micheal Cernia (1999) has identified eight dimensions of impoverishment risk factors in rehabilitation. Of the eight risk factors, four major risk factors have been identified in Melakamanahalli colony. They are landlessness, joblessness, marginalisation and food insecurity, though a number of facilities have been extended to them for sustainable development.

For comparison with the rehabilitated village – Melakamanahalli tribal colony, traditional village namely Chennaikattai colony was taken for the study. It is a mono ethnic village inhabited by the Soliga who are engaged in collection of non-timber forest produce, agricultural labour and forest labour.

Very few are engaged in agriculture and employed in forest department. Many households are living in poverty. The extent of backwardness at the economic level may be attributed to lack of education, food insecurity, joblessness and marginalisation as seen in Melakamanahalli tribal colony. This village is not covered under eco-development programmes which are extended to Melakamanahalli tribal colony.

The following are the strategies eco-tourism for and sustainable development.

1. The natural resources of any kind should be exploited to the extent that ecological balance is maintained.
2. Measures should be undertaken to ensure the renewable of natural resources for future generations.
3. Rights and interests of the local tribals should be protected.
4. There should be emphasis on equity principle while implementing the development programmes.
5. Local people should participate in planning, monitoring and evaluation.
6. There should be better co-ordination between the forest department, tribal welfare department and NGOs.
7. Payment of wage labour should be given as per government rates.
8. Forest protection committees should be formed to protect the biosphere reserve.
9. Empowerment should be given to the local tribals over the tourism management.
10. More employment opportunities should be given to the local tribal women in tourism department.
11. Local crafts should be encouraged.

References

Allen 1980 How to save the World, Kogan Page, London.

Ambhasht 1994Tribal Education: Scope and Constraints, Yojana, January 26, Publication Division, New Delhi.

Arup Ray & D. Mandal 1997 Tribe, Culture and Tourism: An Anthropological Approach Vanyajati, Vol. XIV, No.1.

Barbara Olsen 1997 Environmentally Sustainable Development and Tourism : Lessons from Negril, Human Organization.

Barkin, D. 1996 Ecotourism: A Tool for Sustainable Development in an era of International Integration? Quoted in Anthropology of Tourism: Forging New Ground for Ecotourism and other Alternatives by Amanda Stronza, Annual Review of Anthropology, 2001.

Behura, D.K. 1996 "Development, Environment and the People: An Anthropological Perspective", South Asian Anthropologist, 17(2): 95-100.

Brandon, Katrina, and People and Parks: Linking Michael Wells (1992) Protected Area Management with Local Communities, World Bank, Washington.

Brandon, Katrina 1993 "Basic Steps Toward Encouraging Local Participation in Nature Tourism Project" in K. Lindberg and D. Hawkins (ed) Eco-Tourism: A guide for Planners and Managers, North Bennington, Vt. The Eco-tourism Society.

Burns, Peter M. 1999 An Introduction to Tourism and Anthropology, Routledge, London.

Cernea, M. 1999 The Economics of Involuntary Resettlement: Questions and Challenges; Washington D C : The World Bank.

Chandra P. Gurung and The Annapurna Conservation Maureen De Coursey 1994 Area Project: A Pioneering Example of Sustainable Tourism? (ed) by E. Cater and G. Lowman, John Wiley & Sons Ltd.

Cohen 1979 The Impact of Tourism on the Hill Tribes of Northern Thailand: Int. Asian Forum 10: 5-38.

Colbey 1990 Environmental Management in Development: The Evolution of Paradigms, World Bank Discussion Paper No.80, Washington, D.C; World Bank.

Colchester, Marcus 1988 'The Global Threat to Tribal Peoples: Strategies for Survival' in SM Mohd. Idris (ed), 1988, Global Development and Environmental Crisis: Has Mankind a future? Penang: APPEN (P.459) quoted in Anthropology and Development in Traditional Societies by Hari Mohan Mathur, 1989, Vikas Publishing House Pvt. Ltd., New Delhi.

Elwin, Verrier 1966 Report of the Committee on Special Multipurpose Tribal Blocks, Ministry of Home Affairs, New Delhi.

Fernandes, Walter, Geeta "Forests, Environment and Tribal Menon and PhilipEconomy: Deforestation", in Vierges 1988 Improvement and Marginalisation in Orissa, New Delhi: Indian Social Institute.

Fernandes, Walter 1995"Environmental Deterioration and Sustainable Development", The Administrator, Vol. XI.

Govt. of Karnataka, Project Tiger Brochure, by Field Bandipur, Dept. of Forest Director, Project Tiger Bandipur National Park.

Govt. of Karnataka, Action Plan Report on Project Dept. of Forest Tiger: Bandipur Tiger Reserve(2000-2005) (unpublished report).

Gupta, R. 2003 Report on Jenu Kuruba in "People of India", Karnataka, (Gen. Editor) K.S.Singh; (Editors) B.G. Halbar, S.G.Morab, Suresh Patil, Ramji Gupta, Kolkata: Anthropological Survey of India, New Delhi: Affiliated East–West Press Pvt. Ltd, Part II, 673 – 678.

Kantharaju, K.C. Project Tiger, Bandipur Tiger Reserve, Management Plan ofBandipur Tiger Reserve (2000-2005) Deputy Director, ProjectTiger Division, Bandipur (unpublished report).

Karee Fog Olwig 1980 "National Parks, Tourism and Local Development: A WestIndian Case", Human Organization, Vol.39, No.1.

Mansperger 1995 Tourism and Cultural Change in Small Scale Societies in Human Organization, Vol. 54. No.1.

Mathur, H.M. 1989 Anthropology and Development in Traditional Societies, Vikas Publication House Pvt. Ltd., New Delhi.

Mathur, H.M. 1995 Development, Displacement and Resettlement – Focus on Asian Experiences, Vikas Publication House Pvt. Ltd., New Delhi.

Misra, P.K. 1979 'Jenu Kuruba' Bulletin of Anthropological Survey of India XVIII, No.3, Anthropological Survey of India.

Nanjundayya H.V. and The Mysore Tribes and Castes Iyer, L.K.A. 1928 Vol. The University Press, Mysore.

Nima Manjrekar 2001 Notes from the Wild – An Information Guide to Bandipur National Park, Published by Field Director, Project Tiger, Mysore.

Nunez 1978 Tourist Studies in Anthropological Perspectives in Smith V.L. (ed) Hosts and Guests: The Anthropology of Tourism, Basic Black Well, Oxford, London.

Orlove S. Benjamin 1996 "Anthropology and the Conservation of Biodiversity" in Annual Review of Anthropology, No. 25: 329 –52.

Paige West andEco-Tourism and Authenticity–JamesG. Carrier 2004 Getting Away from It All? Current Anthropology, Vol. 45. No. 4.

Parasuraman 1996 Development Projects, Displacement and Outcomes for Displaced: Two Case Studies, Economic and Political Weekly, June 15.

Patradge, William L. 1989 "Involuntary Resettlement in Development Projects" Journal of Refugee Studies, Vol. 2, No.3, pp. 373.

Patnaik S. N. 2000 Understanding Involuntary Resettlement 384: An Anthropological Perspective, The Eastern Anthropologist, Special Resettlement Number, Vol. 53, No.1-2.

Pottier, J. 1993 Practicing Development, Routledge, London.

Ranjit Daniels 1995 The Nilgiri Biosphere Reserve: A Review of Conservation Status with Recommendations for a Holistic Approach to Management, paper presented to UNESCO, Paris (France)

Sills 1998 Eco-Tourism as an Integrated Conservation and Development Strategy quoted in ARA, 2001.

Singh, K.S. 1994 People of India, Vol.III The Scheduled Tribes, Kolkata: Anthropological Survey of India, Delhi:Oxford University Press, Kadu Kuruba, pp.677-679.

Singh K.S. 1994 People of India, National Series Vol.III "The Scheduled Tribes, Kolkata: Anthropological Survey of India, Delhi: Oxford University Press, Soliga /Soligaru, pp. 1082-1085.

Singh, K.S. 1996 People of India, National Series, Volume VIII-Communities, Segments, Synonyms, Surnames and Titles, Kolkata: Anthropological Survey of India, Delhi: Oxford University Press, 1500-1501.

Smith 1978 Hosts and Guests: The Anthropology of Tourism, Philadelphia : University of Pennsylvania Press.

Stronza 2000 "Because it is ours": Community– Based Eco-Tourism in the Peruvian Amazon quoted in 'Anthropology of Tourism' : Forging New Ground for Eco-Tourism and other Alternatives, Amanda Stronza, ARA, 2001.

Thurston, E 1909 Castes and Tribes of Southern India, Vol. IV pp. 155-177 Government Press, Madras, (Reprint 1975)

Urray 1990 The Tourist Gaze, Sage Publications, London.

Verma 2002 Indian Tribes through the Ages, Publications Division, New Delhi.

World Commission 1987'World Commission Report on Environment and Development our Common Future', Oxford University Press, Oxford, London.

Ziffer. K. 1989 Eco-Tourism : The Uneasy Alliance, Washington, DC : Conserv. Int.

APPENDIX 2.1
DETAILS OF VISITORS TO BANDIPUR NATIONAL PARK FROM 1999-2000

Month	*Indians*	*Foreigners*	*Total*
April	3763	36	3799
May	11027	78	11105
June	4279	58	4337
July	3019	111	3130
August	3207	172	3379
September	3117	85	3202
October	5234	107	5341
November	5730	173	5903
December	8403	119	8522
January	11208	165	11373
February	2933	105	3038
March	1677	85	1762
Total	63597	1294	64891

(Contd.)

DETAILS OF VISITORS TO BANDIPUR NATIONAL PARK FROM 2000-2001

Month	Indians	Foreigners	Total
April	3834	43	3877
May	12757	27	12784
June	5037	38	5075
July	3986	63	4049
August	2845	93	2938
September	2175	57	2232
October	4424	83	4507
November	4277	75	4352
December	5025	93	5118
January	4362	131	4493
February	3268	117	3385
March	2697	87	2784
Total	**54687**	**907**	**55594**

Source: Office of the Deputy Conservator of Forests, Project Tiger Division, Bandipur.

APPENDIX 2.1 (Contd.....)
DETAILS OF VISITORS TO BANDIPUR NATIONAL PARK FROM 2001-2002

Month	Indians	Foreigners	Total
April	6423	42	6465
May	9797	29	9826
June	5827	36	5863
July	4043	79	4122
August	3451	114	3565
September	4002	76	4078
October	6169	115	6284
November	6137	66	6203
December	11817	207	12024
January	5926	133	6059
February	2057	73	2130
March	1264	65	1329
Total	**66913**	**1035**	**67948**

DETAILS OF VISITORS TO BANDIPUR NATIONAL PARK FROM 2002-2003

Month	Indians	Foreigners	Total
April	5760	24	5784
May	12287	33	12320
June	5136	20	5156
July	4187	45	4232
August	4732	107	4839
September	2043	37	2080
October	3696	45	3741
November	4178	75	4253
December	5276	81	5357
January	4072	143	4215
February	1924	127	2051
March	72	-	72
Total	**53363**	**737**	**54100**

Source: Office of the Deputy Conservator of Forests, Project Tiger Division, Bandipur.

APPENDIX 2.2
BANDIPUR NATIONAL PARK
Statement Showing the Elephant Poaching in Last 5 years

Sl.No.	Date	Range	Place	Male/Female	Remarks
			1999-2000		
1.	17.5.1999	Gundre	CPT-89	Male	Tusk missing
2.	18.6. 1999	Maddur	Sulekatte	Male	Tusk missing
			2000-2001		
3.	20.6.2000	Moolehole	Kalkere	Male	Tusk missing
4.	20.6.2000	Maddur	Iron Bridge	Male	Tusk missing
5.	2.7. 2000	Maddur	Bargi	Male	Tusk missing
6.	6.7. 2000	Maddur	Ekkonabetta	Male	Tusk missing
7.	20.6. 2000	Hediyala	Beladakuppe	Male	Tusk missing
8.	20.12. 2000	Moliyur	Devalapura	Male	Tusk missing
9.	12.2.2001	Moliyur	Moliyur	Male	Tusk missing
			2001-02		
10.	11.7.2001	N.Begur	CPT 79	Male	Tusk missing
11.	7.10.2001	Maddur	Bargi Section	Male	Tusk recovered
			2002-03		
12.	20.5.2002	Moolehole	Moolehole Beat	Male	Tusk missing
13.	26.7.2002	Gundre	Basavanabetta	Male	Tusk missing
14.	6.12.2002	A.M.Gudi	Dabbegottu beat	Male	Tusk missing
			2003-04		
15.	12.10.2003	Hediyala	Beladakuppe	Male	Tusk missing
			2004-05		
			Nil		

Source: Office of the Deputy Conservator of Forests, Project Tiger Division, Bandipur.

APPENDIX 2.3

Statement showing the death of Wild animals due to accidents during the period from 1997-98 to 2004-05 Bandipur National Park Area

Sl. No.	Name of the Range	FOC No.	Date	Name of the animal	Remarks
1	2	3	4	5	6
			1997-1998		
1	Bandipur	3/97-98	22/9/97	Cheetal	
			1998-1999		
1	Bandipur	17/98-99	23/3/99	Cheetal	
			1999-2000		
1	Bandipur	7/99-00	1/7/99	Cheetal	
2	Moyar	5/99-00	12/8/99	Sambar	
3	Bandipur	11/99-00	6/3/00	Cheetal	
			2000-2001		
1	Bandipur	1(a)/00-01	29/8/00	Sambar	
2	Moyar	22/00-01	29/9/00	Cheetal	
3	Bandipur	15/00-01	26/11/00	Cheetal	
4	Bandipur	17/00-01	22/3/01	Cheetal	
			2001-2002		
1	Bandipur	2/01-02	21/4/01	Cheetal	
2	Bandipur	7/01-02	22/8/01	Cheetal	
3	Bandipur	9/01-02	29/8/01	Cheetal	
4	Moyar	16/01-02	13/11/01	Sambar	
5	Moyar	16/01-02	03/12/01	Panther	
			2002-03		
1	Bandipur	16/02-03	15/11/02	Jackal	
2	Maddur	38/02-03	19/12/02	Cheetal	
3	Bandipur	31/02-03	05/03/03	Cheetal	
4	Bandipur	32/02-03	20/3/03	Cheetal	
5	Bandipur	28/02-03	06/02/03	Sambar	
			2003-2004		
1	Bandipur	1/03-04	30/4/03	Cheetal	
2	Bandipur	2/03-04	8/5/03	Sambar	
3	Bandipur	3/03-04	21/5/03	Cheetal	
4	Moolehole	1/03-04	21/05/03	Calf Elephant	
5	Bandipur	4/03-04	23/5/03	Cheetal	

(Contd.)

(Contd.)

Sl. No.	*Name of the Range*	*FOC No.*	*Date*	*Name of the animal*	*Remarks*
1	2	3	4	5	6
6	Bandipur	6/03-04	18/6/03	Sloth Bear	
7	Maddur	20/03-04	24/6/03	Samber	
8	Bandipur	7/03-04	24/6/03	Cheethal	
9	Bandipur	10/03-04	22/7/03	Cheethal	
10	Moolehole	7/03-04	01/09/03	Tiger	
11	Maddur	28/03-04	28/7/03	Calf Deer	
12	Bandipur	30/03-04	5/2/04	Female Deer	
13	Bandipur	--	13/2/04	Female Deer	

Source : Office of the Deputy Conservator of Forests, Project Tiger Division, Bandipur.

APPENDIX 2.4
Project Tiger Division, Bandipur
Details of Compensation Amount Paid From Last 5 Years

Year	*Crop Damage*		*Cattle Killed*		*Human Death*	
	No. of Cases	*Amount paid*	*No. of Cases*	*Amount paid*	*No. of Cases*	*Amount paid*
2000-2001	210	119800	34	19800	1	100000
2001-2002	590	272150	32	27000	4	-
2002-2003	28	37000	10	8400	3	700000
2003-2004	1503	742035	11	14050	5	485000
2004 –2005	1794	798305	45	48050	-	-

(Contd. Appendix 2.4)

Year	*Human Injury*		*Permanent Injury*	
	No. of Cases	*Amount paid*	*No. of Cases*	*Amount paid*
2000-2001	5	19654	-	-
2001-2002	1	-	-	-
2002-2003	4	23150	-	-
2003-2004	6	29664	-	-
2004 –2005	6	35645	-	-

Source : Office of the Deputy Conservator of Forests, Project Tiger Division, Bandipur.

3

Ecotourism and Sustainable Development in Nagarhole National Park

B.R.Vijayendra & H.M. Maralusiddaiah Patel

Introduction

The important tourists' areas in the Nilgiri Biosphere Reserve attract many tourists from different parts of the country and also from different countries in the world. Govt. of Karnataka, Forest Department has given attention to provide infrastructural facilities at their places, which include comfortable accommodation, resorts, cottages and guesthouses. These facilities have led to an increase in number of tourists. In 1994-2000, the total number of tourists who visited the area was recorded to be 37,311. In addition, Forest Department employed local tribal as forest guards, watchers, guides and workers at cottages and resorts. In order know the impacts of eco-tourism on the tribes of the area and how eco-tourism can be used as an effective tool to improve the quality of life of the tribal; the present study has been taken up.

The Nagarahole National Park occupies a unique place in Karnataka state. This national park constitutes a part of the Nilgiri Biosphere Reserve. Hence, this tourist centre has been selected for studying the eco-tourism and sustainable development in this park.

Issues

1. Growth and development of eco-tourism in the area.
2. The impact of eco-development activities on the local tribal communities.
3. Involvement of local people, government and NGOs in conservation and development activities in this area.
4. Study of indigenous knowledge of local people in conservation practices.
5. Delineating how tribal exploit the natural resources in sustainable way.
6. Strategies for sustainable development of resources.

Specific Objectives

1. To study the growth of eco-tourism in Nagarahole Area.
2. To study conservation practices observed by the tribal in the protection of the forest resources.
3. To delineate the negative and positive impacts of eco-tourism on the local tribes.
4. To study the tourist perception towards the area, people and local flora and fauna.
5. To study development and cultural change among that local tribal communities due to impact of eco-tourism.

Methodology

The Nagarahole National Park which comes under Nilgiri Biosphere Reserves in Karnataka state was selected for the study. In this area a few tribal communities are living in and around this area viz., the Jenu Kuruba, the Kadu Kuruba and the Yerava.

Fieldwork was conducted for about three months i.e., February to April 2005. Anthropological methods including observation, interview, key informants interview and case study method was used to collect both qualitative and quantitative data. Structure interview was done among the individuals belonging different categories.

1. The first sample includes local tribe who are working in the National Park were interviewed.

2. The second sample includes local tribals who have no connection with the National Parks are interviewed.
3. The third category includes forest officials; local peoples and other officials are interviewed.
4. In addition to formal interviews was conducted with the tourists regarding the place and infrastructure facilities available in the area.

Area and the People: Nagarahole

Karnataka portion of Nilgiri Biosphere Reserve covers a area of 1,527 km^2 and includes the Nagarahole and Bandipur National Parks. This portion is a unique bio-geographic region. In the year 1992 name has been changed to Rajiv Gandhi National Park, but the park is still widely known as Nagarahole.

The forests of this Division are situated between longitude 76° 0′ and 76°15′ E and latitude 11°57′ and 12°14′ N. They lie at an altitude of 792 to 1,224 m above mean sea level. The land is gently undulating, with scattered hills rising to about 300 m, and nallas dividing up the area. Forests of this Division are accessible throughout the year.

Nagarahole is primarily a deciduous forest with the prevalence of tropical semi-evergreen, tropical moist mixed deciduous, tropical dry deciduous forests. The main tree species are *Adina spp.*, *Pterocarpus spp.*, *Terminalia, Dalbergia, Schleichera* and several species of bamboo. It is watered by five large perennial rivers and 40 artificial water tanks. An unusual feature of the National Park is swamps in low-lying areas (locally known as *haadlus)*. The fauna of Nagarahole is said to be compareable with some of the finest natural habitats of the world and some of the endangered fauna include the tiger, leopard, elephant, wild dog, sloth bear, bison, spotted deer, barking deer, mouse deer, four-horned antelope. Nagarahole lies in a belt that boasts of the highest concentration of the Asiatic elephant anywhere in the world. Other important fauna include the Indian Giant Squirrel, jungle and leopard cat, small Indian and Malabar civet and avifauna including a wide range of predatory birds such as the crested honey buzzard, crested serpent eagle, grey headed fishing eagle and falcons as well as the lesser whistling teal, adjutant stork, spoonbill.

A Historical Perspective on the Nagarahole

The temporal scale for this analysis starts with the active intervention of the British in the Nagarahole area in the mid-1800s, which environmental historians unanimously portray as an era of immense change in Indian forest management (Buchy1996; Guha 1989; Gadgil and Guha 1992; Rangarajan 1996a).

Key Events around the Nagarahole Region

Timeline of Events around Nagarahole

- **1832.** Coorg annexed and directly administered by the British (Rice 1908; Thornton1857).
- **1831-1881**. Period of direct British rule in Mysore, followed by native rule in 1881 (Bhatt 1997).
- **1854.** First European coffee plantation established in Coorg (Rice 1908).
- **1869**. Mysore Forest Rules introduced; district system of forests established in 1872 (Stebbing1926).
- **1871**. Coorg Forest Rules introduced (Stebbing 1926).
- **1878.** Passing of the Indian Forest Act 1878.
- **1894-1901**. Reservation of forests in the current Nagarahole Park.
- **1948**. Coorg constituted as a separate (Class C) state of the Union of India (Bhatt 1997).
- **1955.** Nagarahole constituted as a wildlife sanctuary covering 28,416 ha. by Coorg State (Alva1978; Lal et al. 1994).
- **1956**. Kodagu (formerly Coorg) redefined as a district of the former State of Mysore (now Karnataka) (Bhatt 1997).
- **1975**. Notice of intent to upgrade Nagarahole from a Sanctuary to a National Park in 1975 and extend area to 57,155 ha. (Alva 1978; Krishnegowda 1998; Lal et al. 1994).
- **1983**. Final notification to upgrade Nagarahole to a National Park (Alva 1978; Krishnegowda 1998).
- **1987.** Notification of intent to extend park area by 7,814 ha. to the south (Lal et al. 1994).
- **1992**. Name was changed to Rajiv Gandhi National Park, but the park is still widely known as Nagarahole (Lal et al. 1994).
- **1998**. Commencement of Nagarahole Eco-development Project.

1999. Creation of Nagapura resettlement on the Nagarahole boundary and resettlement of 51 tribal families. Broadly, the Nagarahole landscape since colonization went from a commercially exploited landscape, to a landscape protected as a sanctuary for wildlife.

Demographic / Livestock Features

Total population living adjacent to the Reserve as per the 1991 Census was about 72,642. About 7,000 people are also living in about 58 settlements inside the Reserve. People inside the Reserve are scheduled tribes belong to the Jenu Kurubas, the Betta Kurubas and the Yeravas. The main occupation of these tribes is livestock grazing, gathering of non-wood forest products and cultivating dry land crops like ragi, jowar, etc. They also work as labourers in adjacent coffee estates. The cattle owned by these people are of local breeds.

People

Indigenous peoples of Nagarahole consider the areas to be their traditional territory - *Jamma* - and believe that they belong to this land, which has sustained them for centuries, and it is on this land that their Gods exist, where their ancestors were buried. The tribes believe in force of creation *Devaru*. Their sacred sites are important, not in a traditional religious sense but because the sacred sites embody the wisdom of their ancestors from whom they gain advice.

The Jenu Kuruba is mainly depending on forest for their livelihood. They occupy forested regions where for the past known history, they have been living in isolation but in harmony with nature. They draw their sustenance largely from the forests. The forest is not only providing them food, material to build houses, fuel for cooking, but also satisfy deep-rooted sentiments. Their life is connected in one way or the other with forests right from birth to death. The Jenu Kuruba are having major role in capturing the elephants and in their domestication processes. Even today, the Jenu Kurubas are working as elephant's trainers and mahouts in elephants training camp at Murkal. In the Forest Department, many of them are working as mahouts and as daily wage labourer.

On account of various social and political pressures exerted on the Jenu Kuruba, they retreated into forest and hill tracks over the centuries. Many factors have made them to lead a kind of primitive life. They not only know plants, trees, animals of the area very well, but also have established with them a certain kind of cultural relationship. They are as simple as they are fascinating and they are as sincere as they are innocent, as colorful as they are hospitable and lively as they are lovely. Forest had been their well loved home for many generations. In the forests they were collecting honey, wax, soap nuts, roots and tubers, ginger and wild turmeric and selling them in the market. The way of collection of honey is still in primitive stage. Traditionally they used to collect honey in a bamboo container and now a day, they use tins. Some time it is used to fill up their stomach. Honey is mixed with honeybee eggs and some herbal plants and used as medicine for so many diseases.

They have very close linkage with their forest habitats, which they regard as their mother deity. It has been observed that tribal people are not only familiar with the number of biological species found around them but also possess a great deal of understanding of various ecological components of forest. They are emotionally attached to the forest and considered them to be a nature's gift. Their folklore is full of references to the forest. There are several rites and rituals in which one or the other forest produce is used in one way or another. Many of the leaves of either plants or tree or climbers are used in religious rites are procured from the forest. Many trees and plants found in the indigenous forest are consider the abode of deities and are worship on certain occasions. They worship trees, plants and nature. If they want to get ride of from the disease, they mainly depend on forest. The Jenu Kuruba believe in spirits apart from gods and goddesses. At the time of worship, they use forest plants, trees, bamboo sticks and particular flowers and plants for particular worship. To avoid the evil eye, they tie a particular creeper in their waist. At the time of honey collection they make use leaves of a particular plant to make paste and then smear it on the body to avoid the bee's biting. Some times, they put a variety of leaves in fire, the smoke of which can avoid the honeybees.

The Jenu Kurubas mother tongue is *'jenunudi'* (dialect), with large admixture of Kannada, Tamil and Malayalam words. According to 1971 Census the total population of the Jenu Kuruba was 6,623 persons. As per the 1981 Census, they numbered 34,747 persons (17,867 males, 16,880 females). They are grouped under the primitive tribal group (PGT). They live in the interior forest in thatched huts in settlements called: haadi. They build huts on the tree top to watch wild elephants *(manchige)*. In the night, the wild animals generally to enter the *ragi* (a food grain) field in search of food. They are driving away the animals by chasing them with a burning bamboo torch and making the loud noise by beating the tins and drums. Unhygienic condition, lack of access to clean drinking water, under nourishment, malnutrition and their belief in evil spirits and superstition are some of the important factors responsible for their present health problems.

To catch the elephants the new techniques are used now a days. For this they make a big pit inside the forest and bamboo slits and wooden poles are spread on the pit and soil and dried leaves are spread on the wooden poles. The elephants are driven towards the ditches by making sounds and with fire torches and thus are forced to run towards the pits. In this process elephants a inside the pit of which the selected elephants are captured for domestication.

The disease like headache, dysentery, stomach ache, cold, excess of headache, tuberculosis, body swelling etc are cured by giving the local medicines prepared out of herbs, seeds and barks of trees and plants. For head ache they grind the *alalekai* (a seed) with water and apply the paste on the forehead. One who suffers from dysentery is given the medicine prepared by grinding the *dindalu* (bark) with water and hot iron rod is rinsed in it. The liquid thus prepared is given to patient to drink. To avoid the stomachache, bitter gourd leaves are grinded with water and the juice is given to drink. For cold *kippe sundekai* is grinded and is mixed with water; the same is given to drink. To get free from excessive heat, bark of *atti* plant, *biliganake soppu* (leaves), *kariganake soppy* (leaves), *karisundekayi* (seed) and *betta sundekai* (fruit) is grinded and the paste is consumed daily for eight to ten days. For tuberculosis, the paste prepared out of the roots of *karekayi* (roots) is given daily cures tuberculosis. For body swelling, *kolalikesoppu* (a kind of leaves) is boiled in water and patient takes bath with that water to get ride of body swelling.

Table 3.1 The Villages (haadi) near the Nagarahole National Park

1	Gadde haadi	23	06.30	Jenu kuruba
2	Goni gadde	56	15.31	Jenu kuruba
3	Moorkal	40	11.41	Jenu kuruba
4	Siddapura haadi	47	13.21	Jenu kuruba
5	Chandanakadu	27	07.34	Yarava
6	Bommadu	51	15.18	Jenu kuruba
7	Karmadu	09	02.58	Jenu kuruba
8	Thattekere	16	04.58	Jenu kuruba
9	Maranahalli	17	04.43	Betta kuruba/JK
10	Balekuvu	07	02.18	Jenu kuruba
11	Naachi	19	05.44	Jenu kuruba
12	Kodange	23	06.30	Jenu kuruba
13	Kollangeri	20	05.74	Jenu kuruba
	Total		100.00	

Table 3.2 Sex Composition

Sl.No.	*Sex*	*Per cent*
1	Male	51.6
2	Female	48.4
	Total	100.00

Table 3.3 Educational Level

Sl.No	*Educational level*	*Per cent*
1	Anganavadi to 4th std	21.90
2	5th std to 7th	25.20
3	8th to 10th	11.90
4	10th failed	02.90
5	PUC	00.70
6	illiterates	37.40
	Total	100.00

The Table 3.3 on educational status of tribal people leaving in the settlement inside the reserve forest, reveals that 21.90% of the total children are studying in between Anganawadi and 4th standard, whereas only 0.70% children are studying at P.U.C. Illiterates constitute 37.40%, in this category most of them are elderly people. In the middle school level there are 25.20% and it comes down to 11.90% in the high school level. There are 2.90% students who have failed in 10th standard and discontinued. From this table it is revealed that initial level of education is encouraging or well taken by students and as well as parents. But it is gradually reducing. So dropout is very prominent after middle school, it may be due to the non-existence of High School in the nearby area and in case of girls, parents don't want to send them to far off placed. The Table 3.2 supports the above statement as it is indicating 61.40% of children have discontinued study.

Table 3.4 Educational Status

Sl .No	*Educational Status*	*Per cent*
1	Child below age group	13.30
2	Continuing education	25.30
3	Discontinued	61.40
	Total	100.00

Table 3.5 Occupational Status

Sl.No	*Occupational Status*	*Per cent*
1	Estate labours	70.60
2	Watchers	09.10
3	Fire Watcher	03.80
4	PCP/MR	02.90
5	Govt. Employed	01.10
6	House wife	12.50
	Total	100.00

In Table 3.5 shows occupational. There are 6 categories in which nearly of the tribal population are depending on labour work in estates which constitutes 70.60 per cent. There are 9.10 per cent of tribal who are working as watchers in the forest department on daily wage basis during the summer and it continues till rains. In a year they hardly work for 1.5 to 2 months and after that again they have to depend on labour work. Besides, about 1.10 per cent are working as government employees 3.80 per cent of the tribal people are working in the forest as fire watcher and 2.90 per cent as PCP/MR. Both are temporary posts.

Eco-Tourism

Eco-tourism is defined as, that form of tourism that involves traveling to relatively undisturbed natural areas with the specific objectives of studying, admiring and enjoying nature and its wild plants and animals as well as any existing cultural aspects, past or present, found in these areas'. Eco-tourism is distinguished from mass tourism or general resort tourism by having a lower impact on the environment and by requiring less infrastructure development.

The key elements of eco-tourism thus include:

A natural environment as its prime attraction

An optimum number of environment friendly visitors

Activities which do not have any serious impact on the ecosystem

Positive involvement of the local communities

Eco-tourism in India

India is one of the seven mega biodiversity countries of the world, and ecotourism help conserve these resources and assist in economic development which otherwise will remains largely untapped both for the domestic and international tourism market.

Tourism has emerged as the largest industry in the world with an annual revenue of almost $500 billion. Eco-tourism is one of the fastest growing sectors in the tourism industry at present. It has attracted increasing attention in recent years, not only as an alternative to mass tourism, but also as a means of economic development and environmental conservation. However, ecotourism is a frequently debated term. Sometimes it is used simply to identify a form of tourism where the motivation for visitor, centers around the observation of nature. True ecotourism, however, requires a proactive approach that seeks to mitigate the negative and enhance the positive impacts of nature tourism. Being a nature based tourism; it takes into account the natural ecological attraction, their conservation and development. Its main aim is to safeguard the environment and make it beneficial to the local people by generating revenue and education and pleasure for the tourist.

Today, many countries have made significant advances in the field of eco-tourism by creating enabling policy environment, capacity building, marketing ecotourism projects, and supporting research on impact of tourism. Following these international initiates the Department of Tourism, Govt. of India issued tourism policy and Guidelines in July 1998. The policy lays down the objectives for ecotourism and contains operational guidelines for major stakeholder.

India with its varied natural attractions and vast cultural heritage has immense potential for growth in the eco-tourism sector. During our interaction with the stakeholders it was found that a proper understanding of the benefits of ecotourism and awareness about the opportunists available would go a long way in benefiting both service providers and customers. Therefore the workshop was primarily aimed to promote awareness, identify opportunities and showcase the benefits of ecologically sensitive tourism for the tourism industry. The workshop reached out to tour operators, promoters, tourism departments' officials, hoteliers who are important links in the conservation process and focused on ecotourism, policy and planning, challenges with highlight on case studies.

Table 3.6 The Number of Tourists who Visited the Park During 1994-2000

Sl No.	*Year*	*Nagarahole*		*Karapur*		*Total*
		Indian	*Foreigners*	*Indian*	*Foreigners*	
1	1994-95	17005	37	1922	879	19843
2	1995-96	21051	85	6715	895	28745
3	1996-97	16702	91	6518	2253	25564
4	1997-98	26098	80	8001	2873	37052
5	1998-99	25538	60	6775	3006	35379
6	1999-00	26766	150	7989	2406	37311

The park has two tourism zones situated around Nagarahole and Sunkadakatte respectively. The latter, caters to the tourists visiting jungle lodges and resorts, and Govt. of Karnataka Undertaking, based at Karapur at the southern end of the park. Annually, 25,000 to 30,000 tourists visit the National Park.

Table 3.7 Seasonal Distribution of Tourists during 2004

Sl.No.	*Tourist visited the Nagarahole National Park in the Year 2004*		
	Month	*Indian*	*Foreigner*
1	April	Closed	Closed
2	May	2622	32
3	June	592	11
4	July	933	5
5	August	607	21
6	September	914	34
7	October	2943	22
8	November	2259	82
9	December	Closed	closed
	Total	10870	207

Table 3.8 Seasonal Distribution of Tourists during 2005

Sl.No.	*Tourist visited the Nagarahole National Park in the Year 2005*		
	Month	*Indian*	*Foreigner*
1	January	2184	178
2	February	1279	82
3	March	167	32
4	April	841	20
5	May	4368	37
6	June	1354	441
	Total	10193	790

Wildlife Viewing

Department vehicles are available for wildlife viewing. The park generally has a moderate climate with three seasons: Summer, Monsoon and Winter. However, monsoons are often severe and the ideal time to visit the park is between September and May.

Table 3.9 Details of Rest Houses, Rooms, Beds and Rentals

Location	*No. of Rooms*	*No. of Beds*	*Suits*	*Rental per day*	
				Indian	*Foreigner*
Nagarahole	2	4	Cauvery	Rs 1000/-	Rs. 2000/-
	4	8	Gangothri	Rs 750/-	Rs. 1500/-
Dormitories	2	24	-	Rs 50/- per person	Rs. 70/- per person
Kalhalla	2	4	-	Rs 750/-	Rs. 1500/-

Visiting Hours

6.00 a.m. to 9.00 a.m. and 4.00 p.m. to 6.30 p.m. Safari ride by Forest Department Bus : Adult – Rs.75/- per trip, Child – Rs. 50/- per trip.

Approach by Road

- 225 kms. from Bangalore
- 90 kms. from Mysore via Hunsur
- 80 kms. from Mysore to Jungle Lodges, Karapura via H.D. Kote Hand Post

Nearest Airport

- Bangalore – 225 kms.
- Coimbatore – 304 kms.
- Mangalore – 225 kms.

State KSRTC Bus services are available from Bangalore, Mysore and Mangalore.

Other Places of Interest

- Big teak tree
- Nagaraja tunnel
- Irupu falls
- Kabini back waters
- Taraka back waters
- Murkal elephant camp
- Nagarahole information centre
- Veeranahosahally information centre
- Nagarahole watch tower

Regulations for tourists

1. Do not disturb the animals.
2. Movement on the main road, is prohibited between 6 PM and 6 AM.
3. Private vehicles are to be parked in specified places and only departmental vehicles to be used to move into the park.
4. Use of horns, radio's stereo music is prohibited.
5. As far as possible, dark clothes to be worn while moving in the park.

6. No arms or ammunition to be carried within the park.
7. Kindling fire, in the forest is prohibited.
8. Littering the park, is prohibited and dust bins to be used.
9. Moving into the park, without a forest guide is prohibited.
10. Pets are prohibited.

Controversy on Taj Group Hotels in Murkal Range

The Forest Department entered into a lease agreement with the Taj Group of Hotels (one of the leading hotel chains in India) for a period of 18 years, on 28 August 1994, to lease an area of 24 acres of land in the Murkal range of the Park, for the construction of a three-star resort complex comprising bungalows, a conference hall and a bar. Previously the site was leased to a sawmill, upon whose failure the Forest Department had proceeded to construct a few guesthouses for campers. According to *Section 2* of the *Forest (Conservation) Act, 1980*, forest land cannot be leased for non-forest purposes without a Central Government clearance. The Karnataka government did not obtain any such clearance from the Union and hence the lease that was granted was illegal. The adivasis of Nagarahole with the support of people's organizations and other NGOs submitted memorandums to the Prime Minister and President, and held protest marches to pressurise the Taj to quit Nagarahole. Finally, the Samithi filed a Public Interest Litigation (PIL) against the Karnataka government. The matter was argued in the High Court of Karnataka and eventually in the Supreme Court and then it was referred to the Union for the necessary clearance, which was denied. Consequently, the state government was asked to revoke the lease and clear the site within 60 days. Not satisfied, the state government appealed to the court once more, which was subsequently dismissed. If the resort was built the subsequent threat to the habitat and to the adivasis living within the National Park can only be imagined. (*Source*: Forest Peoples Programme Bank Information Center, Washington.)

Tables based on the Schedule Tourist information reveals much valuable information's about the educational, occupation, religious status and place they come from, reason for selection etc. of the tourists. The opinion of tourists' on local infrastructure facilities available, the problems faced by them and their suggestion to improve the same are also explained below.

Table 3.10 Motivation to Visit the Park

Sl.No.	*Who Motivated*	*Percentage*
1	Family Member	22.33
2	News paper	14.56
3	Internet	05.83
4	Friends	48.54
5	Journals/Books	02.91
6	Television	05.83
	Total	**100**

Table 3.10 shows as how the tourists are motivated to visit this place and this have been classified into six categories of whom 48.54 per cent of the total number of tourists are motivated by friends, 22.33 per cent of them are by family members, 14.96 per cent of them are by Newspaper, 5.83 per cent of them are through Internet Websites. 5.83 per cent are through T.V. programmes and 2.91 per cent are through reading articles in journals or books. While friends and family members play significant role in motivating others to visit this place among Indian tourists the Internet facilities motivate the foreigners.

Table 3.11 Mode of Transport

Sl.No.	*Mode of Transport*	*Percentage*
1	Bus	26.21
2	Car	73.79
	Total	**100.00**

Table 3.12 Occupational Status of the Tourist

Sl.No.	*Occupational Status*	*Percentage*
1	Government Employees	10.68
2	Private Services	36.89
3	Businessmen	46.60
4	Others	05.83
	Total	**100.00**

Table 3.11 gives information about the mode of transports availed. It reveals that, 73.79 per cent of the total number of tourists avail car/jeep, whereas 26.21 per cent depend on local transport

like bus. As the frequency of the bus is meager, people prefer to visit either in their own vehicle or hired taxi in order to avoid inconvenience.

Table 3.12 tells about the occupational status of tourists. It reveals that out of the total number of tourists, 46.60 per cent are businessmen, 36.89 per cent of tourists are working in private factories, firms and other institutions and 10.68 per cent are government employees. Research scholars and students who prefer to tour form the least in number (5.83 per cent) when compared to others categories of tourists.

Table 3.13 Reason for Selection

Sl.No.	*Reason*	*Percentage*
1	Natural Beauty	66.99
2	Adventure	07.77
3	Interest to see Animal/Plant or Study	25.24
	Total	**100.00**

Table No. 3.8 indicates that out of the total number of tourists 66.99 per cent of the tourist have opted this place due to its natural beauty, 25.24 per cent of tourists visited to have a look at the natural habitats of wild animals, wild trees and plants grown in the natural environment and 7.77 per cent tourists opted as adventure tourism. Enjoying nature and natural beauty form one of the major aims and objectives of visiting Nagarahole.

Table 3.14 Composition of the Tourist

Sl.No.	*Composition of Team*	*Percentage*
1	Alone	nil
2	Family	36.89
3	Group	63.11
	Total	**100.00**

Table 3.15 Sex Composition

Sl.No.	*Sex*	*Percentage*
1	Male	80.58
2	Female	19.42
	Total	**100.00**

Table 3.16 Tourist on State wise

Sl.No.	*State to which the Tourist belongs*	*Percentage*
1	Foreigner	05.83
2	Karnataka	33.01
3	Tamil Nadu	19.42
4	Andhra Pradesh	06.80
5	Kerala	13.59
6	Maharashtra	05.83
7	West Bengal	03.88
8	Gujarath	04.85
9	Delhi	02.91
10	Others	03.88
	Total	**100.00**

Table 3.17 The Tourist Educational Status

Sl.No.	*Educational Qualification of the Tourist*	*Percentage*
1	Post Graduate	40.77
2	Degree	33.01
3	Technical	07.77
4	Under Graduate	18.45
	Total	**100.00**

Table 3.18 Religion of the Tourist

Sl.No.	*Religion*	*Percentage*
1	Hindu	66.99
2	Muslims	15.54
3	Christian	07.77
4	Buddhist	02.91
5	Sikh	02.91
6	Others	03.88
	Total	**100.00**

The objectives, which have a direct bearing on the indigenous people living in and in the immediate periphery of the Park, improve Protected Area (PA) management with the involvement of local people and Eco-development to reduce negative impacts.

In the case of the preparing plans for improved PA management, it is stated that people living in and around the park are dependent on the resources of the park and are most affected by the establishment of a park. Thus the project seeks to provide opportunity for these groups, including NGOs to take part in park plans by providing them direct benefits which in the long run will strengthen the relationship of sustainability and mutual dependency for the conservation of the park.

Table 3.19 Mother Tongue of Tourist

Sl.No.	*Mother Tongue*	*Percentage*
1	Kannada	25.24
2	Tamil	15.53
3	Telugu	05.83
4	Malayalam	13.59
5	Hindi	03.88
6	English	05.83
7	Bengali	03.88
8	Gujarati	04.85
9	Urdu	11.65
11	Marathi	05.84
13	Others	03.88
	Total	**100.00**

Table 3.20 Types of Problems in the Nagarahole Park

Sl.No.	*Types of Problems*	*Percentage*
1	Transportation	17.48
2	Food	12.62
3	Guide	13.59
4	Accommodation	15.53
5	Others	40.78
	Total	**100.00**

Various works such as building of roads and concrete structures inside the Nagarahole must stop with immediate effect. The tribals reject any development initiative, which destroys the canvas of the wild. The tribal families, which have been forcefully re-located to the fringe forest areas, must be vested with the right to enter the forests for performing their traditional duties and observing their festivals, apart from enjoying their right to collects minor forest produce.

Vigorous efforts must be made to curtail 'fence eating the crop' with necessary vigil on the agencies of the State and tribal and the state agencies should work hand in hand in keeping out the smugglers and the poachers. Forest contractors should be banned.

The State should initiate special efforts at imparting specific training to the tribal in order to blend traditional wisdom with acceptable modern conservation strategies with the ultimate aim of the tribal himself assuming positions such as Conservators and management.

Movement of all vehicles except to meet conservation requirements and emergencies must be banned inside the forests. These vehicles must be solar powered to reduce noise and environmental pollution. All approach roads passing through the forests must be diverted outside the forests on a war footing. Road leading to Kutta and Balele should be stopped.

All concrete structures within a few km. radius of the forests should be demolished and strict regulations must be enforced for any structure which comes up in future. Bricks burning and cultivation of tobacco in this region took off over the last thirty to forty years, with an estimated near doubling of the area under tobacco cultivation since 1981 and need tones of fuel. The encroachment of forest by estate people is also dangerous for the park.

The tribal economy shall be based on sustainable cultivation practices which has been followed over the centuries by these forest dwellers in the form of medicinal plants and forest produce such as gooseberries, honey, tubers, roots and shoots. The tribal should enjoy the rights over inter should cropping without affecting the forest canvas around his *Haadi* and without using any modern machinery or chemical fertilizers. Horticultural produce ought to form a back-bone of the tribal economy and food habits. The tribal shall have the rights over small prey.

The tribal *haadis* need to be established by the tribal in keeping with their traditions and merging with the topography of the forests without any destruction of the forest cover. The tribal should be given assistance for putting up their traditional dwelling structures using dead wood and dry leaves. If the State provides them with community electricity, the tribal may opt for solar electrification for lighting purposes.

During the teak plantation in 1900 the tribals were planting the ragi and jower as an intercrop inside the plantation popularly known as *kumrry* cultivation. Next year they shifted their cultivation to new plantation because they could grow anything there after the teak plants grown bigger. This cultivation was misinterpreted as shifting cultivation. Both the *haadlu* cultivation was also stopped.

The tribal children should be educated in their mother tongue with Kannada being an optional language at the primary level. The curriculum ought to be framed with the help of tribal Yajamans, tribal experts and educationists, based on the inherent conservation idiom of the tribal. After due education, the tribal should be given preference in agencies involved in forest conservation and preservation of indigenous cultures.

The condition of the two vehicles assigned for Safari are very poor. Both vehicles area making lots of sound and emits lots of smoke due to running by diesel. Windows and seats are broken and there is no safety for tourists.

As per the tourist's data, tourist visits Nagarahole not only from different places of our country but also from abroad. Hence guide should be trained properly, so that he should be very enthusiastic and should be well received by talking always atleast three languages i.e., Hindi, Kannada and English. The guide's duty is to give brief introduction about the Park and proper instructions like how to behave while moving inside the forest, maintenance of silence etc. The guide was found giving more prominence for only animals but not for plants and other rare species.

The Nagarahole Park should be free from plastics. It is observed that many tourists through plastic covers of biscuits, chocolates, pans and even carry bags. It is absolute necessary to check in the gate before entering inside the park like it is doing by the zoo authorities while entering inside the zoo.

There is only one bus in the morning and one in the afternoon. One has to wait for quit some time to Safari. The Park does not have proper place for tourist to rest till Safari starts. Especially during rainy season tourist are facing lots of problem and many had reported their bad experiences.

There is no drinking water facility to tourist, except one tap and that too stop if power goes off.

Suggestions

The Murkal is already having all infrastructure facilities like 10 cottages and two big dormitaries, except electricity.

1. Tourist who like to go for safari should get down at Murkal and those who want to stay can book their suits otherwise they can be picked up from Murkal itself, so that safari starts from Murkal and ends in Murkal.
2. Instead of those two old vans, proposal should be made to buy either battery operated buses or buses running by LPG. It would help reduce pollution both air and sound.
3. No private vehicles should be allowed inside the forest especially in the safari road.
4. It not only stops all vehicle movements but also reduce pollution, besides giving relief to the wild animals inside the forest. There is need to control plastic culture and smokers etc.
5. These actions would make Nagarahole National Park with a true eco-tourism site on the world map.

References

1. CES, 1986. *NBR Information System: Preliminary Report*, CES, Bangalore.
2. Daniels, R.J. R., 1987. *On Assigning Conservation Values to Bird Species of Western Ghats CES*, Bangalore.
3. ENVIS, 1987, CES Report CES, Bangalore.
4. ENVIS, 2000, *NBR: An Overview Report CES,* Bangalore.
5. Forest Peoples Programme, 2000. *Nagarahole: Adivasi People Budakattu Hakku Stapana Samithi*, Washington (Unpublished).
6. Gadgil M and et.al., 1985. *A manual of Eco-development with Special Reference to the Western Ghats.* CES Bangalore.
7. Gadgil M and et.al., 1987. *Scientific Programme for the NBR: Report of a Workshop*, CES Bangalore.

8. Gadgil, M., and et.al., 1986. Scientific Programme for the NBR. Proposal for an Action Plan CES, Bangalore.
9. Government of India, 1983. *Ministry of Home Affairs, Report of Committee on Orientation of Forest Education in India*, New Delhi.
10. Jagannatha Rao, R., and et.al., 2001. *Joint Forest Produce and Management in Karnataka: Current Status and Potential* CES, Bangalore.
11. Kothari C.R., 1987. *Research Methodology : Methods and Techniques*, Wiley Eastern Limited, New Delhi.
12. Maralusiddaiah Patel, H.M., 2005. Ethnographic Atlas of Indian Tribes, in P.C. Mehata (ed.) Serial Publication, New Delhi.
13. Maralusiddaiah Patel, H.M., and B.R. Vijayendra, 2005. Primitive Tribes in India, Dash Sharma (ed.), Serial Publication, New Delhi.
14. Ranjit Daniels, R.J., 1996. *The Nilgiri Biosphere Reserve : A Review of Conservation Status with Recommendations for a Holistic Approach to Management*, Working Paper, UNESCO, Paris.
15. Sharma J.K. and et.al., 2002. *Biosphere Reserves in India and their Management*, Ministry of Environment and Forests, KFRI Peechi, Kerala.
16. Singh, K.S., 1992. *Scheduled Tribes, People of India*, Oxford University Press, New Delhi.

Appendix-3.1
Wildlife at the Nagarahole National Park

Common Name	*Scientific Name*	*Local Intensity*
Common Langur	Presbytis entellus	Common
Bonnet Macqque	Macaca radiate	Present
Slender Loris	Loris tardigradus	Present
Tiger	Panthera tigris	Present
Leopard	Panthera pardus	Present
Jungle Cat	Felis chaus	Common
Leopard Cat	Felis bengalensis	Present

(Contd.)

(Contd.)

Common Name	*Scientific Name*	*Local Intensity*
Small Indian Civet	Viverricula indica	Present
Malabar Civet	Voverra megaspila	Present
Common Palm Civet	Pardaoxurus hermaphoditus	Present
Common Mongoose	Herpestes edwardsi	Common
Stripenecked Mongoose	Herpestes fuscus	Common
Striped hyaena	Hyaena hyaena	Very rare
Jackal	Canis aureus	Common
Wild Dog	Cuon alpinus	Present
Sloth Bear	Melursus ursinus	Present
Common Otter	Luthra luthra	Present
Giant Squirrel	Ratufa macroura	Present
Indian Giant Squirrel	Ratufa indica	Common
Indian Porcupine	Hystrix indica	Present
Indian Hare	Lepus nigricollis	Common
Elephant	Elephus maximus	Present
Gaur	Bos gaurus	Present
Four-horned Antelope	Tetracerus quadricornis	Present
Sambar	Cervus unicolor	Rare
Spotted Deer	Axis axis	Common
Barking Deer	Muntiacus muntjak	Common
Mouse Deer	Tragulus meminna	Present
Wild Boar	Sus scrofa	Common
Indian pangolin	Manis crassicaudata	Present

Appendix-3.2 Plants used by tribal people in Nagarahole (Non-Timber Forest Produce)

Local Name	*Botanical Name*
Hunse	Tamarindus indica
Alalae	Terminalia Chebula
Kakkebark	Cassia fistula
Honge	Pongamia pinnata
Seege	Acacia coucinna
Antuvala	Sapindus emarginatus
Bela	Feronia elephatum
Nelli	Rmblica offcinalus
Dhupa	Ailanthus triphysa
Gulaganchi	Abrus precatorius

(Contd.)

(Contd.)

Local Name	*Botanical Name*
Gajjige	Caesalpina bounducella
Thupra	Diospyrus melanoxyion
Dalechini	Cinnanonum zeylanoxylon
Geru	Anacardium occidentale
Muthuga leaves	Butea monosperma
Sagade	Schleichera oleosa
Maggare seeds	Randia dumetorum
Kasarka	Strychnos nux-vomica
Kadugera	Semicarpus anacardium
Lichens	
Wild tumeric	
Wild ginger	
Eachalu	Phonix sylvestris
Makliberu	
Halmaddi	
Kallabale	
Wax	
Horns	
Lac	
Honey	
Bones	

Appendix-3.3
IUCN and Management Objectives

IUCN Category number	*Category Name*	*Management objectives*
I	Scientific reserve / strict nature reserve	To protect nature and maintain natural process in an undisturbed state to permit scientific study, environmental monitoring, education, and the maintenance of genetic resources.
II	National Park	To protect natural and scenic areas of national or international significance for scientific research, education and recreation

(Contd.)

IUCN Category number	*Category Name*	*Management objectives*
III	National monument / natural landmark	To protect and preserve nationally significant natural features because of their special interest or unique characteristics
IV	Managed natural reserve / wildlife sanctuary	To protect nationally significant species, group of species, biotic communities, or physical features of the environment where these require human manipulation for their perpetuation.
V	Protected landscapes	To maintain nationally significant natural landscapes that are characteristic of the harmonious interaction of man and land while providing opportunities for public enjoyment through recreation and tourism
VI	Resource reserve	To protect natural resources for future use and to prevent or contain development activities that could affect the resource pending the establishment of further management objectives.
VII	Natural biotic area / anthropological reserve	To allow the way of life of societies living in harmony with the environment to continue undisturbed by modern technology
VIII	Multiple – use management area / managed resource area	To provide for the sustained production of water, timber, wildlife, pasture, and outdoor recreation

4

Tourism and its Impact on Bokapuram Village in Nilgiri Biosphere Reserve

P.K. Guha

Introduction

The Nilgiri Biosphere Reserve, the first of the fourteen biosphere reserves of India located in the Western Ghats between 76°- 77°15'E and 11°15' - 12°15'N. and established in September 1986. The Biosphere Reserve falls under the biogeographic region of the Malabar rain forest and embraces the sanctuary complex of Wyanad, Nagarhole, Bandipur and Mudumalai the forested hill slopes of Nilambur, the upper Nilgiri plateau, a Silent valley and Siruvani hill spreads over Karnataka, Kerala and Tamil Nadu. The total area of the biosphere reserve is around 5520 sq.kms of which 1240 sq. kms are under core zone, 3239 sq. kms are under manipulation zone (tourism) and 706 sq. kms are under restoration zone.

The Nilgiri biosphere reserve possesses different habitat types, unspoiled areas of natural vegetation types with several dry scrub, dry and moist deciduous, semi evergreen and wet evergreen forests, evergreen shoals, grass lands and swamps. The Nilgiri biosphere reserve includes the largest population of the endangered animal species namely the Nilgiri tiger and the lion –

tailed macaque along with the Elephants, Tiger, Gaurs, and Sambhar. This biosphere reserve is the habitat of a number of tribal groups remarkable for their traditional modes of harmonious use of the environment.

The Nilgiri Biosphere reserve is very rich in plant diversity consisting of 3300 species of flowering plants and 175 species of orchids. The fauna of this Biosphere over 100 species of mammals, 350 species of bird, 80 species of reptiles and amphibians, 300 species of butterflies and innumerable invertebrates, 39 species of fish, 31 species amphibians, 60 species of reptiles occur in this Biosphere. Nilgiri Biosphere reserve spreads over Karnataka, Kerala and Tamil Nadu states.

Conservation Objectives of the Biosphere Reserve

The Nilgiri Biosphere Reserve was established to fulfill the following objectives:

- To conserve in situ genetic diversity of species
- To restore degraded ecosystems to their natural conditions
- To provide baseline data for ecological and environmental research and education
- To function as an alternate model for sustainable development

The conservation and management of the Nilgiri Biosphere Reserve depends on the coordination between government agencies and the local people. Since 1993 intensive training programme for tourist guides of Ooty have been conducted and concepts of eco-tourism, waste management and the role of the Nilgiri Biosphere Reserve are emphasized. Forest guards play a vital role in biodiversity conservation. They are exposed to the concept of biodiversity, endangered and endemic fauna and flora of Nilgiris, forest fire and its impact on the ecosystem.

The Nilgiris are an important tourist centre in South India, and attract a large number of tourists. A large number of hotels, clubs, resorts, gardens and roads have emerged rapidly thereby degrading the natural vegetation. The entire ecology of Nilgiri Biosphere Reserve is affected by extensive pollution and water scarcity. The Ooty Lake has been ruined accumulating garbage and disposal of sewage into it.

Mudumalai Wildlife Sanctuary

Mudumalai Wildlife Sanctuary in Nilgiri hills, the first sanctuary in south India. This 321 sq.km wide sanctuary encompasses a National Park measuring an area of 103 sq. km. The Mysore –Ooty national highway passes through the sanctuary. The Moyar river is flowing along the border of Tamil Nadu and Karnataka, which separates Mudumalai and Bandipur sanctuary. The vegetation is quite varied in this region. The hilly terrain of Mudumalai has 3 types of the forests, namely—

(1) Tropical moist deciduous forests, (2) tropical dry deciduous, and (3) mixed vegetation (where rainfall is higher).

Objectives of the Study

With this backdrop the present study was aimed to understand the nature of the conservation and management of the forest resources by the indigenous population, the impact of tourism and people's perception in the fringe area of Mudumalai sanctuary of the Nilgiri biosphere.

To study the above it was necessary to select a village situated in the fringe areas of the sanctuary in which the villagers are actively engaged in the forest activity as well as in tourism activity. The present study was conducted in Bokkapuram village of Nilgiri district, which is situated in the fringe area of Mudumalai sanctuary of the Nilgiri biosphere among the indigenous population (mainly the Irulas). In 1992-93, the government adopted this village for sustainable development and to find out the indigenous knowledge of local people to protect the forest.

The study was conducted with the following objectives:

1. To find out the use of forest produce in socio-religious and socio cultural functions and to find out the indigenous knowledge of local people to protect the forest.
2. To find out the use of medicinal plants.
3. To examine the various economic variables.
4. To find out the relationship with the forest through the socio-religious activities.
5. To understand the effect of tourism on the socio-economic and socio-cultural fields.
6. Government schemes for protecting the forest.

Methodology

Tentative schedules and questionnaires were prepared before conducting the fieldwork. During the selection of the village for the study, care was taken so that the study may become a representative one. It was decided that fieldwork would be suitable in a village where the forest management strategies and the tourism activities are being undertaken around Mudumalai Wild life Sanctuary, for the micro level. Household census was completed for the village and empirical data was collected through household census, participatory observation, group discussions, interview, focused interview, case studies using schedules and questionnaires and secondary sources. Cadastral maps were taken to show the changing pattern of land use.

To understand the land use pattern of Bokkapuram village, the data were collected on each plot of Bokkapuram village. First the data was collected on each plot of Bokkapuram village for the year 1971 from Sholur Panchayat office, Sholur. Then the details of land use characteristics of 1971 for each number of plots were noted down from the record books (Warangal) along with cadastral map of Bokkapuram village. The informations on land characteristics were collected on 104 numbers of plots of the village. While dealing with the data we came across several units of cadastral map like quantum of land, different elements of physical and cultural environments, lease and patta land. Accordingly, different colours and symbols have been put on different numbers of plot. For the understanding of the land use maps, a standardized pattern of colours has been used like blue for water, yellow for arable land, residential area stands in orange, deep green for forest and so on to get the clear picture on the land use pattern of Bokkapuram village.

Study Village

The Bokkapuram village is located between 76° 38′ 5″ to76° 39′ 7″ E longitude and 11° 31′ 6″ to 11° 32′ 6″ N latitude. The village is located at a distance of 31 kms west from Ooty and 5 kms from Masinagudi. The village is divided into five hamlets namely—1 Thakkal, 2. Thottalengi, 3. Kurumbar Padi, 4. Koelpatti, 5. Kurumbar Parllam where the Irulas and the Kurumbas inhabit.

1. Thakkal section is located on the western part of Bokkapuram village. In the historical past the people of this area used Manvetti (spade) for cultivation. They never used bullocks for cultivation. Since they used spade locally known as Manvetti for cultivation, so this area is called as Thakkal.
2. Thottalengi—This section is located in the northern portion of Bokkapuram. Thottalengi is evolved from the word, *doddalingi*—a name of a lady. *Dodda* means fat and *lingi* was the name of the lady. She was a very influential lady and used to stay in this area. They also informed that she was the first lady of Irula tribe. This area was named after this lady as Thottalingi. Thottalingi is the broken ward of Doddalingi.
3. Kurumbar Padi – It is located on the eastern part of Thottalingi. In the past this area was inhabited by the Irulas. In Irula dialect *padi* means mud where the Kurumbar settled down and the area was latter named as Kurumbar Padi Kurumba-name of the tribe Padi – mud.
4. Koilpatty—Koilpatty is located in the central portion of Bokkapuram village. *Koil* means temple and *patty* means huts. Here the Irulas constructed their houses with bamboo, mud with straw roofs, surrounding the Mariamma temple where the main priest lives. This area is known as Koilpatty since long past.
5. Kurumbarparllam— It is located at the northeastern part of Bokkapuram. *Parllam* means river where the Kurumba people settled down by the side of Modagatta river. The houses were constructed by the state Government.

Bokkapuram village has 120 families. Out of 120 families the census work done on 118 families covering 91 families from Irulas, 24 families from Kurumba and 03 Muslim families. A total of 495 souls were covered of which 248 males and 247 females.

Table 4.1 Distribution of community

Community	*Families*	*Male*	*Female*
Irula	91	193	189
Kurumba	24	57	51
Muslim	3	08	07
	118	248	247

The government had established a hand pump unit and a wastewater recycling unit to provide clean drinking water after having several discussions with the villagers about their way of living and the problems faced by them. A smokeless *chula* unit was put up in the tribal village school to minimize the firewood consumption. The villagers then requested to put up smokeless *chulas* in their houses. About 230 units were installed in the tribal homes. Two biogas units were also commissioned. Since 1995, 124 tribals were benefited through the bee keeping scheme. Every year 25 beneficiaries were selected and were provided with bee keeping units, seeds for kitchen garden and mushroom units for income generation. A major thrust of the environmental education effort was the restriction of cattle grazing in the forest by the villagers. This was done by asking the villagers to feed the cattle on cut fodder and confining them so that their dung could be used as bio fertilizer. Soil and water conservation, grafting, mushroom cultivation, vermin composting and nursery keeping were taught to the villagers, while tribal families produced tree saplings and marketed it to various agencies. The government had also motivated the villagers to register a society called "Bokkapuram Narpani Mandram", to get various beneficial schemes from the government. A survey of the social status, health and hygiene of the tribals of the village was also conducted by the Centre.

Occupational Structure

The occupational composition of a group of population is always influenced by economic, demographic and social factors. The use of the labour force, its distribution into various occupations, sex-wise participation in different economic activities and the difference in participation rates by age, literacy and residence are fair indices of physical resource base the system of social organization and the nature of economy prevailing in a region. (Chandana, 1960).

Traditionally the Irulas of Nilgiri Hills (according to 1871 census) used to cultivate a patch of land by scratching the soil with a hoe and sowing Tenne (*Panecium italieum*), Ragi or kire. They frequently used to attend the Mettapaliam market and barter the jungle produce for salt, tobacco and cloths.

The Badagas have been migrated to the Nilgiri from Mysore about 300 years ago, after the breaking up of the kingdom of Vijaynagar. They are agriculturist race and cultivate various cereals. They held their lands under Government at very easy rates (S.M. Breeks, 1873).

It is learnt from the field investigation that more than 100 years back the Badagas brought 30/40 Irula families to Bokkapuram area to work as agricultural labourers. The Badagas used to shift from one place to another due to the disturbances created by the animals like elephants and bears and in want of fertile land.

Irulas used to collect wild fruits, herbs and roots along with beeswax, drugs, gum, honey and medicinal plants. The collected products were exchanged with lowlanders for cloth or food. (Shortt, 1868:62) Besides the cultivation the Irulas used to collect forest products for their livelihood till the formation of cooperative society.

The Masinagudi Hill Tribes Large Sized Multi Purpose Cooperative Society Ltd, originally started as labour Contract Cooperative Society in 1961 and subsequently converted into Marketing Society in 1976 and finally converted and started functioning as Large Sized Multi Purpose Cooperartive Society (LAMP) from August 1982.

The areas of operation of the society are extended to the entire district of the Nilgiris. Among the various objectives, the society is concentrating mainly on collection of Minor Forest Produce, providing financial assistance to the members by the way of issuing short term, medium term and long term loans and also supply of consumer goods to the members and general public. Principally the Lamp society works with the main objective:

1. To help the tribals by providing integrated credit, and other services and facilities from increasing employment, production and income and by organizing service for distribution of consumer goods.
2. To grant short (1 yr), medium (3 yrs) and long (7 yrs) term loans to member and mainly for productive purpose and also to grant consumption loans.
3. To procure, purchase and supply agriculture inputs like fertilizers, seeds, manures, pesticides etc.

4. To procure, purchase and sell agricultural produce, minor forest produce (list supplied by the forest department), dairy etc.
5. To organize agricultural service activities by owning or hiring agriculture machineries like tractors, power tillers, bulldozers etc.
6. To encourage execute, own and maintain lift irrigation scheme etc.
7. To find suitable and profitable employment for the members by taking of Minor Forest Produce collecting the same through members on payment of wages or otherwise and selling the same to the best advantage of the society and members.
8. To provide basic amenities for habitation, medical help and educational facilities to the members.

In reality the LAMP is presently functioning with few objectives in the area—

1. Issuing loan
2. Minor Forest Produce
3. Supply of Consumer Goods.

Eligibility of the Membership

1. Any tribal over 18 years of age who is competent to contract under Section 11 of the Indian Contract Act 1872 and residing or owning or cultivating lands with in the area of operation of society.
2. Other Cooperate Institutions.
3. Corporate body approved by the government.

Board of Members

Members of board are 7 in total. Five members are elected from the tribal members. One member is elected from the non-tribal and one is elected as Managing Director Ex-Officio.The society takes up lease for collection of Minor Forest Produce in the following areas in the Nilgiri district North divisions as Segur Range, Sinagara Range, Ooty North Range, Northern Estate at Bokkapuram, Gudalur, Bithirkadu Range etc in all Minor Forest Produce viz—

(i)Tamarind, (ii) Soapnut, (iii) Seeyakaai, (iv) Gallnut, (v) Broomgrass, (vi) Honey etc. Only tribal members are allowed to collect the minor forest products and paid wages. In the season time a tribal gets average wages of Rs. 65 and in lean season he gets Rs. 35.

From the year 1982 to 1994 the LAMP got lease of the MFP rights from the Forest Department. But from the 1994 the LAMP is not getting lease from the Forest Department.

After 1996 to 2000 Forest Department supplied the list of non-timber forest product to the private party to collect NTFP by the tribes. After 2000 this practice has been stopped. Wages paid to the tribals for collection of following Minor Forest produce:

1. Tree moss — Rs. 10 per kg
2. Soap nut — Rs. 5 per kg
3. Seeyakaai — Rs. 15 per kg
4. Gallnut — Rs. 4 per kg
5. Broomgrass — Rs. 20 bundle of 2 kg
6. Cotton seed — Rs. 20 paisa per seed
7. Tamarind — Rs. 2 per kg
8. Honey — Rs 20 per kg

After 2000, when the collection of NTFP was stopped, the inhabitants of the Bokkapuram village began diversifying in various occupations.

Since the Irula tribe in Bokkapuram village is the representative group, so the data have been collected on occupation only on the Irulas. The eight different types of occupations are as follows:

1.Daily Labour (DL), 2. Cultivation and Daily labour (CDL), 3. Cultivation(C), Service (S), 5. Own land (not cultivated) (ONC), 6. Landless (LL), 7. Temple work (T) and 8. Business (B).

Table 4.2 Percentage of Occupational Structure (Male)

DL	*CDL*	*C*	*S*	*ONC*	*LL*	*T*	*B*
48.37	2.26	1.75	1.25	10.02	8.02	0.75	0.75

From table 4.2 it is revealed that 48. 37 per cent of people engaged themselves in daily labour activity, followed by 10.02 people percent having land but not engaged themselves in cultivation. It has happened because

(i) There is no irrigation system in Bokkapuram village though it has been mentioned in the objectives of the LAMP society. So the cultivation completely depends on rainfall.

(ii) The landowner of this group does not have so much of money for cultivation. So they go for lending money from the businessmen of Masinagudi at the rate of 10 per cent interest per month, which they cannot afford. If the production is less, they cannot return the principal and interest. So they are very much scared of taking loan. So they keep the land vacant.

This category is followed by landless family. The percent of other occupational activities are negligible.

The following table shows the female participation in different types of occupational activities. The occupational activities are as follows:

Table 4.3 Female Participation in Different types of Occupations (in percentage)

DL	*CDL*	*C*	*S*	*B*	*T*
21.30	03	1.5	0.75	0.25	0.5

The table 4.3 shows that 21.30 percent females are engaged in daily labour followed by cultivation. 1.5 percent females participate in cultivation but in rest of the activities their participation is negligible.

The activities throughout the year:

Chart

The diagram shows the activities throughout the year of the Irulas of Bokkapuram village. The above diagram shows that—

1. January (*Thai*)—In this month they collect the forest products either from self-garden or from bordering forest area. Generally they collect –
   Kadukai (used as soap), Pussakai (used as soap), Nellikai (used for pickle), Unsa – anno and other seasonal available forest produce.
2. February, March, and April—Dry season. This period is mainly utilized for different types of festival. Local name—February (*Masi*), March (*Panguni*) and April (*Chitirai*).

3. May (*Vaigasi)*—Cultivation starts and honey collection season.
4. June (*Anj)*—Cultivation and honey collection.
5. July (*Adi*)—Cultivation and honey collection.
6. August (*Avani*)—Harvesting and honey collection. They cultivate mainly Ragi and different types of vegetables like Chilli, Tomato, Brinjal, Beans, and Cabbage etc.

Ragi grows 15 to 20 muta (bag) in 2 acres. One bag contains 100 kilos. They sell 7 to 12 mutas at the rate of Rs. 7 per kg. Rest they keep for self-consumption. To sell out Ragi either the villagers go to market and sell it directly to the shopkeepers or sometimes shopkeepers come to the village for purchasing from the field. Shopkeepers make the powder and sell it at the rate of Rs. 10.00 per kg.

They also sell chilli at the rate of Rs. 50 per kg. In one acre the chilli grows 30-35 chaks(bag). One chak contains 100 kg.

Another selling product is cabbage. In good condition cabbage grows 7 (seven) tons in one acre. Selling price is Rs. 2.25 to Rs. 2.50 per kg. The cultivators sell the cabbage to Mettapallyam market directly. Rest vegetables they produce for their self consumption.

After harvesting mainly the Ragi they take small amount of Ragi and other agricultural products like—beans, brinjal, cabbage etc and offer worship to any temple like –Dandanmari, Mariamma with coconut and stick. After that they consume the products.

Before sowing they worship the God (any temple) for better production.

When the Ragi is about to ripe they also worship the god to save from the wild animals like elephants, wild bores etc.

From May to August they also collect honey (Jeno).

There are four types of honey. These are as follows:-

1. Kosuthen: Small size beehive. This type of honey is collected from trees/ stones. Very small quantity is available (1 ounce to 2 ounce). This type of honey is used for medicinal purpose. They do not sell it.
2. Kuchiteno: The size of the beehive is not so big, only 1 to 2 litres honey is collected from the bee comb. This type of honey is used to prevent cough. Selling price is Rs. 70 per litres.

3. Adkuten: 2 litres honey is collected from the beehive. Selling price is Rs.60 per litre.
4. Barajeno: Large size bee comb. 50 litres honey is collected from one beehive.
   Selling price is Rs. 50 per litres. They collect this honey from the forest without any permission from the forest office. Moreover, they don't have any licence for the collection of honey.
7. September: (*Puratasi*) Harvesting period continues.
8. October: (*Ipasi*) Collection of Chilli, gram etc. season.
9. November: (*Kartigai*) Different types of roots are being collected.
10. December (*Margadi*)

Besides cultivation they go for daily labour throughout the year. Mainly they work in Westopuri Coffee Estate, Singur coffee estate at the rate of Rs. 50 per day.

Daily labour includes the collection of cow dung. Dry cow dung is collected from the forest for selling purpose. Selling price is as follows:

Basket	Amount of Cow dung	Selling price
	5 kg	Rs. 10.00
	10 kg	Rs. 15.00
	15 kg	Rs.20.00

Dry cow dung is carried out by the trunk to nearby states mainly it goes to Kerala for using manure.

Only 16 Irula families are doing milk business. Selling price is Rs. 9.00 per litre. Out of 16 families only two families have 30 (Thirty cows.) During (May to October) rainy season they get 10-12 litres milk per day. But in other season it reduces to 3 –4 litres per day. Other than the rest 14 families have 3-4 cows. During rainy season (May to Oct) the cow owner sells milk to Mavinalle Cooperative Society. But in dry season they sellout the milk to the local resorts.

Division of Labour

The following diagram shows the division of labour among the adult males and females and minor females throughout the whole year.

Chart

The above diagram shows that the people without land do the daily labour through out the year. Only adult males and adult females go for daily labour throughout the year. The people having land do the daily labour except the cultivation period. From the diagram it is observed that during cultivation period— ploughing is mainly done by adult males, both adult males and females, harvesting and cleaning of the land done by adult females and males, do sowing. After sowing when crops grow the cultivators watch the field to save the crops from the birds and animals. During day time the females watch the field and during night time the males watch the field.

In this village tremendous water scarcity occurs from February to April. The adult males and females along with minor females fetch drinking water from nearby water body covering a distance more than one kilometer.

Forest Management and People's Perception

Scientific Forest Management

The Scientific Management of the Bokkapuram Reserve Forest (779.02 Hec) covering southern and western side of Bokkapuram village and Kollatty Slope Reserve Forest (1993.4104 Hec) covering eastern side of the Bokkapuram village is mainly done by Forest department with the following objectives:

(i) To save the major forest products from the local people, by recruiting forest guards and forest watchman whose main duty is to look after the forests. If any unauthorized person enters the forest for felling the trees and for collection of other products they are immediately caught and proper punishment is accorded.

(ii) Forest department had stopped the cattle (mainly the cows and bulls) movement inside the forest since 1974. From that time, the forest department is charging Rs. 6 per cattle (i.e. cow and bull) from the villagers for grazing and entering the forest. This has restricted the movement of the cows and bulls inside the forest.

(iii) During dry season (December to March) frequently, fire sets in the forest, which damages the valuable trees every year.

For this, the forest department recruits tribal and local people at the rate of Rs.1500.00 per month to watch the forest and protect it from fire. The people are recruited only at the time of fire season i.e.; (December to March). During this season Fire protection committee is also constituted for the protection of forest from the fire. Fire Protection Committee includes the forest personal and the recruited people.

When fire sets they put off the fire by putting the branches of the live trees into the fire. They also identify the fire line and cut the land in such a way that fire cannot spread beyond the fire line. This way the forest people and the locally recruited people save the forest from the fire.

In the year 1998-1999 village forest council was formed in the area to control the flow of forest produce. The Village Council includes:-

1. Membership is given to all the heads of the households. Each member pays Rs 2 to VFC as subscription per month.
2. Member secretary is Range Officer.
3. This committee acts for three years then the new committee is formed.

The activities of the Village Forest Council (VFC) are as follows—

1. The non-timber forest produces are to be collected through this committee.
2. Collected forest produces are to be deposited to the committee.
3. Elected President has the power to sell out the products. The whole amount is deposited to the VFC fund and is being spent for the development of the villagers.
4. Forest product to be sold at the local market.
5. Previously the Government took 10 percent of the selling products from the VFC fund but from 2005 the Tamil Nadu Government has lifted this system.

But the existence of this committee is not seen in Bokkapuram village.

Indigenous Forest Management

The villagers are completely dependent on forest resource for generations. Directly or indirectly they are preserving the forest for their own benefit. This village does not have any health center; they mainly use the medicinal plants for their common diseases. They use some of the plants for their medical purpose since the historical past. They also use different parts of the trees/ plants for the different purposes, which does not hamper the growth of the trees. So the growth of the plants/trees is more than those of extraction. They preserve the forest in the following manner—

1. They never cut the green (living) trees/plants.
2. Since the historical past they also maintain the **sacred groves**. It has been noticed from the villagers that the female members are prohibited to touch sacred trees which are (i) Tankameya (Coconut), (ii) Betlarchi (Betelnut), (iii) Bangamara (Lord Murugan), (iv) Thanimara and Tharamara(Soni lord),(v) Arlimara (vi) Aldomara (Baniyan trees), and (vii)Veppomara (Neem tree) etc. The females do not touch these trees in their pollution period. They believe that if they touch these sacred trees, those will die and the whole village will face misfortunes. So they maintain the tradition of worshipping these trees as sacred objects.

Trees: Utilitarian Values

(a) **Medicine**: It has been mentioned earlier that the Irulas have vast knowledge on medicinal plants. It has also been mentioned that this village does not have any health centre. So, for the minor ailments they mainly depend on trees and plants.

The following trees/ plants are used for different types of diseases.

(i) Kalkanji (*Anogeissus latifolia*) is mainly used to cure from dysentery. They make paste of the inner side of the bark and after mixing with warm water they consume thrice daily. They take this mixture two to three days.

(ii) Vannamara (*Pterocarpus marsupium*)— It is used for body pain, mainly the bones. After cutting the bark juice comes out and this juice is being smeared on the outside of the pain area during night time. Within three days the pain is cured.

(iii) Bugutala (*Govitia rottleriformis*)—This tree is used to prevent stomach pain and urine problem. They consume the paste of the bark mixing with either cold water or cold milk, three times daily for three days.

(iv) Kakka mara (*Cassia fistula*) — It is used to prevent itching purpose. First the bark of this tree is dried up in the sun, and then the dust of the bark is applied either on the bleeding area or on the itching area.

(v) Roza (*Lantana camera*)—It is also used to stop bleeding. The paste of the leaves mixing with tobacco is beina applied on the injured portion.

(vi) Kallianna (*Opuntia delinii*)—
The fruit of this plant is eaten to prevent cough.

(vii) Goneka soppu (*Solanum nigram*) — The leaves of this plant is taken by cooking to prevent the wind and indigestion.

(viii) Tippakida— The leaves of this plant is also taken after cooking to prevent the wind.

(ix) Onagana soppu (*Altenethera physsilis*)—The leaves of this plant also taken as food which prevents eye problem.

(x) Ganaka soppu/Manatakkali—The leaves of this plant is consumed as food to get rid off worm and stomach trouble.

(xi) Ale soppu—In case of inflammation around glands located in the upper region of thigh, the leaves of Ale sappu are heated and applied over the affected area.

(xii) Thumbakira and Parbata—The leaves of these two plants after making paste is smeared on the chest of the child to get rid off the cold.

(xiii) Anna soppu (Celosia Argentea)— Leaves of this plant is taken as food to protect the cough and cold.

(xiv) Veppomara (*Pterocarpus marsupium*) —Leaves of this tree is used for small pox suffering patient and they also eat the leaves to destroy the stomach worm

(b) Superstition

(i) Vannamara(*Pterocarpus marsupium*)—A type of black sap comes from the trunk automatically and it is believed that by application of this sap on the forehead of the baby, one can ward off the magical implications of an evil spirit.

(c) Utility

(i) Worship—The following trees are being worshipped by the Irulas of this village. These are as follows: 1. Bannimara, 2. Thanimara and Tharamara (Soni lord), 3. Harlimara and 4. Aldomara. They also use the leaf of Belpatramara for worshipping of lord Siva.

Other Utilities

House Construction

The following trees are used for house construction. These are—

(a) Bannimara, (b) Aralemara (*Terminalia chebula*), (c) Kamblimara (*Gmelina arborea*) (d) Kaglimara(*Acacia sp*), (e) Sironnai (*Bradelia retusa*), (f) Mukursimara (*Elaeodendron glaucum*), (g) Matti (*Terminalia- tamentasa*) and (h) Kumbli (for door and ceiling purpose).

Firewood

For firewood they use dried wood of the following trees:

(a) Harlimara (*Ficus religiosa*) (b) Aldomara (*Ficus bengalinsis*) (c) Sujjalmara (*Albizzia amara*, (d) Tausth mara/ Taramara (*Terminalia bellarica*) (e) Belaaldu mara (*Albizzia procera*) (f) Oengomara (*Pongamia sp*), (g) Belugundumara, (h) Basirimara (*Ficus tsjakelea*), (i) Chillud mara (*Stychnos potatorum*), (j) Jagluganti mara (*Diospyros montana*), (k) Mukurchi mara (*Elaeodendron glacum*).

They use the wood of Bidamara (*Dalbergia latifolia*) for making the furnitures.

Beverage

They used to prepare a spirited beverage named 'sarayam' from Baldumara/Bhalamara (*Acacia sp*).They used to boil the dried bark of this tree with the dried bark of banana and mollusses and consume after the filter. But presently this practice has been stopped.

They make plough for cultivation from the wood of Sujjal mara (*Albizzia amara*).

They use a special type of grass locally known as Dabbaulu/ Darbai for roofing purpose. They also use bamboo (*Azadirachta indica*).

Musical instrument

The Irulas of this village have musical instrument. These instruments are made of forest products.

Fiute (*Korlu*)—The central long part of the flute is made out of Aldomara (*Ficus bengalinsis*), Gurudmara and bamboo (*Azadirachta indica*).Lower round part is made of Naoladi (*Stereospermum Atrovirens*), Muttu mara (Terminalia-tomentosa) and Achalmara (*Hardivicia binata*).The top most part is made out of soft portion of bamboo which remains inside the mouth at the time of play.

They have two types of drums—(i) Madla and (ii)Thambatta. These two drums are made out of deer's skin.

The women use the leaves or bark of Mailanji for decorating their nails and palms. The cultivators also use the branches of this tree for beating the ragi—an agricultural product.

Life cycle Rituals

When the puberty starts the girls is kept in a secluded place separated from the bedroom. At present the girl is kept in verandah covered by the leaves of either Aldomara soppu(*Ficus glomurolata*) or by the leaves of Laklimara soppu (*Vitex nigunda*).This covered area is known as Gullu.

At the time of marriage, a wooden post locally known as Murthu komba is installed in the middle of the pandal of groom's house. This post is prepared from the branches of the tree named Sasuvarkamba (*Gliricidia sepium*). Before the burial they spread the leaves of Seagaala (*Albizzia amara*) and Ganthaalas/ Ganda (Santulumabum) trees on the scrops. They use the bark of Oengomara for cleaning the Mariamma idol. They rub the idols by the bark of the above-mentioned trees with water and it gives the shining effect. They use the dust of Bensikattu— a white stone available in the forest to decorate the floor during festival. Presently they mix the colour with the dust for more attractive. They also use the following fruits of the trees/plants as soap for cleaning. These are (i) Pussakai (*Sapanduse marginatus*) and (ii) Ongakaya (*Terris indica*).

Edible Forest Products

Fruits

Besides all the uses of the forest products they also consume the following fruits, roots and green leaves. *Anno* means fruit. The name of the fruits are (1) Kambianno (2) Belthanno, (3) Sollianno (*Rubus fragaria*), (4) Chellanno (*Cordia wallichii*), (5) Nerla anno (*Syzygiu mcumnii)*, (6)Sagada anno (*Schleichera-oleosa*), (7) Geggulkanno (*Canissa carandas*), (8) Elsianno (*Zizuphus jujuba*), (9) Nerla anno (*Syzigium cumini*), (10)Unsa anno (*Tamarindus indica*), (11) Nellikai (*Emblica officinalis*) and (12) Mangliberu.

Roots

The name of the roots are: 1. Nooragenusu, 2. Bellaragenusu, 3. Mullu genusu, 4. Nema genusu, 5. Nopra genusu, 6. Alaganda, 7. Odupunnu ganda, 8. Sebu.

Green leaves

The name of the green leaves which they consume after cooking. These green leaves are: Soppu means green leaves, 1. Sega soppu (*Acacia pinnata*), 2. Musta soppu, 3. Munna dagu, 4. Kira soppu, 5. Ala soppu, 6. Gonda kira, 7. Tawakira, 8. Madra soppu, 9. Katmulla soppu and 10. Silkira soppu .

Manner of Worship

Since their traditional occupation revolved round the forest they maintained the legacy of worshipping certain deities for their welfare. Individual members worship their family deities at the entrance of the forest area. This was a pre-hunting ritual. After killing the animal the heart of the animal is offered to their respective family deities after roasting on fire. The rest portion of the animal is divided among the hunters.

Sometimes after cooking, the meat is offered to the god with rice— called EDA and then they eat. It depends on the dangers of the forest. The danger means the danger of either bear or elephant. They roast the heart where the danger is more and they cook the meat where the danger is less. During the time of entrance into the forest three/ four individuals worship sometimes three/ four deities. Presently this practice is not seen among them. So, the family deities should be discussed in detail.

Temples in the Forest

Irula tribe has four territorial divisions. These divisions are as follows:

1. Thai Kattamana—Extension— Kundalpet in the north to Moyar river on the south and Kaninpura Kalini in the east to Kakkanal river in the west. Capital—Kaninpura-Kalini.

Name of the god (Dheeru).

(a) Ballama mani—Head (Female god)

(b) Badrukadi—Female god.

2. Kodugu Kattamana— Extension— Kakkanal river in the north to Gudalur in the south and Tappakadu in the east to Yanad river in the west. Capital—Karguddi.

Name of the god:

(a) Kargudi madi—Head (Female)

(b) Navagal Saranam—(Male deity)

3. Innara Kattmana—Extension—Moyar river in the north to Nilgiri Hills in the south and Jodapalla/Cherrapatti in the east to Teppakadu /Moyar river—Capital—Bokkapuram.

Name of the god:

(a) Saranam—Head—(Male god)

(b) Chinnudukini—Queen (Female god)

(c) Thandunumari—(Male god)

4. Ambaliyur Kattamana—Extension—East—Thengu mara hade. West— Jodpatta, North—Moyar river, South—Nilgiri Hills, Capital—Anaketti.

Name of the god:

(a) Karinpura mari—Head (Female deity)

(b) Budunath mari—(Female deity)

(c) Machikarubantain—(Male deity)

The above mentioned four territorial zone shows that each zone has different gods, which they worship till now. These are mainly located either inside the forest or at the boardering area of the forest. It shows their relationship with the forest, which they do not destroy. The people of each zone have different temples, scatterly distributed in and around the forest within their zone.

Table 4.4 Name of the Temples

Innara Kattamana

SL. No	Name of the temples	Name of the places
1	Saranam (Male deity)	Teppakadu
2	Semgara Earmasthi (Female deity)	2 kms south of Teppakadu
3	Samudra mari (Female deity)	Near Teppakadu
4	Dargol mari (Female deity)	Near Teppakadu
5	Kata satti (Female deity)	Near Singara
6	Urmari (Female deity)	Near Singara
7	Dantanmari (Female deity)	Near the forest check post of Masinagudi.
8	Eda Muttiya (Male deity)	1 km north of Dantan mari temple
9	Masini Amma (Female deity)	Masinagudi village
10	Nili Siddapaji (Male deity)	West of Masinagudi
11	Doganalli Maleswara (Male deity)	3 km north of Masinagudi
12	Goorlu mari (Female deity)	Masinagudi town
13	Chikkama (Female deity)	Moyar
14	Elsimari (Female deity)	Masinagudi
15	Kornatti mari (Female deity)	Masinagudi
16	Basapa (Male deity)	Bokkapuram
17	Kattikal mari (Female deity)	Bokkapuram
18	Karbontiya (Male deity)	Bokkapuram
19	Dombu Ratti mari (Female deity)	Bokkapuram
20	Katra mari (Female deity)	Bokkapuram
21	Kurupada (temple of ghost)	Westopari Estate
22	Gopal Swami (Male deity)	Westopari Estate

Kodugu Kattamana

1	Kargudi mari (Female deity)	Kargudi
2	Navagal Sarona (Male deity)	3 kms south of Kargudi
3	Melkargudi mari (Male deity)	3 kms south of Kargudi
4	Mudu Deora (Female deity)	3 kms south of Kargudi
5	Ombatta madi (Female deity)	2 kms west of Melkargudi mari
6	Embur Mari (Female deity)	12 kms west of Teppaku

Thai Kattamana

1	Badrakali temple (Female deity)	Kakkanalla
2	Kethaliann (Male deity)	5 kms west of Bandipur
3	Mulaprudu Masini (Female deity)	Near Bandipur (west)
4	Onnurain Masini (Male deity)	12 kms west of Bandipur
5.	Elkeri mari (Female deity)	Anuratti
6	Mangala mari (Female deity)	Mangala
7	Mangal mari (Female deity)	Mangal

Ambaliyur Kattamana

1	Machi Karbontyan (Male deity)	Masinagudi (10 km east)
2	Siriyur mari (Female deity)	Anaketti (6 km.east)
3	Anekal mari (Female deity)	East of Balata
4	Chakkanalli .mari (Female deity)	Near Balata
5	Karenpura mari (Female deity)	Near Balata
6	Anegalamma (Female deity)	Anaketta
7	Budinath mari (Female deity)	Moyar (east)

Besides these above-mentioned territorial divisions, the Irulas have eight different ***Kulas*** each having different family god. They used to worship this family god before entering the forest. The eight different kulas are:

From the above table it is revealed that the Irulas have thirty-four family deities. They used to worship these deities, (depends on the number of individual of each family) at the time of entering the forest in the historical past. But presently the entry to the forest has been restricted. But the Irulas of each kula (division) has their own festival at the particular time in one calendar year. At that time the members of each kula (division) go to that particular place to worship located in and around the forest.

The festivals are as follows:

1. Samakula: The people of this kula go to Asanuhu in Periyar district of Kerala to attend the festival in the last week of February.
2. Karittiga kula: The members of this kula attend the festival at Anaketty to worship 'Machi karbontya' in May.
3. Uppiliga kula: The people of this kula attend the festival to worship Karbontya (male deity) and Ombata mari (female

deity) at Kargudi, Masiniamma (festival deity) at Mudumalai in between February to April. But particularly in March they go to worship 'Khetalyan' (male deity) at Bandipur and 'Chinnudu Ermasthi' near 'Singara' in Northern Estate.

4. Kuppa kula: The people of this kula visit Teppakadu to worship 'Kaveri Sarana' (male god) at the time of festival in February.
5. Ongeor kula: The people of this kula attend the festival to worship Bannari mari (female god) at 'Satya Mangalam' (Periyar district) in the month of March-April.
6. Belliar kula: The members of this kula go to Asanur (Periyar district) in the month of March to worship Jadaswmi (male deity).
7. Orgulu kula: People of this kula worship 'Semgara Iyn' located at Northern Estate in the month of March-April.
8. Kurunaga kula: In the month of March the people of this kula worship 'Iraguddi' (female deity).

The largest festival of Nilgiri hills is Mariamma Festival. It occurs in Bokkapuram village in the month of February and it lasts for three days. People from nearby all the villages come and worship Mariamma. Thousands of vehicles come during night time also. The festival is meant to prevent pox.

From the above discussion it is observed that they have selected the festival time mainly in between January to April. They have selected this time because:

1. January to April is the dry period and during this time it is easier to enter the forest and they can stay hither or thither in and around the forest.
2. It is a post harvest season.

The above discussion shows the relationship between the forest and their socio-religious life. So they are in favour of preservation of forest as forest is inticrately associated with the socio- cultural life and sustainability.

Land Use

The value of land depends on its use. The use depends on three factors—

1. Accessibility—includes both time and money costs associated with traveling, as land is an immobile factor.

2. Space—The space factor includes the needs for land depending on its size and quality.
3. Environment—These factors include physical land characteristics and neighbourhood characteristics.

Though land is indestructible, land use can be changed more than once. (Fujita, 1989).

As a major part of cultural landscape, the land use depends on physical environment (which includes—highland, lowland and water bodies and cultural environment (includes settlement pattern, cultural places, public places etc.

So, both the elements of environment, directly or indirectly have been deflected through the land utilization.

To understand the land use pattern of Bokkapuram village, the data have been collected on each plot of Bokkapuram village. First the data were collected on each plot of Bokkapuram village for the year 1971 from Sholur Panchayat office, Sholur. Details of land use characteristics of 1971 for each number of plots has been noted down from the record books (Warangal) along with cadastral map of Bokkapuram village. The informations on land characteristics have been collected on 104 numbers of plots of the above said village. While dealing with the data we have come across several units of cadastral map like quantum of land, different elements of physical and cultural environments, lease and patta land. Accordingly, different colours and symbols have been put on different numbers of plot. For the understanding of the land use

Table 4.5 Land use

Land use Characteristics	*Percentage*
Arable land	68.11
Forest land	11.26
Bush	0.44
Hills	1.80
Rivers	5.28
Waste land, grazing land, settlement, school, temples, burial ground, road and vacant land.	13.11
	100

maps, a standardized pattern of colours has been used like blue for water, yellow for arable land, residential area stands in orange, deep green for forest and so on to get the clear picture on the land use pattern of Bokkapuram village. From the data analysis from the map of the year 1971, the following table has been prepared.

The above table shows that in the year 1971, 68.11 per cent area was under cultivation. From the map it is observed that cultivated lands are located on the southern, eastern and southwest portion of this village because of the following factors:

1. The southern, eastern and southwest portion of Bokkapuram village is comparatively flat than that of north.
2. A number of rivers are flowing from northeast to south and southwest. The cultivable lands are located either by the side of the rivers or between the tributaries. Since the lands of **this** area are located on the river plains so the land of this area is more fertile than that of north. Agriculture of the region depends on rain, so at the time of cultivation river water is also used for the growth of crops.

Forestland is followed by arable land, which is only 11.26 percent. In the past the forests covered the Bokkapuram village. But the people of this village for their own convenience converted forestland into cultivated land after clearing forest. So, in the year 1971; the forest covered only 11.26 per cent of land.

The remaining 20.63 per cent land includes bush, hills, rivers, and wasteland, grazing land, settlement, school, temples, burial ground, unmetalled road and vacant lands. It may be mentioned that in 1971, all the roads were unmetalled and the villagers had to face a lot of difficulties at the time of rainy season.

Applying the same methodology, the details information on land characteristics of each plot has been noted down from panchayat office, Sholur and from my personal observation, the map of existing land use of Bokkapuram village has been prepared. From the data analysis the following table has been prepared.

The above table shows that 25.59 percent of land area is covered by cultivation. It shows the decrease of more than thirty per cent as compared in the data available in 1971. The reasons behind such a drop are that the people of the village are very much reluctant of cultivation because of following facts:

Table-4.6 Existing land use 2005

Land Characteristics	*Percentage*
Arable land	25.59
Grazing land	13.91
Resort	9.92
Farm House	2.65
Settlement	4.39
Vacant land	21.6
Hills	1.80
Rivers	5.28
Forest, Temple, School, Burial ground, Metalled road and Commercial establishment	14.86
	100

1. Non -availability of irrigation system.
2. The villagers are poor so they cannot afford the cultivation. They lend money from the businessmen of Masinagudi at the rate of 10 per cent interest per month. Majority of them cannot repay the loan amount in time. So they go for daily labour in coffee garden and in some other works in the rest of the year to repay the whole amount. Cultivation is so they not profitable to them and so they keep the land vacant.
3. Most of the resorts are constructed on cultivated land.

The existing map shows the increase of vacant land to 21.6 per cent, which has happened due to the people's indifference attitude towards cultivation. The above table shows that grazing land also been increased to 13.91 percent. The grazing land is mainly used by the owner of the farmhouses for the cows. In this village, two Germans have purchased land and constructed farmhouse where more than hundred cows are being kept and are in milk business. Local people have been recruited to look after these cows.

The existing land use map also reflects a new land based activities i.e. Resort, which provides the impetus to the tourism. First resort was constructed in the year 1985. At the time of my fieldwork total 10 resorts have been noticed. These resorts entertain the Indian and Foreign tourists.

The above table exhibits the increase of land in settlement to 4. 39 per cent, which was quite negligible in the year 1971. It is also seen that a few shops (mainly tea stalls) have come up. In these shops the local people as well as the visitors take tea and snacks

It is revealed from the existing map that slowly the area of the cultivable land is getting reduced and this area is occupied by the rich men for the construction of resorts and housing which is very alarming. If trend continues then in future Bokkapuram village will loose its own characteristics, the flora and fauna will be highly disturbed and the dominant tribe of this village, i.e. Irula tribe will loose their own cultural characteristics because of acculturation.

Tourism

Bokkapuram village is located on the lap of Nilgiri Hills, and is famous for its natural beauty and calmness. The village is surrounded by the mosaic of rich flora and fauna. The adventure minded people go inside the forest on foot to see the deers, bears and elephants. But it is very difficult to see elephant during the daytime. The elephants of the area are very hostile and even local tribes are very much scared of elephants. So tourists only can watch deers or bears.

Table 4.7 Reasons for the Selection of Bokkapuram as Tourist Spot

Natural Beauty	*Adventure*	*Natural beauty and adventure*
28 62.22 %	06 13.33 %	11 24.44%

Table 4.7 indicates the reasons for the selection of Bokkapuram village as tourist spot by the tourists. From the above table it is observed that 62.22 per cent tourists visit this village for its natural beauty, 24.44 per cent tourists visit this village for natural beauty and adventure and 13.33 per cent visitors visit for adventure.

Table 4.8 The Motivation to Become a Tourist

Honeymoon	*Relaxation*	*Others*
01 2.22%	39 86.66%	06 13.33%

Table 4.8 shows that how a person is motivated to become a tourist. According to the above mentioned table, 86.66 per cent tourists visit Bokkapuram for relaxation, 13.33% tourists visit for some other reasons, honeymoon visitors are negligible and it is only 2.22 per cent. As it has been discussed earlier that the physical environment, climate and calmness of this village are the main capital for the attraction of the tourists. So, naturally people visit this village mainly for relaxation.

The Hindus mainly visit this village for worshipping goddess Mariamma— a prime deity of Nilgiri Hills. Mariamma festival occurs in the month of February— it continues about three days. During this time lakhs of people come from neighbouring villages to worship Goddess Mariamma, so it is a sacred place for Hindus.

Table 4.9 Showing the Different Religious Groups

Hindu	*Islam*	*Christian*	*Spiritual*
21 46.67%	04 9.11%	19 42.22%	01 2.22%

The table 4.9 shows that 46.67 per cent Hindus, followed by 42.22 per cent Christians. Because the European people visit this village mainly for relaxation and they are Christian by religion. Other religious groups are negligible.

Spiritual—Of spirit as opposite to matter; of the soul especially as acted upon by God.

The above table shows the room rent of the resort, flow of tourists and the introduction of tourist resorts. From the table it is revealed that the room rent is very high and only the high paid people/ business people can only visit this village and stay in the resorts.

The table 4.11 shows that 40 per cent visitors visit this village between 31 yrs to 45 yrs of age group. It reflects that the people of this age group are quite rich and well placed. The table also shows

Table 4.10 The Resort Information and the Flow of Tourists

Resort Information: Flow of Tourists								
Name	*Yr of Opening*	*No of Beds*	*No of Rooms*	*Rate(Rs)*	*Peak Period Oct to Jan*		*Lean period Jan to Oct*	
					Foreign Tourist	*Indian Tourist*	*Foreign Tourist*	*Indian Tourist*
Jungle Hut	1985	24	12	1000 +12.5% tax	80 from Europe	100 families- Bang, Mys, Ch	10 no	20 no
Monarch Safari lodge	1989	48	24	900/- to Rs. 1200+12.5% tax; 1400+ 12.5% tax	500 British and Dutch	3500 Mys, Ch , Coim	30 British and Dutch	1000 from Bang., Kerala, Chennai.
Blue Valley	1995	32	12	1000+ 12.5% tax	75 European	315 Bang; Ch & Kerala	10 European	150 Bang, Ch, Kerala
Forest Hills	1995	18	7	995+10% tax	80 mostly couples from Europe	730 from Bang, Ch	100	128

(Contd.)

(Contd.)

Resort Information: Flow of Tourists

Name	*Yr of Opening*	*No of Beds*	*No of Rooms*	*Rate(Rs)*	*Peak Period Oct to Jan*		*Lean period Jan to Oct*	
					Foreign Tourist	*Indian Tourist*	*Foreign Tourist*	*Indian Tourist*
Casa Deep Wood	2000	24	12	1400 +12.5%tax	200 European	1500 Bang, Mys; Ch; 90 % Bang	50-70	200
Bear Mountain	2004	36	6 cotge. 12	900 to 1200+12.5 %tax	100	1500	10	130
Jungle Retreat	Refused to give any information.							
Belmont	1993	20	10	600 to 1500+10.5 to 12.5% tax	50	130	20	80

that among the Indians, the maximum tourist come from Tamil Nadu and its neighbouring states i.e. Karnataka or Kerala. The tourists of this village mainly come to enjoy its natural beauty and for relaxation. Because after doing hard work throughout the year they select this village for relaxtion. The tourists are also attracted by the above mentioned resorts because these resorts provide almost all sort of modern day amenities, and people of a particular age group (31 yrs to 45 yrs) show inclination to these resorts for their holiday tourism.

Data have been collected from 45 numbers of tourists. Accordingly eight tables on different aspects have been plotted. The tables are as follows:

Table 4.11 Showing the Percentage of Different Age-group of the Tourist

0—15 yrs	*16 yrs to 30 yrs*	*31 yrs to 45 yrs*	*46 yrs to 60 yrs*	*Above 60 yrs*
0	Total no—17 37.77%	Total no—18 40%	Total no—4 8.88%	Total no—6 13.33%

Table 4.11 shows that the age group of 31 yrs to 45 yrs is predominated (40%)among all the age groups of the interviewed tourists,followed by16 yrs.to 30 yrs.of age group which comes to 37.77 per cent. Among other groups 0-15 yrs is nil, 46 yrs to 60 yrs is 8.88 per cent and above 60 yrs.is13.33per cent The calculation shows 13.33 percent, higher than that of 46 yrs to 60 yrs of age group. The table also shows that the tendency of the adults to visit to Bokkapuram village only to enjoy its physical environment and calmness. The percentage of above 60 yrs of age group is 13.33 which is higher than that of 46 yrs to 60 yrs of age group because of inflow of foreign tourists. It is revealed from the schedules that all the above 60 yrs of age tourists came from European countries.

Table 4.12 Showing the Composition of Team

Alone	*Family*	*Party/Group*
Total no.02 4.44%	Total no 17 37.77%	Total no 27 60%

It is observed from the table 4.12 that 60 per cent tourists visit to Bokkapuram village with group or party, 37.77 per cent visitors visit with family and 4.44 per cent tourists visit alone. From the table it is observed that tourists visit this village mainly with group or party. Since in this village the foreign tourists come and they like to visit in a group or party from outside to save their money. Visit to a place with party or group is always cheaper so they prefer this system. They also move in a group as they feel more secured in an unknown place.

Table 4.13 Showing the Flow of Tourist from Different States or Countries

Name of the States

Tamil Nadu	*Pondicherry*	*Maharashtra*	*Uttar Pradesh*	*West Bengal*	*Karnataka*	*Kerala*
Total no 11 24.44%	Total no 01 2.22%	Total no 02 4.44%	Total no 01 2.22%	Total no 01 2.22%	Total no 10 2.22%	Total no 02 4.44%

Table 4.14 Name of the countries

Denmark	*England*	*Netherland*	*Germany*	*Holland*	*Zimbabawe*	*Sweden*
Total no 04 8.89%	Total no 04 8.89%	Total no 05 11.11%	Table no 01 2.22%	Total no 01 2.22%	Total no 01 2.22%	Total no 01 2.22%

Total no of Indian Tourists—28 (62.22%)
Total no of Foreign tourist—17 (37.78%)

Table 4.13 and 4.14 show the flow of tourists, both Indian and Foreigners to Bokkapuram village. The above table shows that 62.22 per cent Indian and 37.78 per cent Foreign tourists visit to Bokkapuram village. This is more than half of Indian Tourists. Table 4.13 shows the flow of Indian tourist to Bokkapuram village from different states. The table 4.13 shows that 24.44 per cent tourist comes from Tamil Nadu because Bokkapuram is located in Tamil Nadu so maximum number of tourists comes from Tamil Nadu, followed by Karnataka 22.22% because Karnataka is the neighbouring states and nearer to Bokkapuram village followed by Kerala 6.4 per cent and Maharashtra 4.44 per cent. These two states are a little distant from Bokkapuram village. Only 6.66 per cent people come from other states/ UT. So, it is seen from the above table that maximum numbers of tourists come to Bokkapuram from Tamil Nadu and other adjacent states. The people of eastern, western and north eastern region do not know the name of Bokkapuram village due to the lack of advertisement in those areas. So proper advertisement is needed to increase the flow of tourist to Bokkapuram village from the distant states.

Table 4.14 shows that 37.78 per cent tourist come to Bokkapuram village and it includes Netherland (11.11 per cent), 8.89 per cent from Denmark or England and 2.2 per cent from Germany, Holland, Zimbabawe and Sweden. They mainly visit this village to enjoy the natural beauty and comfortable climate.

Table 4.15 Showing the Problems of the Tourists in Bokkapuram

Different types of the problems						
Language	*Transport*	*Accomodation*	*Food*	*Cleanliness*	*Any other*	*Did not state anything*
12 26.67%	04 8.89%	01 2.22%	01 2.22%	04 8.89%	06 13.33%	17 37.78%

Table 4.15 shows the various types of problems faced by the tourists at Bokkapuram. It is observed from the table that 37.78 per cent tourists did not state anything— causes are not known. 26.67 per cent tourists faced language problems,8.89 per cent of them also face transport and cleanliness problems and the frequency of bus service in the village is very thin. The tourists are unable to avail the Jeep as it is always packed up. Cleanliness is another problem. The first impression of the village is not encouraging to the tourists as this village is very dirty. It has happened because the Panchayat is not looking after the village affairs as it is located at Sholur far away from Bokkapuram village. So, the village remains almost neglected by the Panchayat office. After the Mariamma festival the festival area becomes full of plastics and other debris. Panchayat does not care for it, it cleans out itself— by the air, rain etc. The percentages of other problems are negligible.

Table 4.16 Showing the Satisfaction of the Tourists with the Local Infrastructural Facilities

Yes	*No*	*Did Not State Anything*
30 66.67%	13 28.89%	02 4.44%

Having all the problems mentioned in table 4.16, the table 4.17 shows 66.67 per cent tourists had shown their attitude towards satisfaction. But the visitors pointed out the following suggestions:

1. Transport system and road condition should be improved.
2. Littering should be stopped.
3. To ban loudspeaker which disturb the wildlife. Loudspeakers are being used at the time of Mariamma festival for 24 hours.
4. To ban fairs in this village, which hampers the wild daily life style.
5. Safari park including elephant ride should be introduced.
6. Guide should have clear information about the local activities.
7. Temporary camping facilities should be deep inside the forest at least for day time without disturbing flora and fauna.
8. To stop building resorts.
9. Care should be taken more for the preservation of flora or fauna.

Effect of Tourism

A lot of changes have taken place into their socio-cultural life.

1. Instead of taking indigenous staple food i.e. Ragi and other forest products, they are taking normal food available in the market.
2. They have abandoned their traditional dresses.

The frequency of daily labour, labour shown in the following tables:

Wage rate: Male gets Rs. 75 per day.

Female gets Rs. 60 per day.

From the table it is revealed that 7.7 per cent male and 3.8 per cent female are working in different resorts

Table 4.17 Males and Females Working in Different Resorts in Bokkapuram Village

Name of the resorts	*Total no of Male workers*	*Total no of Female Workers*	*Total Number of Labourer*
Monarch Safari	14	06	20
Blue Valley	06	02	08
Casa Deep	03	01	04
Jungle Hut	08	06	14
Forest Hills	03	01	04
Bear Mountain	04	03	07

Discussion

The village is situated in the outskirts of the sanctuary; hence the impact felt in the village directly affects the environment of the sanctuary and the biosphere as a whole. The Mariamma temple of Bokkapuram village is lying in the vicinity of Nilgiri Biosphere Reserve becomes a great source of income generation during the festival and which includes also the tourist arrival. Thus the area has the great scope for the development in the field of employment of the local villagers and also in the incoming of the tourist, thereby helping in the total well being of the people as well as of the biosphere. But the tussle between the two local communities, Irulas and the Badaga—centering round the ownership of the temple creates a hinderence. The two communities have their own respective role in worship and maintenance of the temple. Therefore the positive role made by the two communities in worship and maintenance of temple makes the area attractive for tourists. So, the harmonious relation between the two communities needs to be maintained for the betterment of the area. Government should look into the matter to solve the problem. This ultimately would help in reducing the pressure on the biosphere. But care and restriction needs to be taken while organizing the day and night fair during Mariamma festival, because it hampers the faunal movement in the sanctuary. After the fair, the area is littered with non biodegradable items like plastics and other things. Unfortunately the Panchayat is not taking care to clean it out and it disturbs the natural growth of local flora. The high pitched music should be stopped as it spreads the sound pollution. Vehicle movement should be restricted so as to sustain the existing faunal diversity. The Panchayat should take active part in cleaning out the village regularly. The foreign or Indian tourists come in this village regularly, but the village road always remains dirty.

Generation after generation, the forest activities have been entered into their socio-cultural and socio-religious life. It has been reflected in the forest management part, though presently the collection of forest products have been restricted by the forest department but it is true that forest has been entered into their soul. The possibilities of economic activities matching with their socio-cultural tradition and conventional working activities keeping in harmony with the ecological balance should be explored.The tourism may be promoted in line with sustenance of the existing ecological diversity. In this context tourism is required to be restricted so that the disturbance in ecology is prevented. Ecotourism is advocated in this ecological niche.

The local community may be encouraged to introduce host villages for facilitating the tourist in respect of accommodations and other logistic support services. In the process of development the appropriate authority may be requires protecting the heritage of the community against the probable evils of communication/ urbanisation.

Along with this, the development of the villagers and their problems needs to be addressed.

The inhabitants of the Bokkapuram village face the following problems:

Drinking water facility is insufficient. During dry period the people face tremendous drinking water scarcity. Sometimes they travel more than one kilometer to fetch drinking water. During dry period drinking water tap dries up particularly in Thottanlingi area. So, the development should be done in order to get regular water supply.

All the tribals are subsisting on the leased land but their demand is patta land. During dry period the villagers are unable to cultivate the land due to non-availability of water. Organized irrigation system is to be commissioned by the appropriate authority to support agriculture during dry period. Banking and financial institutions are to be introduced to help the cultivators in using the vacant land for the agriculture. There is every need for introduction of the primary market for reasonable disposal of their agricultural products so as to sustain their livelihood on support price basis.

Medical facilities are not available in the village. Even for minor disease they go to Masinagudi—8 kms away from Bokkapuram. The health and educational facilities are to be introduced.

Community participation is to be encouraged in every aspect of development work.

Appendix-4.1

Name of Trees

Sl. No.	*Local Name*	*Botanical Name*
1.	Bangamara	Pterocarpusmarsupium
2.	Bannimara	
3.	Thani mara	Terminalia bellerica
4.	Thara mara(soni lard)	Terminalia bellerica
5.	Harali mara	Ficusreligiasa
6.	Aldo mara(Banyan tree)	Ficus bengalensis
7.	Vappo mara	Azadirachtaindica
8.	Seegala(leaves are placed on the dead)	Albizzia amara
9.	Ganthaalas(Sandal wood)	Santulumalbum
10.	Sasuvarkamba	Gliricidia sepium
11.	Maono mara(mango tree)	Mangnifera indica
12.	Baldu mara(Drinks are prepared)	Acacia Species
13.	Belpatra mara(for worship)	Aegle marmelas
14.	Tarsul mara	Grewia Tilifolia
15.	Sujjal Mara	Albizzia amara
16.	Tausth Mara/TaraMara	Trminalia bellarica
17.	Bida mara	Dalbergia latifolia
18.	Tegan Mara	Tectona Grandis
19.	Arale Mara	Terminalia chebula
20.	Belaaldu Mara	Albizzia Procera
21.	Oengo Mara	Pongamia sp.
22.	Jalda mara (Flower for worship)	Shoreataluxa
23.	Gangula Mara (flower for worship)	Plemera Alba

(Contd.)

(Contd.)

Sl. No.	Local Name	Botanical Name
24.	Jagulandi Mara	Diospyros Montana
25.	Kumbli Mara	Gmelina Arbarea
26.	Sironnai(used for temple construction)	Bradelia retusa
27	.Kagli Mara	Acacia sp
28.	Belunda Mara	
29.	Mukursillara	Elaeodendron glaucum
30.	Basiri Mara	Ficustsjakelea
31.	Mundugalli Mara	Opumtia
32.	Chillud Mara	Stychnos Potatorum
33.	Elsi Mara	Zizyphus Moritiana
34.	Malti Mara	Terminalia Tomentosa
35.	Goni Mara	Ficus rugosa
36.	Iza Mara	Premnatomentosa
37.	Nagamara	Syzigium cumini
38.	Bargutalla mara	Girotia Rottleri formis
39.	Thuma kira	Leucas aspera
40.	Pasa	Licheum fungus algae
41.	Ekkadagida	Terminalia tomentosa
42.	Mutty mara	
43.	Soama Mara (Last portion of the flute)	
44.	Gurud Mara (Middle portion of flute)	
45.	Bamboo	Azadirachta indica
46.	Naoladi (lower & middle portion of flute)	Stereospermum Atrovirens
47.	Mukurchi Mara	Elaeodendran glaucum
48.	Mailangi (Mehendi)	

Appendix-4.2
Name of Medicinal Plants

Sl.no.	Locai Name	Botanical Name
1.	Kalkanji Mara (Dysentry)	Anogeissus latifolia
2.	Vanna Mara (Bone pain)	Pterocarpus massupium
3.	Bugutala Mara (Stomach pain)	Givotia-Rotteri formis
4.	Kakka Mara(Bleeding)	Cassia Fistula
5.	Roza (Bleeding)	Lantana Camera

(Contd.)

(Contd.)

Sl.no.	*Local Name*	*Botanical Name*
6.	Kallianna (fruits)	Opuntiadelinii
7.	Passi	Moss
8.	Goneka soppu	Solanumnigium
9.	Tippa kido	
10.	Onagana soppu	Altenethera physsilis
11.	Ganaka soppu	
12.	Ale soppu	
13.	Thumba kira & Parbata	Jatropha curcas
14.	Anna soppu	Celosia argentea
15.	Veppomara (Pterocarpusmarsupium)	

Appendix-4.3
Name of the Roots

Sl. No.	*Local Name*	*Botanical Name*
1.	Mangliberu	Not available
2.	Noora Genusu	Not available
3.	Mullu Genusu	Not available
4.	Nema Genusu	Not available
5.	Nopra Genusa	Not available
6.	Alaganda	Not available
7.	Odupunu ganda	Not available
8.	Kothiganda	Not available
9.	Thavaragenusu	Not available
10.	Sebu (aram)	Not available

Appendix-4.5
Fruits

Sl. No.	*Local Name*	*Botanical Name*
1.	Aldomara soppu	Ficus Glomurolata
2.	Laklimara soppu (used for covering varanda)	Vitex nigunda
3.	Sega Soppu	Acacia Pinnata
4.	Musta soppu	
5.	Munna Dagu	
6.	Kira soppu	
7.	Goneka soppux	

Appendix-IV.6
Name of the Leaves

Sl. No.	*Local Name*	*Botanical Name*
1.	Aldomara soppu	Ficus Glomurolata
2.	Laklimara soppu (used for covering varanda)	Vitex nigunda
3.	Sega Soppu	Acacia Pinnata
4.	Musta soppu	
5.	Munna Dagu	
6.	Kira soppu	
7.	Goneka soppux	

References

Banerjee, Ajit 2004 Classical and Joint Forest Management and JFM's contribution to Indian Forestry in Desai, Mamta and M.K. Raha (ed) in The Dying Earth Peoples Action and Nature's Reaction, acb Publication, Netaji Institute for Asian Studies, Kolkata.

Basak, Radhagobindo 1964 Bengali translation of Kautilya General Printers & Publishers Private Limited, Calcutta.

Breeks, S. M. (ed) 1873 Primitive Tribes & Monuments of the Nilgiris. James Wilkinson Breeks to the Madra Civil Service Commissioners of the Nilagiris. Cultural Publishing House. 18 D Kamla Nagar, Delhi.

Chandana, R.C. & 1980 Introduction to Population M.S. Sidhu Geography, New Delhi.

Fujita, M. 1989 Urban Economy Theory, Cambridge, Cambridge University Press.

Palit, S. 1996 Indian Forest Department in Transition in Poffenberger, Mark and Betsy Mc Gean, Delhi.

Shortt, John 1868 The Irulas- A. Williamjebadhas and William A. Noble in Blue Mountains—The Ethnography and Biogeography of a South Indian Region. Edited by—Paul Hockings. Oxford University Press. Oxford New York.

Siva, N. 1999 Evolution Study of Masinagudi Hill Tribes Large Sized Multipurpose Co-operative Society at Masinagudi in the Nilgiri distt. of Tamil Nadu. Report submitted to Deptt. of Adi Dravidar and Tribal Welfare, Govt. of Tamil Nadu, Chennai. Directorate of Tribal Research and Development. Govt of Tamil Nadu. M. Palada, Udhagamandalam, Nilgiri.

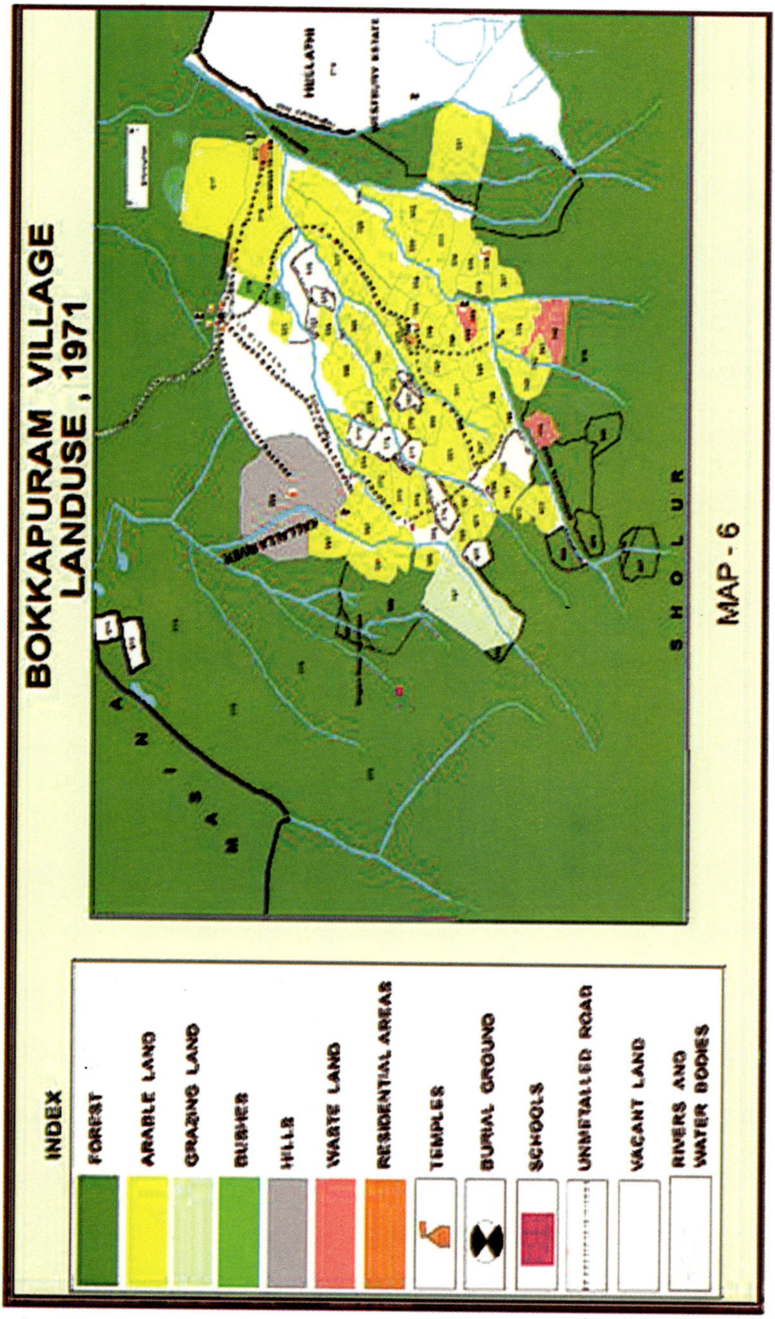
BOKKAPURAM VILLAGE
LANDUSE , 1971
S H O L U R
INDEX
FOREST
ARABLE LAND
GRAZING LAND
BUSHES
HILLS
WASTE LAND
RESIDENTIAL AREAS
TEMPLES
BURIAL GROUND
SCHOOLS
UNMETALLED ROAD
VACANT LAND
RIVERS AND WATER BODIES

MAP - 6

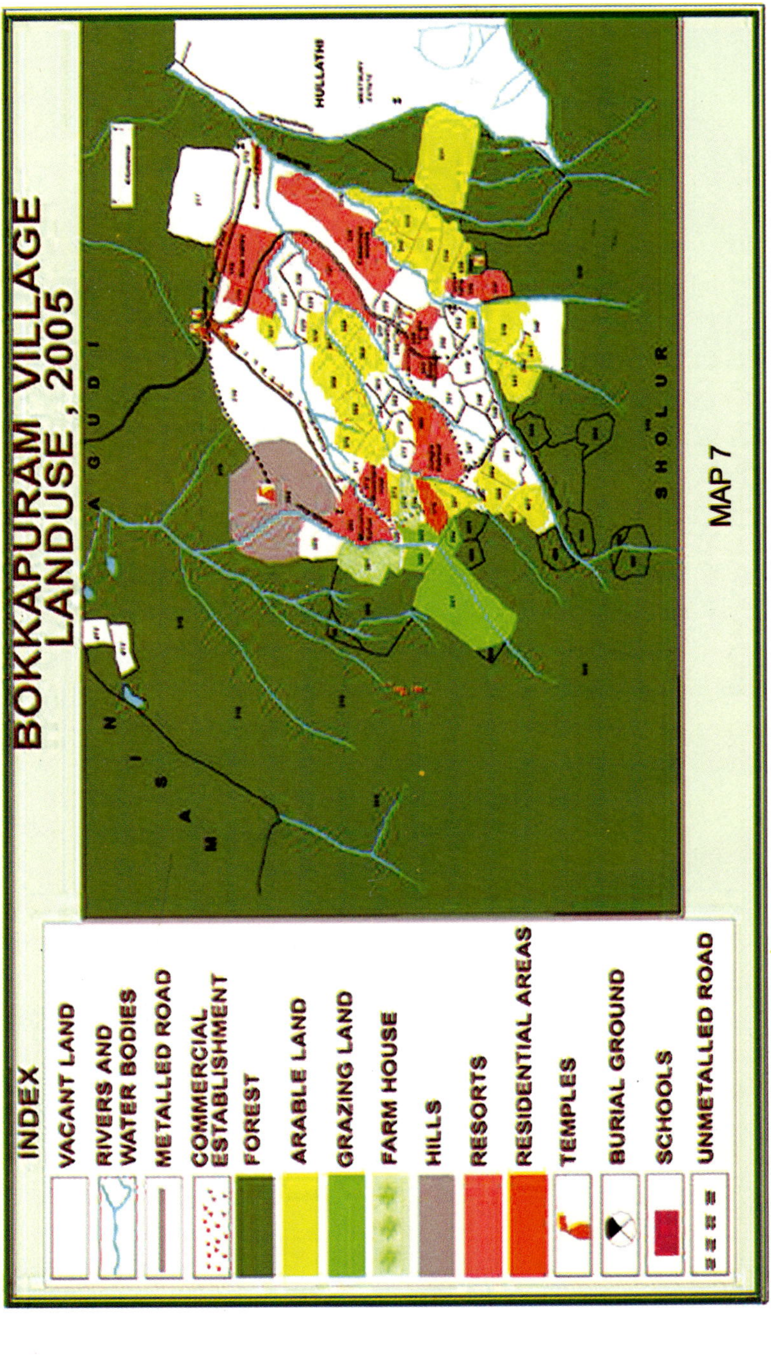
BOKKAPURAM VILLAGE
LANDUSE , 2005
MASINAGUDI
SHOLUR
HULLATHI
MAP 7
INDEX
VACANT LAND
RIVERS AND WATER BODIES
METALLED ROAD
COMMERCIAL ESTABLISHMENT
FOREST
ARABLE LAND
GRAZING LAND
FARM HOUSE
HILLS
RESORTS
RESIDENTIAL AREAS
TEMPLES
BURIAL GROUND
SCHOOLS
UNMETALLED ROAD

THE ECONOMIC ACTIVITIES THROUGHOUT THE YEAR

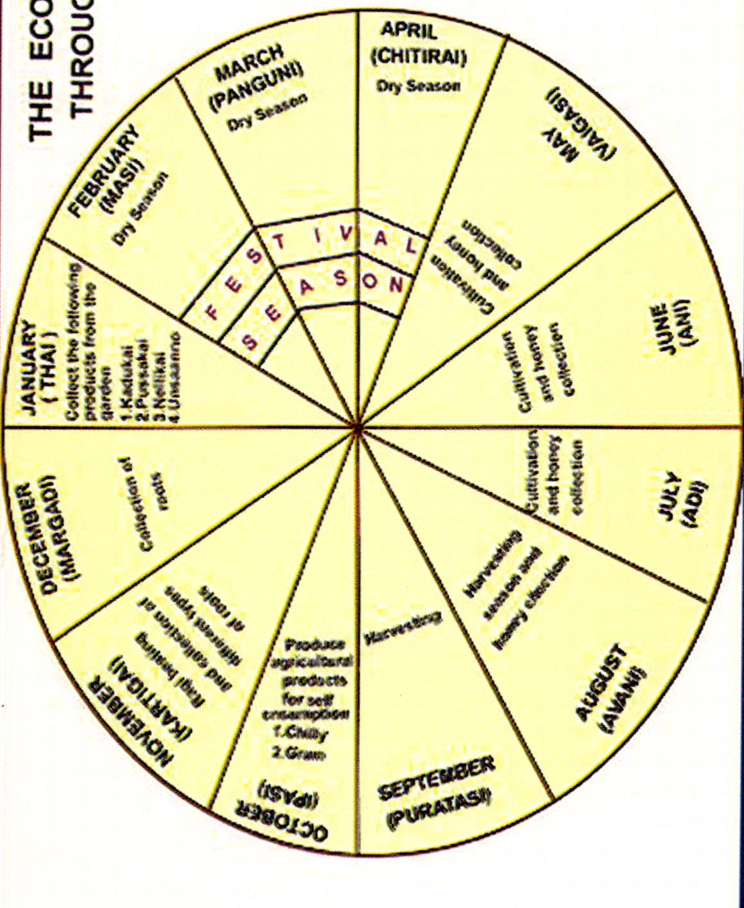

CHART 1

5

Bio-Diversity and Sustainable Development in a Fringe Village in Mudumalai Wildlife Sanctuary Nilgiri Biosphere Reserve-A Case Study

Sanchita Ghatak

Introduction

As a follow up of UNESCO's Man and Bio-sphere (MAB) programme, the Indian National MAB committee designated Nilgiri Bio-sphere Reserve (NBR), which includes part of two of the ten bio-geographic provinces of India viz. the Western Ghats and Eastern Ghats as the first Bio-sphere Reserve of the country in August 1986. Spread between 10°45' N to 12°15' N Latitude and 76°0' E to 77°15' E Longitude, over 5520 sq.km. of which 1240 sq. km. representing the core zone, NBR occurs in the states of Tamilnadu, Kerala and Karnataka. Tamil Nadu accounts for major portion of the NBR with 2537.6 sq. km followed by Karnataka (1527.4 sq. km) and Kerala (1455.4 sq. km). Comprising of nearly 15 forest and wildlife management units of the three states, the NBR is the true representative of bio-diversity abundance of Western Ghats. In 1940 a part of Mudumalai Range of Tamil Nadu State was declared as the first ever Wildlife Sanctuary. The word

Mudumalai means 'Ancient Mountain'. Today it is the most popular Wildlife Sanctuary in the South, situated in the Nilgiri district of Tamil Nadu state.

Study Area

Sreemadurai village is situated in the manipulation (forestry) zone. North of this the village is surrounded by 20 no. compartment of Mudumalai block of Mudumalai Wildlife Sanctury (MWS) and in the east it is 6 no. compartment of Theppakadu block of MWS. It is the fringe or peripheral village of forest manipulated zone. The village is situated in the southern boundary of the MWS and is selected for study as a fringe village located in Gudalur Taluk of Nilgiri district.

Sreemadurai village is a multi-ethnic village. The Paniyans, Mullu Kurumbas, Kattu Nayakans, Mountadan Chetties, Keraloids and the Celoneies are the different ethnic groups. Before the declaration of the Biosphere Reserve in 1986, the villagers of this village especially tribals i.e., Paniyan, Mullu Kurumba and Kattu Nayakan were dependent on the forest of Mudumalai. In the study it is tried to understand how the villagers of Sreemadurai sustain themselves in their own bio-diversity.

Conceptual Framework

The objective of the study is to show how the development is to be sustained at the desire extent through which the biological and cultural heritage is preserved and maintained. Again in order to see the preservation and maintenance of biological and cultural heritage with the development, few indices such as landman ratio and socio-cultural level may be taken as a tool for highlighting the conceptual framework.

Methodology

Data have been collected through:

1. A set of questionnaire
2. Collection of cadastral maps
3. Filling up of the cadastral maps
4. Group interview of the villagers and self help groups
5. Collecting secondary data from different departments at Gudalur taluk

6. Collecting relevant maps from different departments Gudalur taluk

Introducing the Studied Village

Sreemadurai village is bounded on the west by Cherumulli village, on the south by Gudalur and on the north and east by Mudumalai village of Gudalur taluk as well as MWS. Sreemadurai village with 11°30′25″ N to 11°34′28″ N latitude and 76°28′41″ E to 76°31′30″ E longitude is situated on the fringe of the MWS.

Topography of the village shows undulating character with low hills and valleys. Average elevation is 1000 m above mean sea level. The north-eastern portion of the land mass has a narrow passage around Gudalur which facilitates entry of the NE monsoon. This undulating region rises gradually in the north and forms a watershed, dividing the baren forests of Doddakatti Block in the north from the dense wooded Mudumalai Block in the south of Mudumalai Range. The characteristic features of the village are frequent occurrence of swamps of varying sizes at the foot of the hills. Many of these swamps are cultivated for paddy.

The main characteristic features of the village are (a) undulating topography without any pronounced direction of drainage; (b) low hills with gentle slopes (c) impeded but not barred, drainage in various places (d) presence of vegetation on the slopes to prevent rapid drainage (e) the average annual rainfall of over 2500 mm favouring the formation of swamps in this region.

Owing to heavy rainfall the clay colloids are carried down to the foothills and cumulative deposition tends to flatten the ground and gives the ground a permanently swampy character.

The major rock type of Sreemadurai belongs to the Archaean complex of peninsular India Soils have developed from parent materials like charnockite, gneiss and pyroxene granulite rocks occurring here. Soils are shallow on the crest of hillocks and moderately deep soils on the hill slopes. Valley soils are mostly submerged in water for more than 6 months in a year resulting in an aquatic moisture regime. These soils are mostly used for cultivation of paddy. Soils on gentle to moderate hill slopes are extensively used for tea plantation.

In the forest soil and vegetation survey report on Gudalur Forest Division (Sharma and Prasad, 1983), 12 soil series have been identified in Guddalur division falling under four soil orders viz. Mollisols, Alfisols, Inceptisols, Entisols.

Mollisols – Constitute 7% approx of the Reserve Forest area – under either in grass or shola vegetation. It is moderately well drained with slight erosion and moderate permeability. Soils are acidic in reaction and have a sandy loam texture.

Alfisols – It is sandy loam to loamy sand on the surface and sandy clay to clay loam in the alluvial horizon. Conductivity is low. PH varies from 5.3 to 5.8. Brownish to reddish in colour, well drained and deep.

Inceptisols – Developed from basic and acid rock types and occupy about 29% of the reserve forest of the area. These soils are brownish to reddish in colour and more or less freely drained. They are acid in reaction, low in conductivity, sandy in texture.

Entisols – Developed from all rock types, occupy about 10% of the reserve forest area. This is found mostly on hill tops or in localities which are highly eroded. These soils have developed on moderate to strong slopes or on fans and deltas of small stream. They are acid in reaction. PH 5.5±0.4% low in conductivity, sandy loam in textures.

Parent material, climate, vegetation and relief have played an active role in the formation of the soils of this village.

Here soil is known as 'man'. Red soil is known as 'semman' (Sem=red, man=soil). 'kariman' (Kari=blacklike) is black soil. 'Wandalman' and 'manalman' are alluvial and sandy soil respectively where 'wandal' means alluvial and 'manal' means sandy. Alluvial soil is favourable for paddy cultivation and red soil favours tea and coffee plantation.

From the name of the hamlets (see table 1) it is clear that villagers have a deep relation with forest. All names are from plant or animals. Only three names are temple oriented.

Biodiversity

Biodiversity includes two related concepts: (1) Genetic diversity and (2) Ecological diversity. Genetic diversity is the amount of genetic variability among individuals of a single species as also between species. Ecological diversity is the number of species in a community of organisms. For functioning of an ecological system, each kind of diversity is fundamental and hence important for human welfare. Diversity characterizes most living organisms. NBR is indeed very rich in bio-diversity.

The natural resources are product of biological and ecological diversity which ultimately leads to the different ethnic groups to interact with the nature in diverse way. In the following headings natural resources are discussed in three main groups namely forest resources, human resources and land resources including occupation.

Forest resource

Nilgiri district, covering 1350 sq. km of forest area, holds within its fold all the important forest types of Southern India and in fact is unique in the whole of India. Vegetation of the district can be broadly divided into four principal groups:

1. The shola-grassland vegetation of the Nilgiri plateau consists of vast stretches of grasslands with numerous isolated, compact, sharphy defined and usually small woodlands, which fall under a category of tropical rainforests, locally known as 'sholas' derived from the Tamil word "solai" means a tropical rainforest.
2. The open deciduous shrub of Sigur plateau supports a dry vegetation of varying composition.
3. The moist deciduous and the dry deciduous teak forests of the Nilgiri – Wynaad depending on the amount of annual rainfall. Here in areas of high rainfall, patches of evergreen and semi-evergreen forests occur. This group includes West coast tropical evergreen forest, west coast semi-evergreen forest, southern moist mixed deciduous forest, southern secondary moist mixed deciduous forests, moist teak forests, dry teak forest, secondary grassland and teak plantation of Mudumalai.
4. The forests of the south eastern outer slope, below the frost line, the submontane type of forest occurs. A type of evergreen forest at an altitude between 1200 m to 1500 m is noticed. In the lower slopes bear a dry deciduous type of forest with an admixture of dry evergreen species.

Sreemadurai village covering 149.605 hector of forest land is within Gudalur Forest Division. Its forests harbour all the flora and fauna of the neighbouring Mudumalai Wildlife Sanctuary. Forests here are varied and diverse, represent bio-diversity treasure house and are home to many rare, endangered species of plants and animals.

Sreemadurai village is within the forests of Nilgiri Wynaad area. The village is rugged being thrown up here and there into hills. It is a wooded area and has a higher rainfall and much more luxuriant vegetation. The relief map shows the ground rises gradually in the north to a low range of hills. The range of hills of the locality forms the watershed. Wynaad means 'swamps', which is the predominant land form of the area. Many of these swamps are cultivated with paddy. The undulating type of the country without any pronounced direction of drainage, low hills with gentle slopes, impeded but not barred drainage in various places, the presence of vegetation on the slopes to prevent rapid drainage and an average annual rainfall of about 1500 mm. all contribute to the formation of swamps in this region. Due to heavy rain finer particles are carried down to the foot hills and again due to the cumulative deposition of the fine particles flatten the ground at the foot of the hills and gradually by the nature of the deposit give the ground a permanently swampy character.

Forest History of the Area

In 1875 all the forests came under the forest department for effective conservation. In 1882 the Forest Act was introduced for the protection and conservation of forest and from then the selection, mapping and demarcation of the forests was carried out. In 1876 IG of forest advised the planting the forest denuded area in order to increase the fertility of the cultivable valleys, to protect the hillsides from erosion and to conserve the water supply and the few remaining shoals.

Flora

The flora of the Sreemadurai village is of mixed complexion with deciduous plants predominating. Rainfall is the principal factor in determining the character and composition of the flora of the area. But terrain, depth, composition and drainage of soil also play important roles. The striking feature of the vegetation of the plateau is the dominance of grassland cover. The composition, size, height and growth of the sholas vary according to altitude of the area. Sholas are confined to sites where there are good drainage and sufficient moisture and containing shallow soil.

Tall grasses called 'elephant grass' or 'thapai' grow luxuriously over much of the area. Elephants and gaurs are fond of elephant grass. Bamboo, the giant variety called Bambusa arundinaceous is the most important plant of the area from the point of view of wildlife. Elephants eat bamboo. Bamboo grows mostly along the banks of the most streams and ravines and also offers shelter to most forms of wildlife. Bamboo is put to a variety of use by the tribals residing in the locality. After completing its life span, nearly fifty years or so, mass flowering and seedling take place. These seeds are like rice in taste and appearance and animals and birds gather to feast on the seeds.

The area is well known for its valuable timber. Teak (Tectona grandis) is commercially the most valuable tree and grows wild. It has a wide distribution. Other timber species are rosewood (Dalbergia latifolia) locally called Eti-maram, Mathi (Terminalia acrenulate), Vengai (Pterocarpus marsupium), Venteak (Lagerstroemia lanceolata) locally called Venthekku; Sadachi, Karmathi, Thadasu (Grewia titiaefolia), crocodile bark tree (Terminalia tomentosa), jacktree called Palamaram, Vagai etc.

Flowering trees and shurbs light up the jungle when they bloom/Indian laburnum (Cassia fistula), Butea monosperma, coral tree (Erythrina indica), red silk cotton tree (Salmalia malabarica) all bear striking blossoms.

Regarding fruits wild mango, jamun, nelli, zizyphus, jujuba and varieties of wild figs are there. Zizyphu, jujuba fruit is a special favourite with the animals and birds. Jackfruit [Chakkakai (tender rawjack)] is one important food of the Paniyans and also others. When there is scarcity of rice they dig-out roots locally called nootu kizhangu. They boil it and simply take. They also take vegetable curry (chaaru) or dried fish (meen) available in the forest and river side.

Edible tubers are an important source of food for the tribal. Villagers collect many leafy vegetables from the forest and cook for their family. A list of vegetables is given below.

Honey is an important item of their collection. In general they collect honey (theen) in the month of May – June from the forest. They collect it in particular season. The honey is used for different serious also like cold and cough, for stomach upset etc. They sell it in Gudalur market. The price varies from Rs. 60/- to 80/- per kg.

The villagers collect medicinal plants from the forest. The traditional herbalists among the Paniyan, Mountadan Chetty and others of Sreemadurai village, use roots, rhizomes, bark, leaves, flowers, fruits, latex and seeds of medicinal plants that grow in the forest areas of their village. The medicinal components of these plants have been recognized and validated through trial and error process, and then incorporated into an ethno-healing system based on the traditional wisdom of the tribes. There is one institute in the hamlet Putturvayal of Sreemadurai village called "Swamy Saradananda Guru Niketan". They prepare and sell the aurvedic medicine. Usually the Paniyan and the Kumumbas sell these medicinal plants to the Aurvedic shops. Plants have a special place in religious and social ceremonies of every rural society. Tulsi (Ocimum Sanctum L) is sacred plant of the villagers, used in every religious ceremony. Now it is proved that eating a few tulsi leaves in the morning purifies blood and keeps blood pressure normal. Again they use saffron (crocus sativus L) and turmeric (curcuma longa L) in the marriage ceremonies. Here several plants are associated with superstitions beliefs. Alstonia Scholaris (L) R. Br. and Borassus flabellifer L. are associated by the villagers in Sreemadurai village with witches and spirits. Vazaela (banana leaves), Kuvalam (betel leaves), Pachha-Kaya (raw banana), banana, coconut, neem leaves, different types of flowers like chembarathi, chekki etc., are used in their religious functions. Bamboo leaves especially kuruthu, the unopened bamboo leaves and banana leaves are important in puja. Banana leaf has a special importance in religious ceremonies. Sandalwood is considered sacred by the villagers and its paste is used for religious ceremonies in the temples everyday. Coconut is used for ceremonies and its leaves for decoration in Puja pandel.

Allergy is a common complain and in order to treat the common allergic disorders caused by Semecarpus anacardium

L. and Holigarna arnottiana Roxb (both called as 'cheru'), Terminalia bellerica Roxb (called Tanni) is used by many villagers here. Plants are also used by tribals as veterinary medicine in treatment of cattle and birds.

Owing to clearance of forest the medicinal plants are becoming rare. The villagers know that many modern synthetic medicines have side effects perhaps more harmful than the disease itself. But the herbal medicines do not have such bad effects.

Certain plants found here are narrated in mythology such as, Asoka (Saraca asoka Roxb. de willd = Saraca indica Baker) a beautiful garden tree with fragrant flowers. In the 'Ramayana' where Sita is said to have been made to sit under an 'Asoka' tree in Ravana's garden in Lanka.

The economy of the villagers, especially of the tribals, depends on plants. The main item of forest produce needed by the people living here are (a) firewood for domestic consumption, tea factories and other cottage industries (b) timber for construction (c) small timber for building houses and for agricultural implements (d) pasture for cattle (e) bamboo, (f) thorn for fencing, (g) thatch grass, etc. etc.

Firewood: The average villagers never pay for his requirements being met from what is available in patta lands and unreserved forest. With the rapid extension of cultivation, the supply of fuel from private lands has fallen very low. The area under tea cultivation is also increasing day by day. The demand of tea industry for firewood has increased substantially.

Timber: The small timber requirements are met mostly from private forests and patta lands. Since the timber resources of this Division are meager in general, timber is also imported from Kerala markets. For inferior constructional purposes large size Eucalyptus grandis timber are used. Timber is purchased by merchants from outside.

Grazing: The number of cattle grazed is very large. The purpose of villagers maintaining such large herds is for their dairy products and for manure. Grazing fecilities are therefore an important requirement for the people and this is provided at very nominal rates. Grazing is regulated by issuing grazing permits subject to the usual condition noted in the permit. The grazing fee is Rs. 1.00/- per sheep, Rs. 2.00/- per cow, Rs. 4.00/- per buffalo, ass and or horse and Rs. 30.00/- per elephant.

Bamboo: This is the poor man's timber and is widely used by the villagers for roofing and side walls. Cattlesheds and enclosure are built almost exclusively with bamboo splits and bamboo posts. Many poor families cake out their livelihood by weaving baskets, thatties, mats, etc. out of bamboos. The bamboo requirements of local people are met mostly from private forests.

Fodder and thatch grass: The villagers living close to forests require fodder grass for stall feeding. This is permitted to be removed in head loads free of cost for bonafide domestic use. The most popular roofing material for cheap houses is grass. Villagers fell and it and then pack it felt and to a thickness of 10-15 cms. a bamboo reaper mesh. This serves as an ideal non-conducting material, insulating the interior from extremes of heat, cold and rain. This is also a material which is abundant in its supply and removed in head loads. Its removal is regulated under permits issued by the lease of minor forest produce. Under G.O. Ms No. 412 Forest and Fisheries Department dated 5.4.1982, the rate of monsoon grass was 25 paise per head load and Rs. 10/- per cart load.

Minor forest produce: The main items of minor forest produce in this division are Lavangam bark, avaram bark, reeds, shikakai (Acacia concinna), medicinal plants, honey, bees wax, amla or nellikai (Amblica officinalis), gall nuts, wild pepper, wild ginger, wild turmeric, wild mango (Mangifera indica) lemon grass (cymbopogon citratus), kulirma bark (Machilus macarantha), dammar (Shorea, Canarium, Vateria), camphor [distilled from Cinnamomuni Camphora (L)] etc. There is a demand for Eucalyptus citriodora leaves for distillation of eucalyptus oil. Eucalyptus grandis wood and wattle wood need for the forest based industries in this belt. All parts of coconut palm are useful and the plant helps the local people to meet almost all their needs.

Properties of different woods are known by many tribals. They use only, pieces of wood of the Nalpamara trees, namely atti (Ficus racemosa L.), 'itti' (Ficus macrocarpus L.), 'peraal' (Ficus benghalensis L.) and 'arayaal' (Ficus religiosa L.) as cutting boards for cutting medicinal plants.

Here tribals collect sehaikai for bathing. They also use soapnet. It uses like soap. They collect it from the forest in the month of Nov. – Dec.

Use of forest in daily life: Both the tribals and the non-tribals of the study area depend on forest in so many ways. Tribals' especially the Paniyan's huts are erected on raised platforms. The walls are made of stout bamboo and these are plastered with mud. The frame of the roof is made of bamboo or minor timber and thatched with grass. These show that they depend on forest for all these building materials. They use a special type of soil for decorating the huts which they collect from the forest.

Regarding ornaments, the Paniyan women can be easily identified by the ornament worn in the dilated ear-lobes called Olai which is prepared by themselves. For this they bent cylinders black in colour, out of solidified milk of a jack tree. For glittering in red colours, the red seeds of kunthumani (Abrus precatorius) are embedded in the front cross section portion. In some cases scrolls of palm leaf were found to have been plugged in the holes, a diameter of about three inches in diameter.

From birth to death in each ceremony the Paniyans use so many forest items which shows that in ancient time they were within the forest and collected those materials easily from their surrounding. Few examples are given below :

In the Paniyan family after the birth of a child they give coconut oil, betal leaves and tobacco to the mid-wife. After the naming of the child, the maternal grand-mother ties a thread, prepared from forest product around the waist of the child. After the first menstruation in the ceremony "neevedu kkul", the girl stands on banana leaf over paddy, cow urine kept on left-side and she pray for good health.

A head load of firewood present to the girl's house from boy's side for Valli Vekkal or Panam Kettu Kalyana (betrothed ceremony). Again after betrothed ceremony the would be bridegroom visit his father-in-laws house with a head-load of firewood, betal leave, nuts and tobacco once in a week. In funeral ceremonies a bier is made of bamboo sticks and banana stems. With a leaf spoon the lineage people of the dead person pour a few drops of coconut water into the month of the corpse.

Forest management by people of the village: The inhabitants of Sreemadurai were poor gatherer and cultivators in the past. Any direct influence of the early history on the forests was mainly due to the inhabitants of the Nilgiris and not due to the invaders. They have always been a gatherer people and had not been known to have caused any destruction of the forest except causing injurious effects on the sholas because of their custom of annual burning of grasslands for fresh pasture.

Forest has an important role in the study area. Here several communities have settled and evolved unique interactions between themselves and nature. The Paniyans or other tribals of the study area never cut any green tress. Groves are the last remnants of the native vegetation of that area. This is an effort by local communities to protect and preserve their natural forest tracts against clearing of forest for cultivation and settlement. It is for the preservation of native species of plants, animals, insects and micro-organisms. Here the sacred groves are known as *Kolikadu or Kaavu*. These scared groves have been protected due to religious and traditional beliefs. Some endangered, rare and threatened medicinal plant species found in the sacred groves.

Among the female deities Mariamman is common and worshipped in groves. Within male deities Aiyanar is common and worshipped in the groves.

The sacred groves can be considered as a part of forests left untouched by the local inhabitants and protected by the local village folk deities. These sacred groves are the only remnants of the original forest and now play a vital role in the conservation of biological diversity.

In Kanchi kolly hamlet there is one tree called Maduraiveeran. 2/3 stones are kept there serially. Villagers pray here for the good of the family and village. The deity is the watching god. The tree is a thick wood. If one cut it, the result is full growth within a few days. So they never cut it. No climbing is allowed in this tree also. On every Friday and Tuesday evening they worship Lakshmi Valliyamman. Vengai is a sacred wood. They preserve it for puja purpose.

The Paniyans of Sreemadurai village are still animists. They believes in spiritual beings. Here they have shrines consists of layers of stones under the foot of a tree. The spirits of the deities or the stone images are the source of the inner power to the Paniyans. They also worship a jungle-dwelling Bhagawati.

The Mullu Kurumbas and the Kattu Nayakan worship their Gods in a hut like secret place. This place is known as Dvarmanai. Dvar means god and manai means house. But the Paniyans do not construct a hut like shed, they only worship their god in open space both within and outside the forest. They sacrifice cock and coconut for good harvest, welfare and good health and also for the well being of the community, before the sacred place.

Forest administration: Sreemadurai village area is divided under two forest blocks i.e., Melambalam and Odakolli. These two forest blocks are under Sreemadurai beat. Again this beat is under Gudalur section which is again under Gudalur Range and also under Gudalur forest division. Reserve land in Sreemadurai beat is 87.230 hector. There is no scope for further regeneration of forest in this village. The village has very little forest land.

Fauna : The diversity of animals, birds and insects life associated with the forest is equally high. These animals occupy specific forest ecosystems where their needs are met and their breeding potential is enhanced or in other words their healthy survival is guaranteed. Even the private plantation of tea, coffee and other agricultural crops attract animals such as elephants, leopards, barking deer and various other species either for food or other forms of cover. The common mammalian species found here are Sambhar, Barking deer, elephant, black napped hare, etc.

Sreemadurai beat within the Gudalur forest division is located in the middle of a very important wildlife zone traversing the three states of Tamil Nadu, Kerala and Karnataka. Therefore it is as important as a wildlife sanctuary; however the highly complicated nature of the problems of this area does not permit its being declared a wildlife sanctuary or being made part of Mudumalai Wildlife Sanctuary.

The important management principles that are suggested for this Division are the following :

(a) Lessening and resolving man animal conflict

(b) Taking immediate punitive action against wildlife offences
(c) Maintaining the existing elephant corridors and preventing their destruction
(d) Liaising and co-operating with the staff of Mudumalai and other sanctuaries
(e) Dedicated patrolling

As mentioned earlier man-animal conflicts are very common in this Division. Preventive and post occurrence operations must be promptly carried out. Efforts must be made to contain wild animals within forests.

Nature-Culture interface in the area: Linkage between the indigenous people (Paniyan, Mullu Kurumba and Kattu Naicken) and natural ecosystem of the area had been long, intimate and harmonious. For all the local communities the hills are "life-giving and sacred". Most of the social and cultural practices of the local communities of the area are traceable to the usage or practice of natural resources. In their local prayer they identify all the samples of trees and thickets, streams and swamps, slopes and summits and pens and pastures in the neighbourhood and wish them well. The bio-diversity is also illustrated in a gratitude ceremony at the culmination of their calendar year.

Domestic cattle bio-diversity is also evident here. The grass turns tasteless after the heavy rains. So salt is offered to the animals in that period by the tribes. Water courses are also ritually purified during these observances.

The interface between the human and bio-diversity is still reflected here. The sacredness of the environment is still part of their ethos, ritually adhered to in their cultural practices e.g., in name giving economy.

Human Resources: One of the major environmental strategies should be to stabilize population. Due to demographic pressures, economic pressures build up and cropland, woodland and grassland which support the human population by supplying goods and services can no longer remain unaffected. Resources shrink as people multiply.

Other factors responsible for the presser on land are decline in death rate and increasing of working class population.

Table 5.1 Population break up according to Hamlets and Communities in Sreemadurai village - 2005

Name of hamlets	*Paniyan*			*Mullu Kurumba*			*Kattu Nayakan*			*Mountadan Chetty*		
	Total	*Male*	*Female*	*Total*	*Male*	*Female*	*Total*	*Male*	*Female*	*Total*	*Male*	*Female*
Kanchikoli (1)	33	15	18	77	39	38	0	0	0	250	118	132
Kanchikoli (2)	103	52	51	0	0	0	0	0	0	91	45	46
	136	67	69	77	39	38	0	0	0	341	163	178
Manimoola	56	29	27	0	0	0	0	0	0	70	32	38
Kozikandy	52	27	25	30	14	16	0	0	0	217	105	112
Kozibazar	23	12	11	0	0	0	0	0	0	44	18	26
Manvayal	0	0	0	0	0	0	0	0	0	311	158	153
Parankolly	38	20	18	0	0	0	0	0	0	248	120	128
Kundithal	0	0	0	50	21	29	0	0	0	316	157	159
Odakolli	33	19	14	25	12	13	11	5	6	37	18	19
Ambalamoola	0	0	0	0	0	0	0	0	0	54	26	28
Kungoormoola	0	0	0	0	0	0	0	0	0	260	128	132
Kutchimuchi	0	0	0	0	0	0	0	0	0	33	15	18

(Contd.)

(Contd.)

Name of hamlets	Kerala Christian Chettas			Kerala Muslim			Kerala Hindu Malayalam			Ceylony		
	Total	Male	Female	Total	Male	Female	Total	Male	Female	Total	Male	Female
Kanchikoli (1)	33	15	18	0	0	0	48	25	23	0	0	0
Kanchikoli (2)	22	10	12	0	0	0	30	18	12	0	0	0
	55	25	30	0	0	0	78	43	35	0	0	0
Manimoola	5	2	3	0	0	0	0	0	0	0	0	0
Kozikandy	5	2	3	0	0	0	35	16	19	0	0	0
Kozibazar	13	5	8	0	0	0	25	13	12	0	0	0
Manvayal	107	77	30	25	12	13	30	18	12	68	32	36
Parankolly	27	12	15	0	0	0	14	8	6	0	0	0
Kundithal	13	8	5	0	0	0	15	8	7	0	0	0
Odakolli	21	9	12	0	0	0	15	8	7	0	0	0
Ambalamoola	143	78	65	48	25	23	34	13	21	120	60	60
Kungoormoola	28	12	16	51	25	26	29	15	14	0	0	0
Kutchimuchi	8	3	5	153	73	80	9	4	5	0	0	0

(Contd.)

Name of hamlets	*Paniyan*			*Mullu Kurumba*			*Kattu Nayakan*			*Mountadan Chetty*		
	Total	*Male*	*Female*	*Total*	*Male*	*Female*	*Total*	*Male*	*Female*	*Total*	*Male*	*Female*
Kundoor	63	36	27	0	0	0	0	0	0	328	168	160
Kalikunnu	40	14	16	0	0	0	23	11	12	52	25	27
Khamati	0	0	0	0	0	0	0	0	0	127	65	62
Mel Chemundi	22	10	12	0	0	0	0	0	0	57	28	29
Kiz Chemundi	9	5	4	0	0	0	0	0	0	23	15	8
Arakadavoo & Nambalakotta	0	0	0	0	0	0	0	0	0	20	8	12
Keechalur	0	0	0	0	0	0	0	0	0	5	3	2
Echamvayal & Kunil	0	0	0	0	0	0	0	0	0	77	38	39
Narimoola	66	34	32	38	16	22	45	22	23	22	10	12
Melambalam	44	22	22	19	8	11	0	0	0	30	15	15
Vadavayal	42	19	23	22	11	11	12	5	7	45	20	25
Total	**624**	**314**	**310**	**261**	**121**	**140**	**91**	**43**	**48**	**2717**	**1335**	**1382**

(Contd.)

Name of hamlets	*Kerala Christian Chettas*			*Kerala Muslim*			*Kerala Hindu Malayalam*			*Ceylony*		
	Total	*Male*	*Female*	*Total*	*Male*	*Female*	*Total*	*Male*	*Female*	*Total*	*Male*	*Female*
Kundoor	13	5	8	62	32	30	26	13	13	0	0	0
Kalikunnu	14	8	6	87	44	43	13	5	8	0	0	0
Khamati	13	5	8	33	15	18	22	10	12	0	0	0
Mel Chemundi	28	12	16	0	0	0	37	18	19	0	0	0
Kiz Chemundi	5	2	3	0	0	0	0	0	0	0	0	0
Arakadavoo & Nambalakotta	22	10	12	0	0	0	26	12	14	0	0	0
Keechalur	142	70	72	22	10	12	30	15	15	0	0	0
Echamvayal & Kunil	33	15	18	39	18	21	23	12	11	0	0	0
Narimoola	16	8	8	0	0	0	0	0	0	0	0	0
Melambalam	17	9	8	0	0	0	0	0	0	0	0	0
Vadavayal	5	3	2	0	0	0	15	8	7	0	0	0
Total	**733**	**380**	**353**	**520**	**254**	**266**	**476**	**239**	**237**	**188**	**92**	**96**

Education: The total village picture shows that 68% of the villagers of Sreemadurai are literated. 74.7% are male literate within male population and female literate within female population is 61.3%.

From the education table it is clear that the Mullu Kurumbas are more educated than the Paniyans. Regarding the Kattu Nayakan they are minor in population as well as education. Though Cylone people are less educated. Now-a-days the tribals are sending their children to the schools. The Mountaden Chettis are educated. Most of them are going to schools. There are two women with post graduation degree this community. But Kerala Christians are ranked first in education in this village. Graduate (12 no.) and Master degree holders (3 no.) are also in this village. There are few Govt. schools in the village.

Kungoormoola High School is situated at the highest altitude of the Sreemadurai village. Manalikunu is the old name of this school. 'Kunu' means highest and 'Manali' means sand.

In Sreemadurai village there are three Ananganvalwadi – (1) Kungoormoola near panchyet, (2) Manvayal and (3) the third one is Vadavayal. Actually Valwadi is like our nursery school. It is under H.A.D.P. (Hill Area Development Programme) and controled by panchyet from Govt. side. One teacher and one cook are appointed by Govt. for each Ananganvalwadi. Food, salari and other requirement are met by the Govt. the children in the age group of four to six years are coming to this Valwadi.

Beside Ananganvalwadi, there are 4 Govt. school and one private school is Sreemadurai village. Regarding Govt. school two are in Kungoormoola of which one is upto X standard and another is upto VIII standard of the remaining two Govt. schools one in Manvayal and another in Kanchikolli. Both are upto V standard. The teaching medium is in local language (Tamil and Malayam). In Govt. school teaching is free including mid-day meal. But there is one private English medium school in Ambalamoola. It is upto X standard. Gudalur town is adjaceant to Sreemadurai village. So many students are going to Gudalur for both English Medium and local Medium school are there.

Beside these, there is one free computer centre at *Kamati* and one tailoring and type writing institute in this village. One Retd.

Headmaster of Badaga is running this institute. It runs from 9-11, two hrs. in the morning for computer and two hrs. in the evening for tailoring and typing there are 30 students in the institute.

Due to exploding population soil is being used increasingly which posses threat to its productivity. Crop land is fast losing fertile top soil at a rate which is undermining long term crop production. Loss of top soil affects the productivity and makes farming costly.

Action regarding stabilizing population has to be taken on the basis of inter-relationship between population, environment and natural resources development.

Land Resource

Due to population growth village heading towards a situation where natural resources are getting depleted at much faster rate than they are being regenerated which reduces productivity and ultimately rate of development itself.

The wet land has remained same. Dry land is more due to physiographic condition. The area under plantation is nil in Sreemadurai. Parmboke is only 0.22 per cent.

Punjai both in patta and anadinum shows a high percentage (30.56+26.60=57.16%). It is due to the fact that plantation (tea and coffee) has been undertaken by the villagers. The uplands cover bigger area where plantation agriculture is undertaken on commercial scale with the help of immigrant population.

Nanjai is only (18.47+3.82) 22.29 per cent. The physiography is responsible for it. Again the Nanjai are rain fed which is very important for agriculture. Both south-west monsoon and north-east monsoon bring rains here.

There are two types of forest land one is Othuku/Kadu which is reserve forest. It covers 0.77% of land another is forest land under section 53 covering 12.68%. In future this type will be converted to reserve forest. Forest department trying to preserve this forest land for the benefit of the area and its naturalness.

Type of land: There are two types of land

(A) Patta land:

(1) Nanjai – It is wet land. Patta land and taxable land.

(2) Punjai – It is dry land as well as Patta land.

(B) Govt. land :

(1) C.A. Nanjai – It is conditional assignment wet land fit for cultivation. It is also patta land but not for sale, ten conditions are there. It is govt. land. Some encroachment is here. For govt. purposes the land may be used.

(2) C.A. Punjai – It is conditional assignment dry land. It is partly encroached dry land. Conditions are given by the Govt.

(3) Anadinum wet land – It is govt. wet land, fit for cultivation. This is access waste wet land but now encroached upon.

(4) Anadinum dry land – This is govt. dry land. It is access waste dry land and now encroached upon.

(5) Tharisu land – It is govt. vacant land and not fit for sale but cultivation is going on and now it has been encroached upon, though it is barren land.

(6) Othuku/kadu - Reserved Forest.

(7) Forest under See 53 – Reserved land.

(8) Arasunilam (Porumbuk) - [Arasu = govt. nilam=land]. This is govt. land used for public general purpose like roads, temples, burial ground.

(9) Estate Thottam – It is plantation Estate land.

Cropland : Sreemadurai is predominantly an agricultural village. The cultivable land of the village has been divided into two categories.

(i) Wet lands which are situated in between the hillocks and are drained by several hill streams and channels. These lands receive water from the hill streams and are wet during most part of the year. Due to the undulating topography and uneven distribution of water the field size is small. This land restricts one crop in a year and generally local variety of rice which takes 10 to 11 months to grow.

(ii) Dry lands which are situated on the hill slopes and mainly depend on rain. Due to moderate to high undulating topography, run-off of rainwater is high which results inadequate moisture for the crops and more areas under plantation crops. Now various vegetables, fruits, pepper have been introduced by the HADP (Hill Area Development Project) in these lands.

Kurumilagu or pepper is the most important crop. Nearly 32% of cropped land is under this head. It is introduced in this village with the immigrant population from Kerala. Pepper is "Black Gold" of Kerala. It requires red dry soil with good slopes. A pepper blossoms at the end of June and harvesting starts at the end of January and carry on till the 1st week of March. A pepper vine begins to bear fruits in the third or fourth year and continue its production for twenty years. Different types of pepper are grown in Srimadura.

Chayai/Tee (tea) is the next important crop. It covers more than 21% of cropped land. It grows on the hill slopes in dry land. It require 2/3 years for full growth and give production. From tea bush plucking of tea leaves may be for more than 100 years.

Tea leaves plucking. It varies from 8 to 13 days duration in one bush. One lady labour can pluck 30 kg leave, per day in rainy season. It decreases to 20 kg per day in dry season in the months of February – May. General rate of production is 500 kg per month per acre. Per acre one labour is required in a day where as in rainy season plucking is done in every eight alternative days. In dry season it is every 12 – 13 days. The labour wage is Rs. 50/- per day with two tea and meal. Tribals of the village are the source of labour, though some are coming from the neighbouring villages also.

Tea fields are kept clear of weeds, shade trees are regularly pruned. Silver oak is the most important shade tree in the tea estates. It also supports creeper like pepper. Fertilizer used for tea are urea, tea mixture, chanakm (cowdung). All these give separately in rainy season. In the month of June – July they give ammonia and potash as manures and In July – August, September they give urea and potash 2 – 3 times to tea field.

In Sreemadurai there is one tea factory in Kamaty hamlet area. The name of the factory is Hill Grove Tea Factory Pvt. Ltd. Workers are also coming from Gudalur to this factory.

NELLU (Paddy) : After pepper and tea, nellu is the important crop in Sreemadurai village. It coveres 150.39 hectare which is 20.54% of cropped land. Traditional agriculture of Sreemadurai is paddy cultivation. The local population of the village i.e., Mountadan Chetis and Paniyan, Mullu Kurumba (minor Pop) and Kattu Naicken practice this. The Paniyans are agricultural labourer, and they are attached to the Mountadan Chittis and cultivate their land. About 63% of paddy land is under the Mountadan Chettis.

The best quality paddy grown in this village is *Gandhasala*. They prepare 'pollau' by this paddy and also keep it for special occasions and rituals. But the popular variety is *Karuvailli*. Though it takes longer period to grow, its resistence capacity is very high. It is the only variety used by broadcasting method (bittu). Its production rate is also high. Weeding is abcent here for heavy rain and swampy nature of the wet land (voyal) Panchakavia (waste materials) is use for manure purpose. It includes waste pepper, vegetable waste, cowdung etc., Prior to their use, these materials are covered closed for nearly one month then it is used as fertilizer. Villagers follow some traditional knowledge. They use parenga marra, a kind of plant in the paddy field for killing the insects.

House construction – the villagers thatch the frame of the roof by paddy straw. So here also paddy has a big roll for construction of huts.

Food – Rice is their staple food which they take in the form of *Kanjee* (grue). They also take different types of roots, tubers and other vegetables like carrot, beetroot, radish, potato, seppam kelangu, cabbage, cauliflower, beans, broad beans, cluster beans, green chilly (mulagu), pumpkin, bottle gourd, papaya tender, Jack tender, tender bamboo shoots, plantam, raw fruit, plantain stem, tapioca, sweet potato, brinjals (vasthrutale), cho-cho marrow, elephant yam, cucumber (matten), ordinary and wild yam.

Putri is the ritual for the first harvest and the first paddy crop to be harvested is *Thondy*.

Kapi (Coffee): Next important crop is *Kapi* (Coffee). It occupies 13.01% of total cropped land. Ecologicallly Sreemadurai is suitable for coffee cultivation. Two types of coffee grown here like other villages. These are Robusta or coffee canephora and Arabica or coffee arabica. A new variety, Kaveri is introduced here. It is a small bushy type. The production rate of coffee is Rs. 18/- per kg with cover and is a yearly crop. In the month of March villagers plucke coffee seeds. Ecological conditions like slopy area, with more rain (1200 mm to 3000 mm) and moderate temperature 12^0 to 26^0 C are ideal condition for coffee cultivation. All these factors are available in this zone with soil condition of deep, well drained and slightly acidic in reaction. Moreover red dry soil in some parts of Sreemadurai village is suited for coffee plantation. Of the two varieties Arabica is grown on the higher elevation over 900 meters and Robusta on the lower elevation below 900 meters. It many be mention here that the kitchen garden round the settlement has been transformed into coffee garden which is an important change in this village.

Vazhai (banana) : *Vazhai* or banana is one of the most important fruit in this area. They take both green and ripe banana. All parts of the banana from leaf to the innermost part of the stem is used by the villagers.

Inji (Ginger) : It was an important crop in Sreemadurai in the past. Now due to the plantation of tea and coffee by the immigrants, the land area of inji is decreasing. The gentle slope, red loam soil, are favourable factors for ginger cultivation. Here two types of ginger are growing. (a) 3 odi, it is used as vegetable. It's juice is used and also used in medicine. (b) Maran – it is very good quality, used for dry ginger. Locally it is called *Chuko*. In one acre of land 5 bags (i.e., 60 x 5 = 300 kg.) seeds are required from which 6000 kg of ginger is produce.

Livestock: Increase in human population is accompanied by increase in livestock population. As livestock population represents family wealth which helps in food supplies.

Here cow is the important livestock. There are 485 population of cattle in Sreemadurai village of which more than 50% is with the Mountadan Chettis. Tribals have less livestock. The Paniyan have 42 cows and 4 goats.

In Sreemadurai village the land available for grazing is reduced but the number of grazing animals have increase. Naturally it is a sure cause of overgrazing, which follows soil erosion and desertification. Human and livestock population have outgrown the biological system that sustains them.

Woodland and aforestation of marginal land: Forests are renewable resource. It contributes substantially to the economic development by providing goods and services to the people and to industry and also generate substantial volume of employment. In this village immigrants came from other states and districts and changed the landscape. We know that there is an inverse correlation between reduction of forest area and the growth of population. Minor forest products (MFP) which are obtain from the forests and enable to sustain a large number of rural cottage and other industries are totally stopped by the forest Department from 2000.

From the previous discussion it is clear that agriculture, forestry and animal husbandry form an interrelated, interconnected and interdependent area as all these are dependent on land. Conservation and wise management of biological diversity must receive due importance in our planning process and economic development.

Changes in the Structure of Employment Opportunities

An analysis of occupational structures of a region unfolds its diverse economic, demographic and cultural attributes and provides a background knowledge for formulating plans for its social and economic development.

The Paniyans, according to earlier literature, cultivated hill rice in patches of forest which they cleared by burning and shifting from year to year. Naturally they have a good knowledge of sowing, transplanting and harvesting of rice. As they were in the forest they also have a good idea of forest. They were also employed as wood cutters. They were also elephant mahouts and were considered as good hunters.

Here in the study area the tribals are all agricultural labourers. Only 5% of the Paniyans, 2% of the Mullu Kurumbas and 2% of the Nayakam practice dairy farming. Forest collection, though illegal, yet the practice. Most of them uses by them to go to the forest for collecting minor forest produce. During the field work it was noticed that one Paniyan was arrested by the forest department for illegal of forest collection. Usually of forest produce Paniyans live near the Mountadan Chettis' agricultural fields. They are excellent agricultural labourer. At present the chief occupation of the Paniyans of this village is agricultural labourer.

The Paniyans know the agricultural work of ploughing, pudding, transplanting, weeding and harvesting. Govt. of Tamil Nadu gave land to the Paniyans in Sreemadurai village as they are fit for raising tea, coffee, interspersed with fruit trees like jack tree, guava etc. and topica, ginger and also paddy depending on the location of the land. But in this village most of the Paniyans who own lands do not cultivate their own land. They give it to other communities for cultivation. Some Paniyan women collect firewood and sell it at co-operative society in the village and at Gudalur for higher price, though collection from the Reserve Forest is totally banned.

Education needs to be regarded as investment of the highest order which in time to come, becomes an asset. Regarding conservation and sustainable development the spotlight would be on utilization and not exploitation. Utilization has an element of long term sustainability implicit in it. Resources need to be used in a wise manner as we know that all resources are finite and there is also a limit to the growth of living systems.

Environmental Education and Awareness: It is very urgent factor in sustainable development. Environmental education can be divided into two categories (a) Formal and (d) Non-formal. Formal education includes school, college and university education. The table of education of the study area shows the village picture and the shows the requirement.

Awareness includes making the individual conscious about the physical, social and aesthetic aspects of environment.

A crash education programme is needed at various levels to make the villagers, particularly children. Aware that the environmental decadence inevitably weakens economy, which in turn leads to social disintegration.

Sustainable Development: Kautilya, the wise minister in the court of Chandragupta Maurya said that "Stability of an empire depended on the Stability of its environment."

Sustainable means ability to be maintained at a fixed level without exhausting natural resources or damaging the environment both physical and cultural as far as practicable. Sustainable development has to be interpreted against our social, cultural and economic milieu and this development should be at par with the preservation and maintenance of cultural heritage and biological diversity.

Environmental problems facing the country where priority action is needed and if solved could as well lead to sustainable development. Sustainable development depends on the quality and quantity of resources. The village Sreemadurai having hill slopes and swampy land on the foothills and 13% of forest land has been selected in order to see how the people of this fringe village of M.W.L.S. tries to maintain sustainability and how alarming is situation over maintaining biological and cultural diversity.

Therefore, it is an urgent need to raise forests/plantations in all areas that may become available. Another aspect is that the good land is shrinking both in quantity and quality. The former is due to the unexpected demands and the latter is due to whole, spectrum of factors ranging from erosion, desertification, water logging, alkali soils etc. The only solution is to raise land resources by reclaiming and developing degraded land such as land infested with unwanted bushes and shrubs, stony and gravelly land etc.

For the ecological sustainability of the study area a integrated land use planning is necessary. There is no such record in this area. Besides, healthy crop lands and grass land is required. To raise the production, increasing area under cropland is urgent for the enhancing productivity per unit area. Though there is Forest Conservation Act (1980) but still transfer of land from forest to agriculture is going on. Revegetation of marginal lands are urgent. The most important one is conservation of bio-diversity.

With reference to the above discussion it can be stated that the village is within Nilgiri-Wynaad area lies west of the Nilgiri plateau. The curve shows that the village is rugged, being thrown up here and there into hills. Wynaad means the swamps, is also a predominant character of the village. The ground rises gradually in the north to a low range of hills.

Land use profile shows forest land covering 13% of the village are in the 960 m altitude, having mostly swampy soil though in some corner red soil are also available. Anathinum dry land is covered on the slopes of the hills. Dry lands are mostly on the hills and on the other side wet lands are in the flat area. The land use varies from hills to slope to swampy lands.

Soil profile of the village indicates red soil is the predominant character of the area. Next category is swampy soil. Red alluvial and swampy red is also noticed. In the valley area swampy and swampy red soil are prevalent but in the other areas red is predominant.

Crops profile indicate plantation crops are in the hills and hill slopes related with the soil character and swampy land with alluvial soils covers paddy cultivation. Due to exploding population soil is being used increasingly which poses threat to its productivity.

Community over space shows that forest area in the north is the occupied as by tribes and other area by the Mountadan Chettis and people from Kerala though some Paniyans live with as Mountadan Chettis near paddy field daily wage labourer.

From the composite profile it is clear that the demand of land for various purposes is on the increase and agricultural and forest land cannot be spared for obvious reasons like continued self sufficiency for food and long term ecological security. In fact with escalating population more land is needed both for agriculture and forestry particularly the latter because forest cover is very low (13%) much below the envisaged 33%.

The inhabitants of this village show that the Paniyans and the Mountadan Chettis were the original people of the area. After the immigration flow of people from Kerala including Christian, Muslim and Hindu the area got multi ethnic character.

The per hectare of land-man dependency is increasing day by day. Last 50 years of records from Census of India shows land -man ratio in Sreemadurai village is very high. In 1961 it was 0.95 and in 2001 it is 4.8 here as in Gudalur taluk land man ratio is 2.39 in 2001 and it was 0.91 in 1961. The district picture is, Nilgiri enjoys 2.99 land-man ratio in 2001 where as it was 1.6 in 1961. From the above statistics it is clear that the pressure of population in the study area is increasing day by day. Again where when land-man ratio is 4.8 in Sreemadurai village, it is 2.99 in the Nilgiri district and 2.39 in the Gudalur taluk. It proves that immigrants is more in the study area in comparing to the taluk and district itself.

People from Kerala (Christian, Muslim and Hindu) understand that plantation crops are more important and suitable in this ecology and they will get more return in cash. So they have adopted those crops. They were earlier planting ginger in a large scale in this village. But after the introduction of tea and coffee, they have understood that they will get more profit from tea and coffee. Again ginger is only one year crop. But tea will give leaves for hundred years.

From the above discussion it is clear that planning for sustainable development has necessarily to be multi-disciplinary and trans-sectoral in character involving at all levels of Govt, public and private agencies. The gains in productivity can be sustained only when resources are managed in a manner which permit continuation of socio-economic development in the long run.

From the above discussion it is clear that here the traditional bio-diversity is changing. Their trend is towards synchronization of diversity. Traditional order is misbalanced. The changes in the sphere of religion, food habit, dress, education even cropping pattern and infrastructure (like roads, transport, electricity etc.) shows this traditional misbalance.

Villagers are now going to the temple in Kerala and other places and at the same time going to their traditional shrine and observing animisms also. They are also taking fast food with the traditional *Kanji*. Now they have accepted the modern dress also with the traditional dress. Regarding education it is seen that they are also taking English medium teaching though it is very less and absent within the tribes. In the cropping pattern it is noticed that ragi cultivation which was prevalent in the past in the dry land is totally stopped and ginger which was a principal cash crop of the village has now decreased due to the more attention towards the tea and coffee plantation from which they are earning more cash.

Roads increasing day by day. It is due to the need of the market. The tea leaves collected daily require to be sent to the factory otherwise the quality will deteriorate or will be a waste. A good number of jeaps and lorries are noticed here. Electricity is there in the village. There are 120 electric polls controlled by Government. Modern computer system is also introduced here though now it is very negligible. All these development shows that it is essential from development and thus making the development compatible with traditional ordering.

Now the villagers are in a transition. Keeping the traditional order, they have adjusted themselves with the development trend of the surrounding. So the equilibrium with reference to the surroundings shows the tendency towards equilibrium in the study area. Owing to the development to sustain themselves in relation with the surrounding require equilibrium.

Now the villagers sustain themselves with the modern development matching with the originality, i.e., traditional system. The more the development will be compatible, with the order of the things accommodating with their culture that was working upto now the more the development will be sustainable.

The Land use shows that the Sreemadurai village cover 149.6.2 hectare of forest land which is 13.45% of the total land coverage. It is clear from the table that forest coverage is not a major share in this traditional village. But we know animals or wildlife do not follow any political barrier. So they move from one forest area to another specially to the fringe village of Mudumalai wildlife sanctuary. Naturally all animals pass through this area freely.

There is a growing realization and the urgent need to conserve the bio-diversity. There is an ecological crisis which has threatened the whole life support system and the large number of habitats and species both plant and animal, have been progressively on the decline.

It is, therefore, in our own interest to conserve our plant as also animal and micro-organism wealth.

Infact human survival on any part of the earth depends upon conservation of bio-diversity resources.

Biodiversity means the number and diversity of distinct living species within the world or a particular environment. The present reduction of biodiversity will be the largest setback to life yet.

According to Global Forest Resources Assessment 2000, the key to sustainable development in any forested regions of the world lies in :

1. Empowering indigenous communities to co-exist with biological diversity.
2. Protecting biological wealth.
3. Preventing the erosion of people's knowledge system related to biological protection and conservation.
4. Ensuring sustainable use of eco-health.
5. Promotion of a wider application of community knowledge, practices and innovation related to bio-diversity with their approval and participation.
6. Ensuring equitable sharing of benefits arising from the utilization of indigenous knowledge systems, innovation and practices.

The Govt. of India has recognized the significance of the indigenous knowlege system relating to the conservation of biological diversity and sustainable development and has enacted various programs and proposals on its behalf.

Conclusion

In Sreemadurai village preservation of biological diversity, is reflected more in areas of forest and where subsistence economy where traditional cultural institutions and indicator are still playing greater. This is much more prominent in the area occupied by the Paniyans in the hill top and hill slopes.

Environment is the sum total of all conditions and influences that effect the development and life of organisms. Associated with any development there is always some amount of environmental degradation. Sustainability in development has to enter in our planning process as one of the basic and permanent objectives. Important steps for sustainable development are: (1) population stabilization as and shrinkage of resources demographic pressures lead to economic pressure. (2) Integrated land use planning because land is one of the important components of the life support system and has been over used and abused. Being an agricultural country land is very important and its use will have to be related with soil quality. It is also connected with watershed management and water conservation. (3) Healthy cropland and grassland is an urgent need to boost productivity per unit area per unit of time. For this the gap between actual and potential yield should be minimize by going vertical rather than horizontal in agriculture. Here the problems of grasslands and overgrazing has not received the deserved attention. Increasing number of livestock in ecologically fragile areas, like the hills of this area leads to very serious environmental consequences. (4) Woodland and revegetation are essential as woodland is destructed for the demand of wood for diverse use like firewood, timber, industrial raw material etc. For this conservation, production and social forestry need to be practiced, (5) Conservation of biological diversity is urgently required for all conservation efforts have to be directed to keep the species away from decline. For this we need to have a strategy based on principles of genetics and evolutionary biology. Again we need the conservation effort on an eco-system basis and not on species basis. (6) Development of non-polluting renewable energy system like biomass, solar energy etc. Here govt. has tried for the betterment of the village specially in the tribal belt where solar energy is introduced in this village for the protection of crops from the animals specially elephant. A solar wire line fencing has drawn for this purpose. Bio-mass also introduced here for fertilizer.

(7) Environmental education and awareness regarding, conservation and management, environmental health and social ecology should be introduced in both formal and non-formal education and awareness. So sustainable development is deeply integrated in planning process.

Sustainable development would increase the moral standards of people living any, which might spill over into the realm of economics.

References

Batta, R.N., Tourism and the Environment: A quest for sustainability; Indus Publishing Co; N. Delhi, 2000.

Breeks, James Wilkinson., Primitive Tribes and monuments of the Nilgiris; Cultural Publishing House; Delhi 1983.

Chockalingam, K., Census of India 1971, Series – 19, Tamil Nadu, Town Directory – The Nilgiris, 1972.

Chockalingam, K., Village and Townwise Primary Census Abstract Part X-B.

Census of India 1981, Series – 20, Tamil Nadu, Part – XIII-A and B, Village and Town Directory, Nilgiri District Census Handbook.

Census of India – 1981, Series 20 Tamil Nadu Part II A, General Population tables.

Census of India 1991, Series-23, Tamil Nadu, Part-XII-A and B, District Census Handbook, Nilgiri, Village and Town Directory.

Census of India 1991, Series 23, Tamil Nadu, Part-XII-A, Coimbatore District, Village and Town Directory.

Chawla, Romila (ed.), Tourism and Development Series, Sustainable Development and Toursim, Sonali Publications, New Delhi – 110 002, 2003.

Chawla, Romila (ed.), Wild life tourism. Sonali Publication.

Chawla, Romila (ed.), Tourism research planning.

Chawla, Romila, Tourism and development series, Global Tourism, Sonali Publication, N. Delhi, 2003.

Chawla, Romila, Tourism in the 21st Century, Sonali Publication, N. Delhi, 2003.

Dadnich L.K. and Hooja Rima; (ed.) Environment Degradation Strategies for Control; Aalekh Publishers, Jaipur - 302001; 1992.

Francis, W., Madras District Gazetters, The Nilgiris Part I and II, 1908.

Modi, Shalini, Tourism and Society, Rawat Publications. Jaipur and New Delhi, 2001.

Nambiar, P.K., Census of India 1961, Vol. IX, Madras, Part X-X, District Census Handbook, Nilgiris, Vol. I and II 1965.

Saxena, H.M., Environmental Geography; Rawat Publications; Jaipur and New Delhi, 2nd edition, 2004.

Sethi, Praveen, Strategies for the future of Travel and Tourism, Rajat Publications. Delhi-110 031, 1999.

Sharma S.K. and K.G. Prasad (1983). "Forest Soil and Vegetation survey report on Gudalur Forest Division, Tamil Nadu." Forest Research Institute and Colleges, Forest Soil cum Vegetation Survey Southern Regional Center, Coimbatore.

Sharma, Subhash Chandra. Geography of Tourism, Vol. I and II, Rajat Publications, N. Delhi, 2002.

Sinha, P.C., Geography and Structure of Tourism and Travel; Anmol Publication Pvt. Ltd., N. Delhi.

Singh, Arun Kumar. Ecology and land use Pattern in Gudalur Taluk, Nilgiris, a Geographical Study; Anthropological Survey of India, Calcutta. 1991.

Weaver, David B. The encyclopedia of Eco-tourism. CABI Publishing, 2001.

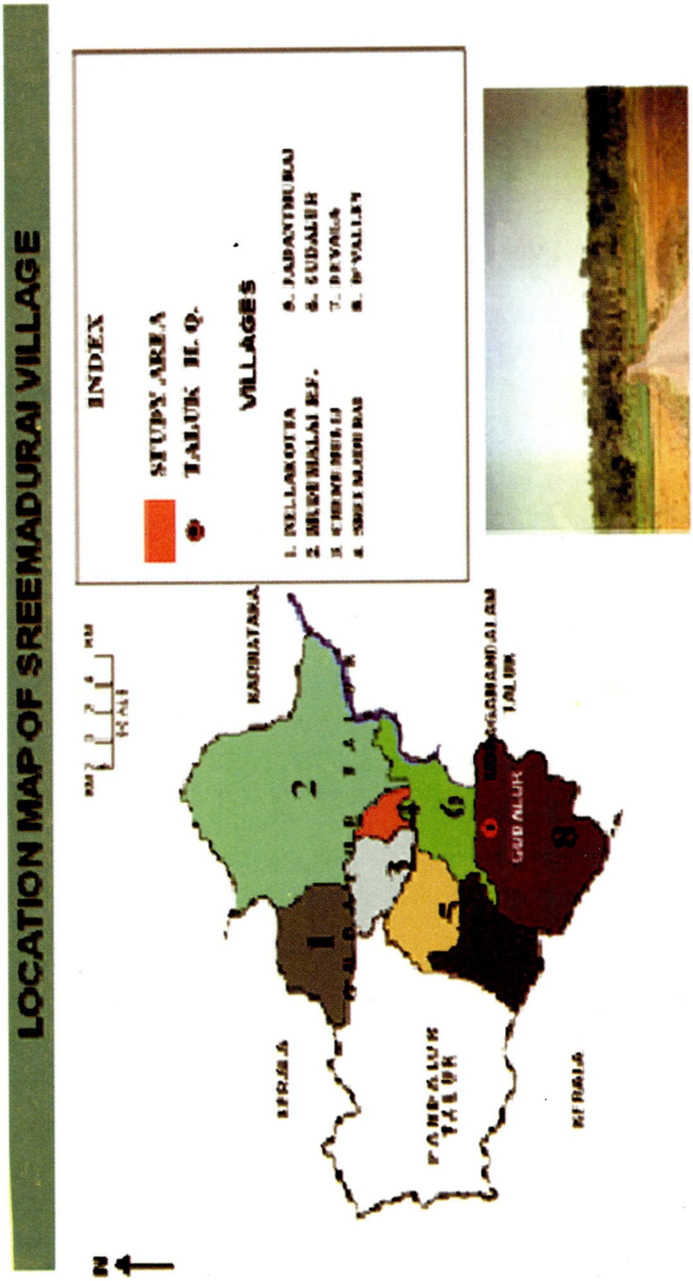
LOCATION MAP OF SREEMADURAI VILLAGE
INDEX
STUDY AREA
TALUK H.Q.
VILLAGES
1. NELLAKOTTA
2. MUDUMALAI R.F.
7. DEVALA
8. O'VALLEY
KARNATAKA
KERALA
GUDALUR
N

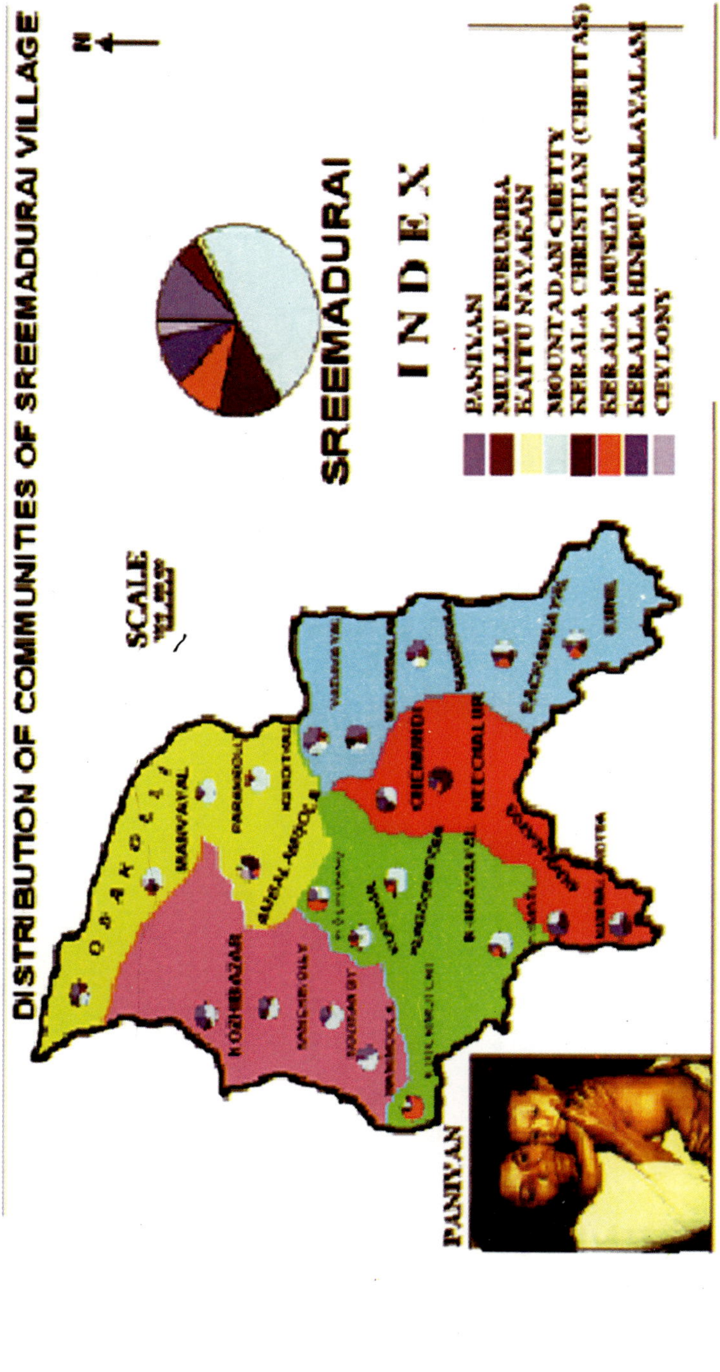
DISTRIBUTION OF COMMUNITIES OF SREEMADURAI VILLAGE
N
SCALE
SREEMADURAI
INDEX
PANIYAN
MULLU KURUMBA
KATTU NAYAKAN
MOUNTADAN CHETTY
KERALA CHRISTIAN (CHETTAS)
KERALA MUSLIM
KERALA HINDU (MALAYALAM)
CEYLONY
PANIYAN

LAND RESOURCES :

Table : 2

Land classification of Sreemadurai village 1886

Sl. No.	Land Classification	1886 (%)
1.	Wet land	18.18
2.	Dry estates land	0
3.	Holding other than (dry) estates land	79.85
4.	Assessed dry land	0
5.	Unassessed Parambokes land	1.97
Total		100.00

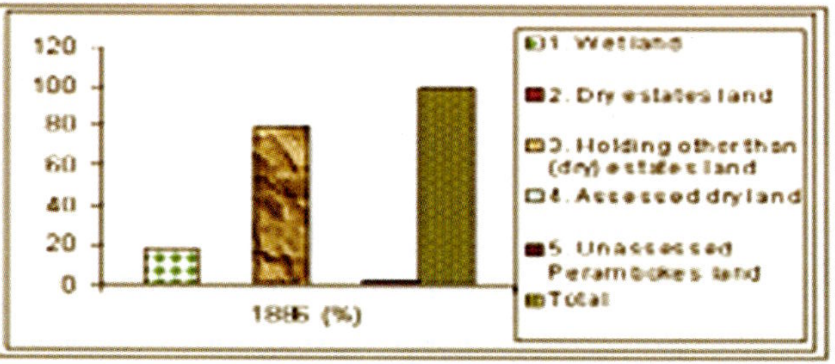

Table : 3

Land classification of Sreemadurai village 1928

Sl. No.	Land Classification	1928 (%)
1.	Wet land	18.94
2.	Dry land	80.84
3.	Estates	0
4.	Unassessed	0
5.	Parambokes	0.22
Total		100.00

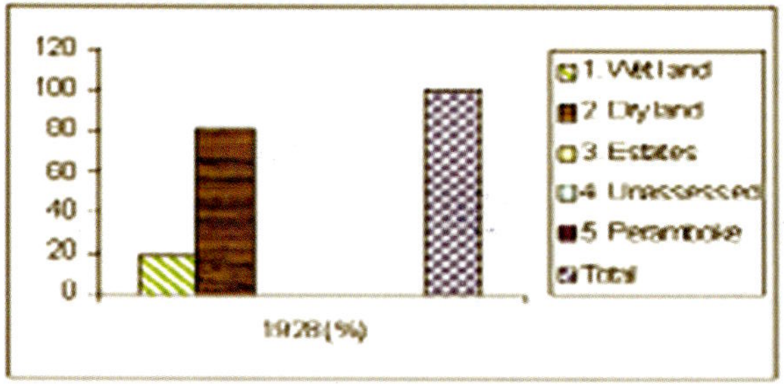

Land classification of Sreemadurai village 1979

Sl. No.	Land Classification 1979 (%)	
1.	Wet land	22.28
2.	Dry developed	56.03
3.	Dry undeveloped	0
4.	Estate developed	1.65
5.	Estate undeveloped	0
6.	Unassessed waste	1.74
7.	Forest	13.46
8.	Paramboke	4.83
Total		100.00

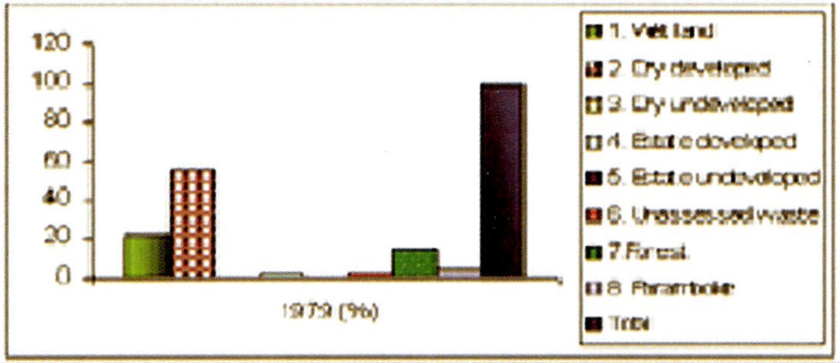

Land classification of Sreemadurai village 2005

Sl. No.	Land Classification 2005 (%)	
1.	Nanjai and C.A. Nanjai	18.47
2.	Punjai and C.A. Punjai	30.56
3.	Anadinum Nanjai	3.82
4.	Anadinum Punjai	26.60
5.	Tharisu	1.76
6.	Oilhulai / Kadu	0.77
7.	Forest land under sec. 53	12.68
8.	Arasunilam / Parambok	5.01
9.	Estate Thottam	0.33
Total		100.00

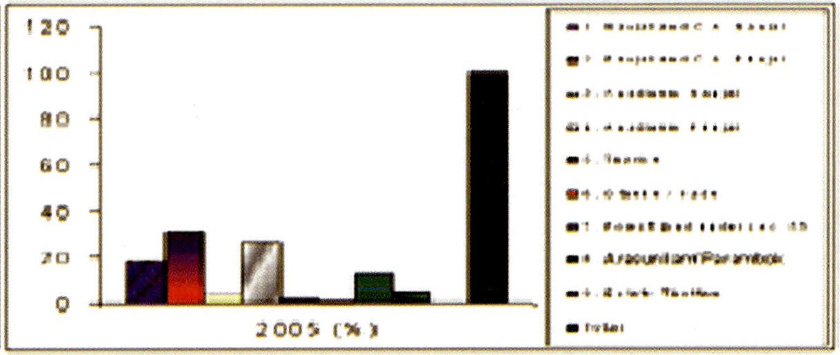

LAND RESOURCE OF SREEMADURAI VILLAGE - 2005

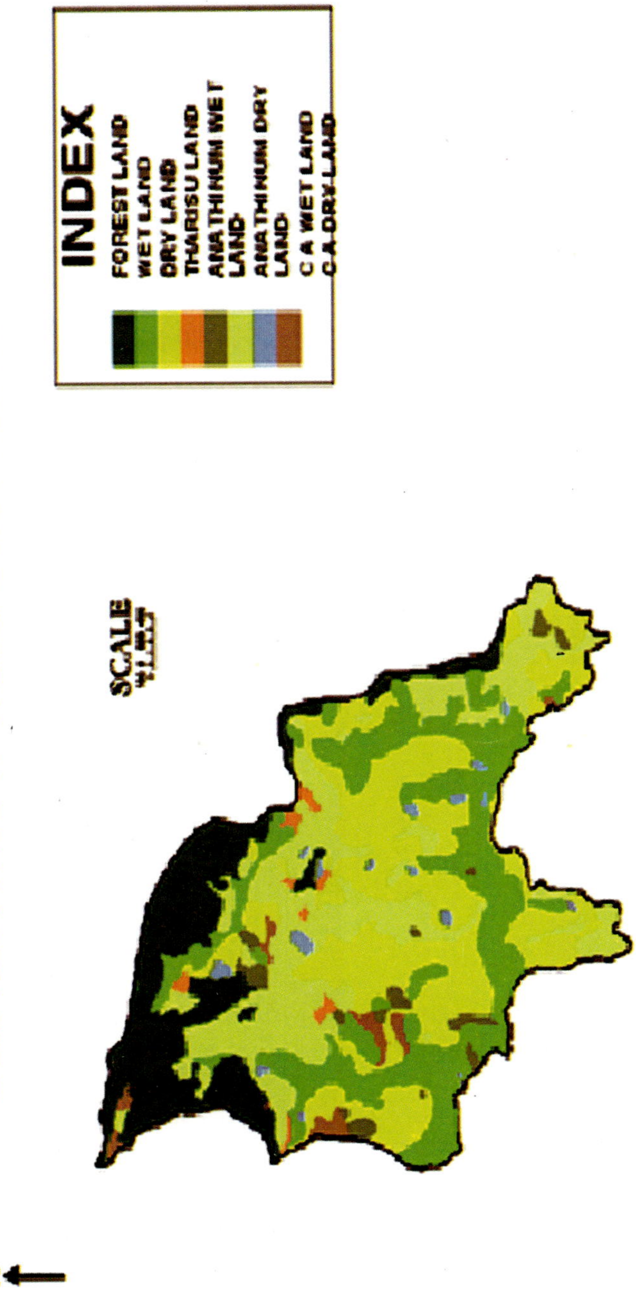

List of Contributors

Arun Kumar Singh, Senior Ecologist, Anthropologist Survey of India, 27 Jawaharlal Nehru Road, Kolkata-700016

K. Ravi, Anthropologist(C), Anthropological Survey of India SRC, Mysore

G.V. Ramana, Research Associate (C), Anthropological Survey of India, SRC, Mysore

B. R. Vijayendra, Anthropologist (C), Anthropological Survey of India, SRC, Mysore

H.M. Maralusiddaiah Patel, Research Associate (C), Anthropological Survey of India, SRC, Mysore

P.K. Guha, Cartographer, Anthropological Survey of India, 27 Jawaharlal Nehru Road, Kolkata-700016

Sanchita Ghatak, Cartographer, Anthropological Survey of India, 27 Jawaharlal Nehru Road, Kolkata-700016

Index

N

T

U

V

W